W9-BTR-101

Software Interpreters for Microcomputers

Software Interpreters for Microcomputers

THOMAS C. McINTIRE *NCR Corporation*
Dayton, Ohio

John Wiley & Sons

New York • Santa Barbara • Chichester • Brisbane • Toronto

Library of Congress Cataloging in Publication Data:

McIntire, Thomas C   1942-
   Software interpreters for microcomputers.

   Bibliography: p.
   Includes index.
   1. Microcomputers—Programming.   2. Interpreters
(Computer programs) I. Title.

QA76.6.M323   001.6'425   78-6608
ISBN 0-471-02678-6

Printed in the United States of America

10 9 8 7 6 5 4 3 2

Preface

Microprocessor technology has come of age. The computer-on-a-chip is being used in an ever-widening variety of applications. The data processing industry in particular is benefiting from the favorable price-performance ratios possible with microcomputers—computers that have a micro as the central processing unit. Business data processing generally favors the use of high-level programming languages, and interpreters provide a software method for interfacing various languages to microcomputers.

For the systems architect we present the arguments, both pro and con, for selecting the appropriate software architecture. For the software designer, the significance of different language attributes is described along with the considerations necessary for an interpreter-driven system.

In concept at least, programming a microcomputer is not very different from programming other computers. Thus, much of this book applies to interpreter designs for systems other than micros, although many of the specifics to be considered for microprocessors are identified. Also, the software engineer of the microcomputer interpretive system must eke out the maximum of performance, often in the minimum of space. For this reason the final chapters of this book are devoted to optimization techniques.

This book should also be useful to the applications programmer. How do interpreters work? Why are certain functions slower than others? Why do some routines consume large amounts of memory? In general, the answers to these questions can be found here, and more optimum programs can result.

Before modifications or improvements to an existing system can be attempted, the maintenance programmer must understand the overall philosophy of interpreters. In this case, study should include the rationale that influences the design of such systems. Therefore, many of the trade-offs that may be made in the design of an interpreter are discussed.

The basic principle of software interpreters is simple, but individual component routines may be complex and the overall size of the system may be large. For the benefit of the software engineering student, then, material is included on how to approach the design phase and on how to begin implementation and testing. Some suggestions are included on systems documentation.

The choice of the tutorial model (BASIC) was made with particular concern for that rapidly growing market: the home computer hobbyist. A number of BASIC interpreters are commercially available, or the hobbyist may wish to attempt his own design or modify an existing system. The model described here should provide the basis for many forms of experimentation.

Although the discussion is not complete in every area, almost every facet of interpreters, their use, and their design, is touched upon.

Thomas C. McIntire

Acknowledgments

The writing of this book was an arduous undertaking, and the thoughts, efforts, and expertise of many people contributed to its completion. I am unable to ascertain the origins of many of the concepts and methods I have described, but I wish to acknowledge the contributions of the professionals of the industry and of computer scientists in general.

I also thank those people whose personal assistance to me made this work possible.

For both stimuli and critique, I must thank my friend, associate, and boss, Keith Lohmuller. I express my gratitude also to Bill Bird, Assistant Vice-President, Marketing Software Programs, for inviting me into the fold of the NCR Corporation; association with the many professionals of this prestigious industry giant has provided a valuable research vehicle and has enriched my life.

It is often said that behind every man stands a woman—and so it is with me. Notwithstanding her continuous help, encouragement, and confidence, I can offer here only a simple "thank you" to my wife, Gloria for her many hours of typing.

As to the practice of programming, I must attribute eons of experience to Steve Clark. Our years together in the bit-bending business leaves me forever in his debt for the knowledge and help he has so freely shared. His technical critique of the manuscript merely adds to my continuing indebtedness.

No writer is truly self-sufficient, and my thanks also go to Ken Sessions as my editor and mentor.

To the readers doing the final tally: where you are enlightened and informed, it is due to the efforts of many; any ambiguity is entirely my own.

T. C. McIntire

Author's Note

The organization of this book attempts to enfold the many topical ramifications into a usable form. Throughout I have sought a reasonable balance between thoroughness and brevity. The intent has been to provide sufficient detail for the interested student without trying the patience of the professional.

The background material in Part 1 may appear very basic to veteran readers, but it is necessary to establish a mutual ground for communication. Interpreter usage rationale is examined, and microprocessors are explained.

The categorization of interpreter types in Part 2 is for the benefit of later discussion. Since no finite scheme of description is fully suitable for naming different types of interpreters, this part provides a base address for indirect referencing.

In Part 3 I enumerate all the various aspects the designer of an interpreter must consider. The critical user of an interpretive system may gain insight as to the scope of the designer's task. For those embarking on interpreter designs, I have included material on a methodology for problem definition. The template form of block diagramming is my own interpretation of a technique that is actually employed in some software development shops.

The model described in Part 4 was selected to show implementation techniques for solving certain interpreter design problems.

Part 5 discusses some of the many "tricks of the trade" in the programming profession. Since entire textbooks can be and have been written on these subjects, it was necessary to limit this part. All programming efforts must contend with speed and overhead tradeoffs. Interpreters are at least one step removed from the primary function of using a computer to do a problem task, and it is especially important to practice economies in their design. Although placed physically last in the book, techniques and methods for programming specific functions must temper many decisions early in the process of design.

In the same context, I offer this advice to the novice designer: Every effort expended during design and problem definition will be well repaid in the final analysis.

T.C. McIntire

X

Contents

PART 2 Interpreter Architectures

Software Interpreters for Microcomputers

PART

Background

Interpret . . . to translate nonmachine language into machine language.

Interpreter . . . a software routine that, as processing progresses, translates a stored program expressed in pseudo-code into machine code and executes the intended operations.

A thorough discussion of computer interpreters must include the *why* function. Since computers are problem-solving machines and their programs constitute a part of the total system, we must examine the solution capability of interpreter programs. Interpreters are generally considered as part of the software. To appreciate the role of interpreters it is necessary to identify those processing problem attributes that are common to the use of all computers, regardless of specific job tasks.

In interpretative software systems, as in all technologies, there are advantages and disadvantages associated with various implementation techniques. We shall therefore examine several alternative methods of system design so that we may judge when interpreters should be used.

In advancing our theme that microcomputers tend to motivate the use of interpreters, we must appreciate the nature of these stimuli. The widespread usage of microprocessor-based systems attests to their acceptance and need. Representative micros are included in this part to show the causative factors that influence the popularity of interpreters.

Chapter

Why Interpreters?

The fact that interpretive software systems are so commonplace in the world of computers implies that there are decided advantages to their use. There is often no perfect single solution to a large group of problems. Since interpreters are not used by every system, we can infer that there are some disadvantages. In the selection of choices we must analyze both the positive and the negative aspects.

In addition to the good and bad points, alternative possibilities must be identified and examined in order to arrive at a sound conclusion. This chapter deals with the favorable aspects of interpreters, the unfavorable aspects, and some of the alternatives frequently used.

1.1 Advantages

The owner of a computer system once asked me what the impact would be if he decided to replace his system with that of a different manufacturer. Much to his chagrin, my answer implied bad news. This problem is not atypical, and it is useful to introduce one of the most favorable arguments for interpreters: case of migration.

In Figure 1.1, the location of the interpreter between the application programs and the computer implies an insulation function. The physical placement of an interpreter between the programs and the processor can, in fact, result in insulation. In the case of the system owner mentioned above, all of his application programs had been written in an *assembler language*. Assemblers are usually designed such that for a given source program statement, a single machine-language object code is generated. The output from the assembly process is machine code, and this restricts the use of that code to a processor that can properly execute it. The portent for users contemplating switching "engines" is the possibility of having to scrap and rewrite their entire program library, which may have evolved over a long period of time and at considerable expense in labor and dollars.

2

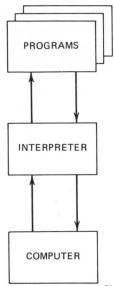

Figure 1.1 An interpreter can function to insulate programs from hardware changes.

Technological advances by the computer industry have generated this dilemma with such recurring frequency that many methods have evolved to make the problems of migration less severe. These solutions involve compromise, however, and are therefore discussed further in the section dealing with alternatives.

System architectures based on the use of interpreters makes it possible to change the processor with virtually no impact on the users of the system. But to exploit fully this switching capability requires that all aspects of the original implementation be biased in favor of interpretive schemes. In this instance, the languages used for application programming must be oriented to produce an object code that is not sensitive to a particular computer's machine structure. This is achieved through the use of assemblers and compilers that produce as output a *pseudo-object code.*

The advantage of interpreters stems from the use of an artificial object code and strings of instructions written in machine language that translate their meaning during execution. It is necessary, however, that the interpreter program itself be written in the native machine code of the using computer. However, only a single native language program is required, permitting the use of all programs whose artificial object code agrees with the structure expected as input by the interpreter.

It is far less costly to develop a single interpreter than to rewrite entire libraries of programs. This has long been recognized by the manufacturers of data processing systems, who frequently employ interpretive methods to their own benefit.

The vendors of many systems on the market today offer various types of software products in conjunction with their hardware. The leaders in the computer industry offer complete data processing systems, consisting not only of the hardware but of system software and application program product sets as well. Even those companies specializing in smaller systems or in primarily the hardware products offer such software as language compilers and common utility programs.

Software development many times exceeds the cost of designing new computers and peripheral devices. As a consequence, developers have taken advantage of the migratory qualities of interpretive concepts in the design of the software products they offer. As an example, the compiler software for COBOL may have a price tag of several million dollars. By comparison, development of an interpreter may cost as little as 10% of that of a compiler alone. And the interpreter can work with all of the other programs as well, not just the compiler.

The advantage of migration to the developer lies in the fact that he too can change his hardware without suffering the burden of new software library development. The histories of hardware manufacturers reveal numerous instances where new processors were shelved, not because of hardware cost impacts but rather because of the costs involved in developing new supportive software. By adopting interpretive types of architecture throughout, *virtual systems* can readily be achieved.

The prospective purchaser of a computing system can take advantage of the interpretive strategy of those offering such systems. Within a given company's product line, upward migration to larger and faster computers can be simply achieved. In fact, the use of interpretive architectures is often a deliberate marketing tactic. By offering their present users an effortless migration path, vendors tend to restrict the practical choices available for switching products. However, when a competitor does not offer an interpretive capability for the artificial object code of another make of equipment, it is feasible for a user to develop his own interpreter, provided he has sufficient design expertise available.

The migration advantages of interpreters are real, not only to the developers of systems but to the end users as well. It is far less costly to write a single interpreter program than to have to rewrite many application programs.

A natural extension of the subject of migration is program transportability. The ability to exchange between users entire suites of application programs is considerably enhanced through the use of interpretive software schemes.

There are methods employed to achieve transportability goals that allow programs written for a given machine environment to be used on other systems. Just as with migration, not all of these methods are fully efficient, and interpreters can enjoy certain specific advantages.

The burgeoning software industry is largely motivated by the fact that their application program products may be used with systems of different companies. This form of transportability results from the extensive use of *high-level languages.* Languages such as COBOL, FORTRAN, and BASIC are common throughout the computer industry, and most system manufacturers provide compiler software for at least one of these. Since there are mutual benefits to the use of common language semantics, tremendous progress has been made over the years in achieving commonality.

There are industry organizations and associations that exist for the express purpose of standardizing languages, but the dynamics of electronic technology sometimes work in opposition to their efforts. The goal of rigidly defining specific forms of expression is aimed at a moving target. (Innovative developments in processor and peripheral designs can require additions and modifications to the programming languages used.) State-of-the-art efforts by each of the "systems" companies necessitates each providing its own unique modifications to the languages used by its programmers.

Here again the role of the interpreter is obvious. Where two systems, a giver and a receiver, can process the same pseudo-object set, there is virtual exchangeability.

The indirect advantages of interpreters are twofold. Those charged with standardizing languages are often tempted to bias their feature selection process. Many of the provisions of approved language standards include forms of expression that are sensitive to certain processor architectures. The proper orientation of the higher-level languages is to provide programming methods that facilitate *problem definition* without special regard to a particular computer's attributes.

Companies wishing to maximize the benefits of standardized programming languages may employ interpretive techniques to satisfy their strategic goals. In effect, interpreters can mask the differences between computer command sets and the instruction conventions of the various languages.

A frequent ploy of system designers is to add new instructions to an existing language to accommodate new features of system design. Through the use of interpreters, however, additions to languages can at least partially be avoided.

Omissions from language implementations occur for the same reasons that languages are extended. A given processor design may not lend itself to accomplishing some language provisions. Interpretive software can be used to lessen the incompatibilities between standard language features and unique processor functions.

The amount of effort required to transport user programs from one system to another is in proportion to the degree of standardization of the programming language used. It is the function of a language compiler (or assembler) to translate program commands into machine-executable code strings. Where a one-for-one correspondence exists, the task is relatively simple. When there is no machine-code counterpart for a program-language command, the compiler/developer is tempted to modify the language itself. The use of software interpreters allows modification of the machine-code set to accommodate the provisions of the programming language used. Thus, interpreters benefit language standardization, and ultimately, user program transportability.

Language expansion capability through the use of an interpreter is provided by the addition of commands. By increasing the number of commands available, the programmer expands the vocabulary available with which to describe processing requirements. Generally speaking, the greater the number of commands, the more powerful the programming language.

In speaking of a computer as having a powerful language capability, the reference is usually to the machine-language code set and structure. An advantage of an interpreter, then, is to increase the power of the processor through expansion of the programming language.

Listed here as the last advantage, but certainly not the least of significance, is the source code interpreter. Source code translation processes such as compilers and

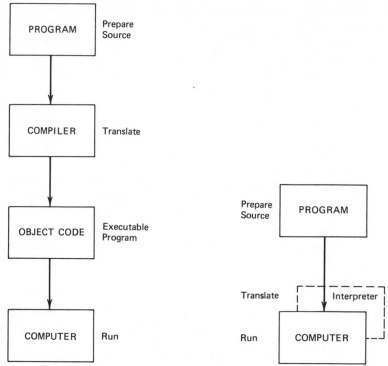

Figure 1.2 Source code interpreters eliminate compilation processing steps by translating "on the fly" at execution time.

assemblers can be completely circumvented through the use of intepreters. Those interpretive designs offering this advantage accomplish the source statement translation during program execution.

Translation of the textual statements provided by the programmer to machine-level object code is necessary in all systems. The difference in methodology inherent to the source interpreter is that it does not require any preprocessing of the programmer-supplied instructions. The nature of this advantage is shown in the block diagram of Figure 1.2, which compares the traditional compiling process and the source code interpretive scheme.

The amount of time required for program compilation varies by system and language (and compiler or assembler architecture), but in all cases there is an overhead factor. In those applicational environments where frequent program changes are necessary, the ability to forego dedicated time for program compilation may prove sufficient reason to select a source code interpretive system.

1.2 Disadvantages

The self-appointed user surrogate's depth of knowledge and eloquence may vary, but his theme will be the data processing euphemism for poor performance: *degradation*. The main problem is the conflict between speed and storage.

In discussing the overall performance of a computing system, speed has two connotations. To the system designer the emphasis on speed is restricted to *processing* speed. The meaning here is the relative timing of the internal operations of the computer during instruction execution. The real concern of the user, however, is overall throughput. In this context, speed encompasses the total time involved in using a computer to accomplish a processing problem.

The increased storage requirements of interpretive software systems are usually a secondary argument, but such systems are generally conceded to include larger memories and greater media capacities. By definition, software interpreters are computer programs, and they must be stored in the memory of the computer. Since the very utility of computers requires the ability to change programs, the interpreter program must be further stored on some external media. The purist will also recognize a nominal disadvantage in the time required for software loading, that is, in copying the software from external media to memory.

Viewed strictly on the basis of cost considerations, there is a temptation to discredit the increased storage concerns. Increasing the available memory of a microcomputer (at least to the addressing extent of the microprocessor) represents a small percentage of the total cost of some systems. And a net system cost increase of as much as 10-15% could be a fair price in exchange for some of the benefits of an interpreter-based system.

System media costs for the external storage of interpretive software must be reconciled, but a number of technologies can be applied successfully. It is relevant that the peripheral devices used with computers often suffer a larger cost burden than the computer itself—especially in the case of microcomputers. For those systems whose applicational requirements dictate media peripherals for data file storage, no cost factor should be attributed to the interpreter for such devices.

Inexpensive magnetic media such as tape cassettes, cartridges, and flexible or *floppy* disks are used on all but the smallest microcomputer systems. The disadvantage of interpreters, with respect to external storage, is the cost of the medium. But with the high capacities achieved in even the smallest of these units, this burden is considered inconsequential in choosing a software architecture. In the absence of a medium, *read-only memories* are cost-effectively employed to house the interpreters for those systems that do not have requirements for magnetic peripherals, further negating the storage arguments.

The view of the software maintenance analyst must be appreciated. The placement of another level of programming within the system tends to increase the complexities of fault isolation whenever failures occur. In addition to the debugging efforts involved, the usual consequence of a software error portends another level of maintenance.

The marketing strategist may suggest that the migration advantages of interpretive systems can be construed as disadvantages. Possible competitive threats can result from an opposition tactic based on the ease with which a user may be enticed to a different system. Since a considerable advantage of interpreters is isolation of the user's programs from the hardware, an interpreter may be the only thing required to launch a trade-out campaign. This is a competitive posture problem; but whether ease

7

of migration should be properly considered a disadvantage of interpreters is arguable.

The perspective of system analysts is application uses. System analysts readily concede that there are speed and storage disadvantages to interpreters, but the degree and severity is sensitive to the intended use of the system. In some instances these factors are sufficiently compensated by offsetting advantages to negate the argument. The emergence of the small, desk-top computer has been enhanced by interpretive concepts. The assumed user profile suggests applicational requirements best suited to such designs.

For example, consider an engineering student who has a problem of calculating the various stress factors of steel structural beams. The computations necessary can involve as many as several hundred iterative calculations. In an interpretive system, a speed degradation estimate of 50% is extremely generous, but is offered in comparison to instructions programmed in machine code. Even if a native-language program could halve the processing time, this saving would not be significant for this user situation. The expense of "two" minutes, in a theoretical four-minute processing run, is a weak argument, especially when tempered by the suggestion that this sytem is idle more than it is used.

The degradation potential first becomes significant when we expand the applicational scope of microcomputer systems to accomplish data processing jobs assigned to the small business system. The basic difference is in attempting to use a relatively small engine to pull what might be a very long train.

The orientation of business applications processors is for bookkeeping and accounting problems. As compared to the supersophisticated calculator, the relative mix of calculations and input and output tasks is considerably different. The real burdens of the accounting computer involve bulk movement of data in and out of the computer.

The internal execution speed of a processor is often cited in terms of *instruction cycle time,* that is, the time required to fetch an instruction from a memory location, execute the command, and cycle to the point of access of the next sequential instruction. Although the cycle time of the average microprocessor is perhaps only one-fifth that of its more expensive cousin, the minicomputer, brute force is not always of the highest priority in the small- to medium-priced business system. Typically, peripheral units—printers, tape, and disk drives—are slower than for their mini counterparts. The extension of this is that microcomputers are sufficiently fast for those applications that are predominantly input/output bound. Some statistics show that in high-volume input and output runs, the processor may be underutilized to as little as 30% of its true speed potential.

Before abandoning the speed argument, we should consider another problem of the system analyst. In operator-oriented applications, overall throughput of the system is stimulated, controlled, and paced by the operator. Consider the time necessary for a keyboard operator to go through a source document. In an equivalent amount of time, the computer can execute several thousand machine-language instructions. A message output to the operator that requires an input response will cause processor idle time of at least 300 milliseconds, which is the approximate time for a rapid response. This minimum can escalate to a minute or more in those instances requiring a judgment decision, such as selection of a seldom used routine or an alternate processing task.

Before any credence can be allowed the speed degradation arguments, a thorough examination must be made of the intended application of the computing system. Not only is it possible that speed inefficiencies may go unnoticed, but given the opportunity to choose, the user might well trade a few minutes a day for other benefits that can accrue through the use of interpretive software systems.

In the strictest sense, with an interpreter there are two programs stored in the computer. The first program is the application program and the second is the interpreter. During program execution, the application program commands the interpreter, which in turn commands the computer. On the surface it would appear, because it must run two programs, that the computer must go through twice as many instructions. With two programs in memory, it would also seem that there is a doubling effect as to the amount of storage required.

The heart of an interpreter is a small routine that sequentially accesses the pseudo-coded instructions that constitute the user program. As each command is fetched and decoded, control is passed to individual routines or *microstrings* that effectively interpret the intent of the pseudo-code and cause computer execution.

The processing steps to execute the command fetch and decode tasks are in excess of the number of executable problem-solving steps provided by the application program. The degree and extent of this *overhead* burden is sensitive to a number of factors, but one of the most significant is the correlation of the user's language and the native command capability of the microprocessor employed.

As a general premise, the higher the level of a programming language, the less efficient is utilization of the processor and memory usage allocation. Like most rule-of-thumb axioms, this one is not very accurate; but there is an identifiable effect, and the degree is related to the language level implemented. An inherent weakness of this theory is in assuming that a program written in native code will always be more efficient because only those commands will be used that accomplish the explicit requirements. Even in programs where exacting care is employed to preclude redundancy, design optima are not always achieved.

If we accept the generality that the higher-level languages connote a degree of inefficiency and we add a further degradation factor within an interpretive architecture, the cumulative result could be unworkable. But consider the converse: The nearer the language level is to assembler types, the less will be those inefficiencies attributed to the higher forms and the better will be the performance of an interpreter-based system.

Not only can language selection influence performance but, more important, the pseudo-code object representation of the programming statements can have significant impact. The closer the syntactical form of the intermediate object is to that of the processor machine code, the less severe are the overhead burdens.

In summary, then, there are inherent disadvantages associated with interpretive software systems. If properly identified and factored into the overall system architecture, however, an interpreter-based system can be used to full benefit without suffering recognizable degradation. Conversely, the cumulative effect of poor design decisions may be unacceptable.

9

1.3 Alternatives

Many factors must be considered in the selection of a software system architecture, including applications requirements, operating environment, hardware capabilities, and language attributes, among others. Modern computer products are extremely reliable and capable of long service lives. But they are machines, and as such they are subject to replacement. There is also a strong tendency for system users to place ever-increasing workloads on their computers. These increases emanate both from increased volumes of data to be processed and from recognition of new applications.

Notwithstanding the probability of eventual system replacement due to wear, many users remain dependent on their original equipment vendors. Being "locked in" to a single source for new products and services, as well as for the maintenance of present hardware and software, is a precarious position at best.

A major advantage of interpretive software systems is machine independence. The added advantage of language expansion capability can permit initial installation of microcomputers with an upward migration path inherently provided.

Where the pro and con arguments for interpretive software are insufficient selection criteria, alternative software schemes must be examined. In those instances requiring changed programming languages, translator programs prevail. Translators are usually applicable when the languages involved are high level. The high-level languages are oriented toward problem-solving definition and tend to be insensitive to hardware characteristics. Where two different vendors do not offer compilers for the same language, or when the language varies considerably between two implementations, translators at least partially solve the migration problems.

The basic intent of a translator is to provide a substituted statement for each of the original-language source statements. Once the translation process is accomplished, the new source file is compiled using the software of the destination computer. The degree and extent of fully automatic translation achievable is sensitive to a variety of influences.

The most favorable circumstances for language translators are those where the language is the same and the hardware configurations are approximately equal. In this case, highly automated translation can be achieved since the only substitution required results from syntactical instruction differences.

Another level of complexity for the translator designer is different languages. Where the old and the new are high-level languages, translators can be quite successful, although considerable effort is required in the design of such translators. Further, differences in system configurations add to the sophistication of translator designs. A difference in peripherals requires different file and media accessing logic, and extreme changes—such as from serial to random-access devices—can impose changes on the problem-solving structure of the original program.

Translators that provide for changing peripheral and system features must do more than just substitute lines of coding on a one-for-one basis. Where problem-solving structures and procedural logic are subject to change, it is necessary to substitute algorithms, data definitions, and sections of procedural code.

In theory, translator programs can be designed with sufficient provisions to accommodate virtually any requirement. Practicality tends to constrain the scope of translators to levels consistent with majority requirements. Because it is imprudent to apply an 80% percentile effort to accommodate a less-than-20% anticipated occurrence, few translators promise 100% capability. When a translator is inadequate for a specific circumstance, it is necessary to resort to manual programming modifications to achieve complete translation.

The applicability of translators for automatically exchanging assembler languages is usually nil. Since machine languages are specific to each processor, it is rare for the substituted processor to have much in common with the original insofar as their respective native commands are concerned.

Emulation is another migration solution in some instances. Emulator capabilities are either of a hardware facility or they are provided through software routines. The intent of emulators is to permit the imitating system to achieve nearly identical results as the original system, usually using programs written for the replaced system. Not all emulation schemes, however, address the problem of transporting the original programs. When replacing a system the user expects to achieve at least a comparable level of performance with the new equipment. Where a new system is touted to be superior to a predecessor this may be true overall, save for an isolated feature or two. Emulator provisions can enhance the newer design to raise a particular deficiency to a level where no performance degradation is visible.

Transportation of application programs from one system to another of different design can be achieved with software simulators. In the strictest sense, the simulator as used here is an interpreter. Instead of interpreting a psuedo-object code,the original program is loaded into the destination system and an interpreter equates this object to the user machine's commands. Although the simulator solution precludes any immediate need to rewrite programs, optimum performance on the replacement system is rarely achieved. Inefficiencies can be attributed to such factors as differences in object code structures, system features, and the dual-program aspect of one program commanding another. When optimum performance is required, it is necessary to rewrite (or at least to modify) and recompile the original programming with the software tools provided on the replacement system.

Filter programs are another type of software solution in certain migration problems. Filters are most typically used when only an isolated, recurring, or constant change is encountered. A filter program is quite practical to solve problems associated with replacement of peripheral devices or when adding hardware features to a system. Filters are written to accept as input the object code for an application program, generating as output another version of the program by substituting specific characters or codes.

An example of filtering is one where the system change involves a change in peripheral address codes. The filter program copies the original object program in mirror-image form. During processing, at each occurrence of a code denoting a device address, a substitute code is inserted to reflect the new address assignment. Since the filter represents a post-compile process, at some point the filter can be phased out,

11

assuming that the necessary modifications are made to the compiler to make it generate the correct results.

The preceding discussion addressed alternatives to interpretive software architectures only insofar as interpreters offer migration advantages. Not all microcomputer implementations can suffer the overhead of software interpreters; let us therefore look at some alternative strategies. Circumstances may not tolerate the speed and overhead inefficiencies of interpreters, but any alternative scheme must reckon with the potential of migration problems.

In very small systems there may be insufficient memory and media to accommodate compiler or assembler programs. Hosting is one solution: The compiler or assembler software is resident on a different, larger system, and the programming operations are accomplished on this host. The object program generated by the host is then copied to a medium common to the end-use microcomputer. The obvious disadvantage to this strategy is dependency. New supportive software may be required if the host system is replaced or if the microcomputer is exchanged for one of a different architecture. Where the owner of the host and the microcomputer is the same, the risks are considerably reduced.

The first-choice alternative to interpreters, for those microcomputers with sufficient capacities, is assemblers or compilers that generate their own native object code. Of these two (assemblers or compilers), the preference is for higher-level language compilers. Even though the compiler may not offer the extremes of optimization possible with machine assemblers, a migration strategy can be formulated around the possibility of a new compiler program for the chosen language to execute on a replacement system.

Macrolanguage generators are another alternative to interpretive software systems. A macro is a subprogram or routine written in native code to accomplish a particular data processing problem. Each such routine is identified by a unique symbolic name. The programming language consists of these macro identifiers. A program generator is used to bind the programmer-supplied list of names together into a run unit. One form of implementation is to prepass copy the specified routines from the library of macroprograms. The output thus generated consists of object code modules arranged in the intended excution sequence. An alternative design method is to delay the binding process until run time. The symbolic names of the macroroutines are loaded directly into memory, and the associated routines are called into play as each name is encountered. This method of implementation avoids replication of the macroroutines, but presupposes random-access file media and the avaiability of the entire macroprogram library at run time.

When considering macrolanguages as an alternative to interpreter implementations, the relative merits of each must be recognized. The use of macroroutines tends to be favored where the variety of applications is relatively small. Overhead burdens for large macro libraries rapidly exceed that of interpreters. These two software architectures have much in common. The primary difference is one of functional orientation. Macroroutines are written to accomplish particular processing problems; interpretive strings are designed to equate programming-language commands to specific machine sequences.

While macrolanguages can be a viable alternative to interpreter-based software systems, the problems of migration and program transportability must be reconciled. Migration of applications written with macrocommands is dependent on a library of macroroutines in the machine language of the replacement system. The exchanging of application programs is restricted to users who are equally familiar with the macrolanguage and who have available the necessary macroroutines for their respective systems.

In reviewing these alternatives to interpreter architectures it is important to note each has disadvantages associated with hardware replacement and restrictions on user exchange of application programs. Some of these alternatives result directly from the technological dynamics of the computer industry. Others have evolved from the desire of users to remain independent of absolute hardware choices. Although interpreter systems suffer speed and overhead burdens, they should not be dismissed lightly in favor of their alternatives.

Chapter

Microcomputers

At the crux of a microcomputer is the *microprocessor.* The cumulative effect of large-scale integration (LSI) technology has resulted in low-cost manufacture of complete microcomputers about the size of this book. Although the processor chip and its related integrated circuits (ICs) constitute a complete computer, effective data processing for business applications requires larger (and usually more expensive) peripheral devices.

Notwithstanding the boxy-looking attachments, it is still the microprocessor component that determines all that can occur. The birth of this commercial bonanza can be traced to the release of the Intel Corporation 4004 in 1971. Barely three years elapsed until the advent of the Intel 4040, a hopped-up successor to the 4004. All during the early 1970s, the highly competitive electronics industry released many technological copies of the Intel 4004, at least in concept, and sometimes in function. The geometric expansion of this innovation led to a 1977 offering of more than two dozen commercially available microprocessors.

From the viewpoint of the software designer, the distinguishing characteristic of microprocessors is their word length. Generally, there are 4-bit micros, 8-bit micros, and 16-bit micros. Two advantages may be ascribed to the successively higher-bit quotations. Larger command sets are possible with a greater number of bits—literally, more bits can be parallel transported through the processor in a given amount of time. The larger-capacity processors also have greater speeds and additional features, mainly because they represent more recently developed technologies than their smaller cousins.

As an example of this maturing process, Intel Corporation's 1975 micro central processing unit (CPU), their third-generation processor (Intel 8080), is more than five times faster than the original 4004. This fivefold increase (from 10.8 to 2 microseconds cycle time) is indicative of the acceleration of electronics engineering; and this snapshot spans only a four-year era.

14

This chapter is divided into three sections, with the orientation of each aimed at the programming facets of 4-bit, 8-bit, and 16-bit micros. The appropriate selection of a specific micro is a task of the computer system designer. The software architect is not always able to contribute to this choice, but it remains to his advantage to know what is available. Since there are genetic and family ties between some of the commercial processor chips, adolescent software systems have some potential for migration. By the same token, an appreciation of the evolutionary aspect of modern microprocessors can only have salubrious consequences for the professional software writer.

2.1   The 4-Bit Micro

The Intel 4004 is the first micro discussed because it was the forerunner of modern microprocessor products. Although somewhat stilted when compared with later editions, the 4004 is still quite heavily used in commercial appliances. Full-fledged microcomputer systems have opted for more powerful CPU chips in recent years, but this primitive granddaddy is holding its own for certain specific applications.

Compared to state-of-the-art electronics, the instruction cycle time is no longer viewed as particularly fast. Engineering specification sheets for the Intell 4004 cite a 10.8-microsecond instruction cycle time, that is, the average time to fetch, decode, and excute one machine-language instruction. While 92,000 instructions per second may seem slow to some, Ptolemy would have been suitably impressed.

The native command set of 46 instructions includes conditional branching, subroutine jump capability, and indirect fetching. Both binary and decimal arithmetic are provided for.

The 4-bit internal data bus provides data pathways between an accumulator, a work register, the ALU (arithmetic logic unit), the instruction register, an address stack, and a scratchpad index register stack. The accumulator, its associative temporary register, and the ALU are 4-bit units. The instruction register is 8 bits wide, and the scratchpad stack is composed of eight pairs of 4-bit multiplexed registers. The multiplexed address stack includes the program counter and three additional 12-bit registers, which operate like the scratchpad stack in a push-down, pop-up manner.

The 4-bit bidirectional data bus provides access to both the read only memory (ROM) and random access memory (RAM) storage. Up to sixteen 4-bit input ports and sixteen 4-bit output ports may be directly addressed. The CPU can directly address 4096 8-bit instruction words of microcode program memory and 1280 4-bit words of random-access data storage.

Eight clock periods constitute one machine cycle. Machine-language instructions are either one or two words in length. A one-word instruction is divided into two 4-bit fields. The upper 4 bits are the operation code and the lower 4 are the operand or command modifier. For two-word instructions the second word contains either memory address values or immediate literal data. To fetch a one-word instruction requires eight clock periods (one complete machine cycle). A double-word instruction requires two instruction cycles (16 clock pulses).

Only five of the 46 native-language instructions are of the two-word variety, and four of these are jump instructions. The remaining double-word instruction is an immediate direct fetch from ROM instruction that permits a destination designation for one of the eight index register pairs.

Eleven additional instructions are categorized with the five double-word instructions into a group known as the machine instruction class. The programmer's friend, the NOP (no operation), is included. An addition and subtraction command provides for register-to-accumulator operations complete with carry or borrow capability.

Any one of the 16 index registers may be incremented by a single command that has register-specification capability. Three instructions involve register-to-accumulator moves. One of these, the load command, will copy the contents of any of the 16 scratchpad registers to the CPU accumulator. The exchange instruction provides for swapping the contents of any of these registers with accumulator contents.

The branch back and load instruction loads data to the accumulator and effects a one-level (down in the stack) branch. A load accumulator from memory and an indirect register load from ROM complete the list of commands associated with the machine instruction group.

The input-output and RAM instruction group comprises another 16 machine-language commands. Included in this group are four read and four write instructions, which work in conjunction with the accumulator to transferr data from or to previously selected random-access memory status characters. A previously selected RAM character may be read into or written from the accumulator with one of two commands provided for this purpose.

Addition with carry and subtraction with borrow against the accumulator, designating a RAM address, involves two additional instructions. Input-output port operations involving accumulator contents use either of two separate commands. The remaining two instructions within this group are associated with RAM ports and the accumulator and provide for read or write functions, referring to previously selected port designations.

Fourteen commands make up the accumulator instruction group. Two of these are clearing instructions, one affecting both the accumulator contents and the carry status, the other affecting the accumulator only. Values contained within the accumulator may be incremented or decremented by use of individual commands for this function. Two instructions provide for complementing either the carry status or the accumulator contents. Two accumulator rotation commands (including carry) facilitate either right or left shifting.

Three instructions provide for program management of the carry status. A *set carry* command does just that, and the *transmit carry* instruction works against the accumulator, with the carry being cleared upon execution. Similarly, a *transfer carry* for substraction clears the carry. Binary-to-decimal adjustment of accumulator values substantiates the dual arithmetic capability of this processor. The remaining two commands include a command line designator and a binary code converter (accumulator contents, from one-out-of-four code).

The newer, more popular, Intel 4040 microprocessor is an enhanced version of the 4004 that retains all of the functional capabilities of its predecessor. The entire command set of the 4004 is available with the 4040, and an additional 14 instructions serve to bring the repertoire to 60. Especially significant to this bigger brother of the first 4-bit CPU is logical operation commands, input-output interrupt, and direct-from-program-memory read capability. Single-step execution provisions are inherent to the newly added halt command. Other enhancements include memory addressability to 8-kilobyte (8192-byte) ranges, eight more scratchpad registers, and an increased limit of seven nested subroutine jumps.

The 14 new commands were added to the machine instruction group of the 4004 set, covering the binary range 0000 0001 through 0000 1110, and they are all one-word commands. Leading the list is the halt command, which when executed causes a programmed stop of CPU cycling.

Registers 4 and 5 may be used for logical OR operations and registers 6 and 7 can involve logical AND operations. All four of these commands use the accumulator in conjunction with a designated register. Command register content can be copied to the accumulator and a *branch back* with *send register control* are two more additions.

The increased memory addressability and the larger register stack depend on bank selector commands (two each for memory and registers). The *read program memory* instruction will fetch half-byte increments per command execution, and simple interrupt capability is provided by the remaining two command additions—one to enable and one to disable the interrupt status.

Although restrictive in terms of power, capacity, and speed, the two Intel microprocessors described here are representative of several that are available, and their versatility is exemplified by an ever-increasing application base. A cursory survey of the surplus market indicates that these units can be purchased in small quantities for well under $5 each. Depending on end-use requirements, the total on-board cost of all of the components necessary for a complete computer, disregarding power supplies and peripherals, may be as low as $50—a very impressive figure when compared to the several thousands of dollars that would have been required for comparable capabilities 20 years ago!

2.2 The 8-Bit Micro

This section also leads off with the Intel Corporation's products, as they tend to be representative of 8-bit processors. Technological leapfrogging is characterized by similarity comparisons of the 4-bit micros and the 1971 follow-on release of the Intel 8008. The most singular difference between the 8000 series and the 4000 series is the 8-bit-wide internal data bus. Although the 8008 offers slower cycle times than the 4000 series, double the data can be parallel-transferred during CPU execution.

Manufacturers of data processing equipment soon took advantage of the 8-bit architecture, primarily because of the direct compatibility with traditional 8-bit-byte subsystem devices. Another significant implementation restriction of the 4000 series was no longer imposed; with the 8008, 14-bit addressing permits direct access to 16,384 words of memory, consisting of any mix of RAM, ROM, or shift register type. A speeded-up 8008 (20-microsecond cycle time) was designated the 8008-1, and its 12.5-microsecond instruction cycle time compares favorably with the 4004 and the 4040.

The chip price is higher for these models, but a READY control signal enables

17

interfacing of the 8008s to any type or speed of semiconductor memory components.

Instruction formats for the Intel 8008 are either 1, 2, or 3 bytes in length. The single-word instructions are typically for register-to-register commands, memory reference, input/output (I/O) arithmetic or logical operations, and the rotate and return commands. The immediate mode commands use one byte for the operation code, the succeeding byte contains the related operand. Jump or call instructions use the first byte for the op code, and two additional bytes to contain the low- and high-order address values.

The 48 instructions in the command set are data-manipulation oriented and are grouped by the designations: index register, accumulator, basic set, program counter (and stack control), I/O, and the machine instruction for halt. The halt command works to cause the CPU to suspend execution until an interrupt is signaled.

Index Register Group, Seven Commands

A one-word command provides for register moves between any of the six 8-bit data registers. Two additional register move commands affect content transfers between the scratchpad registers and the memory address register; the only difference in these commands is for directional designation. An increment and decrement instruction may be targeted for any of the data registers. The only two-word register commands are for direct loading of either the memory address register or one of the data registers with an immediate operand literal.

Accumulator Group, 12 Commands

The ALU instructions all affect the flag flip-flops, but the rotate commands (the next group) affect only the carry flip-flop. This group is equally divided into addition and subtraction commands, six for each type of function. Basic arithmetic functions can involve pairs of data registers, or the memory address register and any of the others, or one of the registers and an immediate literal operand. In all such processes, an overflow sets the carry flag and an underflow sets the borrow flag. It is significant to the software writer that all arithmetic is in binary, and decimal conversions when necessary require subroutines of machine-language code to accomplish them.

Basic Instruction Set

The basic instruction set consists of four groups of logical operations (three commands each) and four instructions for rotational shifts. The logic group provides for AND, exclusive-OR, inclusive-OR, and compare functions. Within each, separate commands can denote register pairs, any register and the memory address register, or any register with an immediate 8-bit operand. Two pairs of rotate commands are provided for left or right shifting, either with or without the carry, all otherwise affecting the accumulator contents by bit incremental designation.

18

Program Counter and Stack Control Group

An *unconditional jump* and an *unconditional call* command is provided, and their function can be derived from their name. Eight *conditional jumps* and eight *conditional call* commands are available, with each group of eight evenly split between true and false qualifications. The four conditions that may be specified reference the flip-flops, one each for *carry, zero, parity,* and *sign* content. The *return* and *reset* are counterparts, *return* working to push down the stack and *reset* triggering the pop-up operation.

Input-Output Instructions

Each of these two commands is a single-word instruction, relating selected input or output ports to the accumulator (implicitly designated) for character-level data transfers.

The inherent limitation of this architecture is still the CPU's internal restriction of seven nested jumps, and the lack of any automatic decimal conversion is noticeable. System-design cost considerations still make the Intel 8008 attractive, as it requires only two voltage levels for power—power supply units often escalate total computer costs.

The Intel 8080, a cousin of the 8008, was until late 1975 the leading 8-bit micro. Although more expensive, this *n*-channel LSI chip offers the user a high-performance solution for both control and data processing applications. Founded somewhat on the same architectural principles as the *p*-channel Intel group, there is no special comparison between them in terms of electronic design criteria.

The Intel 8080 has six 8-bit general-purpose registers and a single 8-bit accumulator. Four program test flags are associated with arithmetic and logic operations, and a fifth flag controls decimal arithmetic functions. Especially significant is the external stack feature, which permits any section of memory to contain the last-in, first-out stack to store or retrieve the accumulator, flags, registers, and the program counter. A stack pointer (16 bits) is used to control memory addresses, ranging up to 65,536 8-bit words. Input-output port addressability can include 256 each, input and output, and all are capable of 8-bit-byte (character) transfers.

The accumulator instructions include provisions for both basic arithmetic and logical operations, with direct, indirect, and immediate addressing capabilities.

The *move, load,* and *store* groups can handle either 8- or 16-bit data transfers between memory, working registers, and the accumulator, again with direct, indirect, and immediate modes possible.

Program branching is provided with *jump, jump conditional,* and *computed jump.* The ability to call and return from subroutines is provided both conditionally and unconditionally. The *restart* command is used for interrupt vectoring operations.

Double-precision operators for stack manipulation and double-add instructions are versatile facilities inherent to this microprocessor. Incrementing and decrementing commands can affect memory, the six general-purpose registers, and the accumulator, and an extended mode works for register pairs and the stack pointer. Shift rotations affect the accumulator, left or right, with or without the carry bit.

19

Input and output operations may involve memory addresses as ports, or by direct access to selected I/O ports. The last group includes special instructions such as the NOP and HALT. Both the accumulator contents and the carry bit have unique instructions to effect complementing them, and binary-to-decimal conversion is a provided command. An *exchange* instruction completes the list; its utility provides for swapping the contents of register pairs.

All in all, the Intel 8080 is powerful, considering the range of versatility packed into one LSI package. The memory stack capability removes all restrictions on the number of nested jumps possible, and double-precision arithmetic capability for both binary and decimal values is comparable to many minicomputers.

Vectored interrupts and DMA is implemented by some product vendors, and when available they offer distinct advantages to the software writer. The physical limit on memory addressing of up to 65,536 bytes poses a restriction for some applications, and the programmer must be cognizant of this constraint. Depending on the speed of the various components contained within the total computer design, instruction speed of execution can approach the physical limit of the CPU, which is rated at 2 microseconds—highly satisfactory for a wide variety of microcomputer applications.

2.3 The 16-Bit Micro

By the 200th anniversary of the United States there were over two dozen micro CPU chips available for general computer-manufacturing use, including highly enhanced versions of the early 8-bit types, at least two 12-bit, and a half dozen 16-bit varieties.

Zilog Incorporated is the maker of the Z80, an 8-bit software-compatible substitute for the Intel 8080A. Of special interest to software system designers is the jump to 158 machine instructions for the Z80 (from 78 for the 8080A). Increased addressing modes (indexed, relative, and bit) and memory-to-memory block moves are significant advantages. Similarly, a *load and increment* instruction is character-oriented and permits moving up to 64,000 bytes with only one command. And a *byte search and compare* (or exit on decrementing to zero) function can be accomplished with another of the Z80 powerful instructions.

A cursory review of trade journals indicates a PDP-8 (Digital Equipment Corporation) population in excess of 70,000 systems. This highly popular minicomputer, first released in 1964, now faces a micro CPU imitator: the IM6100, a 12-bit microprocessor offered by Intersil Corporation. And, most important, existing PDP-8 software can run on a microcomputer based on the IM6100 chip CPU.

The intent of these brief remarks is to intimate technology trends toward incorporating into microprocessors features and functions traditionally available only with minicomputers.

Texas Instruments, Inc. (of calculator fame), offers the TMS9900 a 16-bit microprocessor. Fast interrupt response and programming flexibility are provided through the use of a memory-to-memory architecture, including memory-resident multiple reg-

20

ister files. And as would be expected from a pioneer of LSI calculator technology, the TMS9900 includes an on-chip multiply and divide command capability.

This 64-pin IC has an advanced instruction set comparable to many minicomputer designs. The unusually large number of pins allows fully parallel 16-bit data bussing with a separate 15-bit addressing bus. Direct addressing of memory ranges to 65,536 bytes, with a word length of 2 bytes. All word boundaries begin on an even byte address, and either the even or odd byte may be accessed by byte-oriented instructions.

Sixty-six main memory words are reserved for CPU requirements. The first 32 words of memory (64 bytes) are used for storing interrupt vectors. The second block of 32 words (contiguous to the first block) are for the extended operations involving software *instruction trap vectors.* The high-order two-memory words (hex address FFFC and FFFE) are used to contain the user program base address information, and these values are established during program loading and initializing operations.

A unique implementation of scratchpad registers with the TMS9900 is especially advantageous to the system programmer. Multiple register files may be established in main memory, and a special CPU workspace pointer is used (program alterable) to identify the base address of a specific scratchpad file. Saving work register values merely requires changing the pointer value to a different file area. This capability is useful for programming operations such as servicing interrupts. When jumping from one subroutine to another, it is sometimes necessary to save register values in most systems, but to do so often requires numerous programming instructions. By simply designating a different register file area upon entry to a subroutine, register values are maintained in the previous stack until a return sequence is encountered. Prior to executing a subroutine return, the workspace pointer address is restored to the value that was in force at the time the call was initiated.

The 16 contiguous memory words that are used for each storage stack may be used for temporary storage, as accumulators, address, and index registers. Several of these registers have special uses for subroutine and interrupt linkage functions. Internal CPU logic uses the workspace pointer value as a base for incremental access to each of the associated register words.

Fifteen levels of priority interrupts are possible; code zero is the highest and is reserved for interrupt resetting, with level 15 being the lowest priority. By masking the priority level with an interrupt, the CPU will acknowledge a less-than-or-equal I/O service request. Upon completion of an instruction in progress, the pending interrupt will cause the program counter and the workspace pointer register to obtain new values from the *interrupt vector table* area (reserved in low-order main memory). The *software trap table* values are used to control the return to the calling sequence that was exited to service the interrupt. When the interrupt trap-out is invoked, the interrupt mask is decremented by one to ensure that only a higher-priority interrupt can be acknowledged while in an I/O servicing routine. Return calling sequence integrity is maintained by the depth of the reserved storage space in low-order memory.

The TMS9900 instruction set consists of 67 instructions. Included are commands for arithmetic, logic, comparison, data manipulation, register operations, I/O, and processor control. Although not all commands may use all of the addressing modes available, eight different forms of program address calculations are possible.

In summary, the TMS9900 offers many features traditionally available only on the larger minicomputers, and it is interesting to note the similarities of the multiple memory register stack concepts with that of the IBM 360/370 computer series.

Future Issues

Beyond the present super-16s it is difficult to forecast the upper limits of sophistication to be offered for LSI microprocessors. There are some indicators to suggest a reasonable prophecy, however. Because of the tremendous front-end costs of designing LSI circuits and the expensive processes necessary for their manufacture, only a limited number of high-technology companies pursue micro CPU development. Another economic limitation is the rapidity with which new designs may become obsolete.

Another limitation on too-rapid advances in microprocessors is their dependence on other LSI components. From a bare-bones minimum of perhaps 20 additional chips, upwards of a few hundred may be necessary to support a complete microprocessor-based computing system. It would not be very prudent to develop a micro for which there is no ready source of support components.

Within the computer products manufacturing industry, identification of reliable second-source suppliers of all critical components is essential. Before the maker of a CPU product is willing to commit to new systems tooling, adequate sources of supply must be known; to be dependent on a sole supplier is extremely risky. For a new microprocessor design to be readily accepted in manufacturing markets, alternative suppliers of identical units must be established. This is traditionally accomplished by licensing agreements between the patent holder and companies in the business of mass producing electronic parts. There again, to entice such companies with a new design requires reasonable prospects for a high-volume production forecast.

A relatively new micro technology is emerging that has also tended to thwart extremely innovative micro CPU pioneering: multiple processor systems. Quantity mass production and competitive pressures have tended to erode the unit prices of many of the earlier high-volume microprocessor products. Due to the relative inexpensiveness of these units, it can be more cost-effective to use multiple CPU chips in one product than to opt for more powerful single CPU designs.

High-performance processing requirements can often be satisfied with relatively slow microprocessors by using two or more, each dedicated to performing tasks that may be logically overlapped. In fact, this methodology has proven so effective that micros are being incorporated into peripheral units of minicomputers and large mainframe systems. This *distributed tasking* concept has the advantage of removing menial responsibilities from the central processor and delegating simplistic control functions to the more intelligent peripherals.

It is reasonable to assume that newer and more powerful microprocessors will yet emerge, but it is likely that the pace of breathtaking announcements is on the wane. Various commercial and economic indicators tend to suggest that long-range trends are toward standardization of a few of the most worthy designs, and increased use of multiple processors to satisfy high-performance system requirements.

Dual CPU system designs offer some tremendous advanced software possibilities. By dedicating one CPU to operating system functions and another to rote functions of program execution, a considerable amount of overlap can be achieved, effectively enhancing the speed of program execution for the user. Similarly, and more germane to the subject of interpreters, a micro could be assigned to interpreter processes, and a second CPU could manage the housekeeping tasks of the application program. The natural extension of this concept is to use additional microprocessors as intelligent controller adapters for the peripherals, thus distributing the processing workload and permitting all units to operate at optimum speeds.

And finally, by use of common-machine-language processors and software interpreter systems, a single common high-level programming language can be used for applications and base software development as well.

Chapter

3 Languages

The subject of programming languages is relevant background to the study of software interpreters. Since the primary role of an interpreter is to translate programming instructions into machine functions, an appreciation of the various language types is necessary to select the appropriate interpreter design.

The two basic categories of languages are commonly denoted by their respective translation processes: *assemblers* and *compilers*. A further distinction of compiler languages is made according to their descriptive methods. Where the primary emphasis of a language is in its ability to define processing requirements in terms of problem-solving steps, that language is said to be of a *procedural* type. The *problem*-oriented languages differ insofar as their facility for programming by problem definition rather than by processing sequence. For either of these types of high-level languages, the effect of compilation is the eventual reduction of programming expressions to machine-language code.

Assembler languages also generate machine code, but they differ from the compiler languages. During translation, each machine instruction generated is the direct substitute of a single programming statement.

As can be seen from the above, the thinking processes of the programmer differ for each of these types of languages. When programming in a problem-oriented language, the process of design is one of describing the elements of the problem. To write a computer program in a procedural language is to describe each of the computational steps to be accomplished without special regard for machine sequences. When writing in assembler language, the programmer's orientation must be to write each of the machine instructions and their processing sequence in such a way as to solve the computational problem.

The end product of all programming processes is native object code. In this section we first examine machine languages. While there is considerable variety as to the number, type, and composition of machine instructions that make up the command sets of different computers, there is a high degree of commonality in their basic functions.

The advantage of assembler languages is programming ease. It is far easier to write lengthy lists of instructions using abbreviated forms of textual commands than as series of numbers. In the discussion of assemblers their manner of working is also explained, since many of these processes are common to interpreters.

The significance of the high-level languages is twofold. First, they are artificial; that is, they are independent of any machine code in their syntactical structure. Second, the advantage to the programmer is in being able to concentrate on solving problems without specific regard for the internal operations of the computer. An understanding of compiler languages is essential to the successful design of their interpreters.

3.1 Machine Languages

At the risk of oversimplification, we can describe computers as being capable of only four basic functions:

- Arithmetic
- Data movement
- Equality comparisons
- Changing execution sequence

The essence of the modern digital computer is the stored program. A computer program as internally stored consists of sets of codes, each code denoting a specific function or processor task. During execution these instructions are accessed in sequence, resulting in one process per machine cycle. Each of the discrete tasks possible within a particular computer is a function of the electronic circuitry provided by the designer of the processor.

The electronic brain connotation erroneously ascribed to computers stems from one of the four basic functions. This seemingly intelligent function is that of *changing execution sequence.* The normal program flow during execution begins with the first instruction. With each successive machine cycle, the programmed instructions are fetched one at a time in ascending sequence, with one discrete task accomplished per command. The normally sequential execution can be altered by, in effect, jumping around entire segments of a program or by repeatedly executing the same series of instructions for a defined number of times.

By performing *equality comparisons* on various data elements contained in the memory of the computer, decisions can be made as to when to alter the execution sequence, and as to which series of instructions should next be accessed. Because one of the basic functions of the computer is data manipulation, and another is making decisions by means of equality comparisons, it would appear that conditionally altering the sequence of execution is a process of thinking.

Without arguing further as to whether or not computers can think, let us examine

25

the composition of machine-language instructions. A component of code that is common to all machine commands in any system is the *operation code.* It is this code that constitutes the root command that causes the computer to execute a specific task.

The operation code (often written as *op code*) may be physically located in various places in relation to other codes, the sum of which constitute a *machine-language command.* A machine command may contain no other codes than the op code, but all commands must contain at least one unique code that denotes the operation to be performed during one machine cycle.

Examples of operation codes that are common to many machine languages are ADD, LOAD, STORE, SHIFT, COMPARE, BRANCH, and HALT. The HALT command is typical of those instructions that have only an operation code. The intent of this instruction, when used by the programmer, is to cause the processor to suspend program execution. The only way the computer can resume processing is through some external stimuli, such as the operator triggering a RUN function.

In the case of the HALT command no data is processed, so the machine-language instruction contains only an operation code. As each program instruction is serially fetched, decoded, and acted upon, electronic circuits are triggered on the basis of the operation codes. Where the command encountered is HALT, the cyclic operation of fetching, decoding, and executing simply stops.

Most of the instructions that make up the command set of computers contain more information than just an operation code. When issuing a command such as ADD, it is necessary to establish what data is to be acted upon. Consider the following problem:

$$X + Y = Z$$

The operation code of the ADD command denotes the function of addition. What must also be known is the respective locations of the data values for X, Y, and Z. That is, it must be established what two data items are to be summed and where the result should be placed.

In the most primitive processor design, a simple operation code of ADD could be sufficient, assuming the following programming conventions.

1 Before issuing an ADD command it is necessary to preload two hardware registers with the respective values to be acted upon.

2 These two registers are denoted as X and Y, respectively.

3 Upon execution of the command ADD, the values contained in X and Y are summed and the result is stored in a register denoted Z. Any previous content of Z is lost.

4 After execution of the ADD command, the values of X and Y remain unchanged.

The *parameters to be associated with the operation code in this example are said to be implicitly* defined. That is, the locations for data are preestablished by processor architecture. It is the responsibility of the programmer to establish the contents of these registers through the use of a command such as LOAD. The program coding sequence must be of the order: LOAD X, LOAD Y, ADD.

More sophisticated microprocessor commands permit designation of one or more parameters in conjunction with the operation code. *Operand* values, denoted by codes within the machine command structure, are said to be *explicitly* defined. An explicit parameter is programmer supplied, therefore the processor makes no implicit assumptions.

The sizes and numbers of explicit designations permitted by language commands is referred to as instruction *bandwidth*. Typically, a microprocessor with an 8-bit architecture employs a hybrid form of parameter specification capability. Depending on command type, some commands permit either one or two explicit definitions. Any operand that is required that cannot be explicitly identified must be established implicitly through conventions of design.

Three locations are possible for data, without regard to whether they are explicitly or implicitly accessed. The first of these possible locations are those called *registers.* The word *register* refers to *memory cells* that are physically contained within the CPU circuitry. Another term, *accumulator,* is semantically synonomous with register, although some manufacturers use this word to refer to a particular register.

A second location for the storage of data is the computer's memory. Memory organization and addressing schemes run a considerable gamut, but it is sufficient for the discussion of machine languages to define *absolute* and *relative. Absolute,* as the word implies, is the *actual numeric address* of a memory cell location. *Relative* refers (at least implicitly) to some given *base.* The *effective address* is the amount of relative offset (plus or minus some numeric quantity) added to the base address. This base address value may be contained in a register (*indexed addressing*). During processing, a special hardware register, called the *program counter,* contains the address from which the presently executing command was fetched. This address value may also be used in a relative fashion, as an operand of the command then in process.

A third possible location for values to be associated with a command is referred to as *immediate.* In a byte-oriented system, an immediate value is that of the byte immediately following the byte that contained the operation code. In effect, in this case at least, the complete command (operation code plus parameter) is actually 2 bytes wide.

The value to be acted upon by an operation code is one of two possible types. *Literal* values are those quantities that are imbedded within the coded content of the program when it is created. *Variable* data values are those that are subject to change during program execution. In the earlier example of the ADD command, the sum that would be generated in register Z constitutes a variable data value. The values stored in register X or Y (or both) could have been either variable or literal. Consider:

$$X + 13 = Z$$

In this instance, X suggests a variable data value and it is to be added to the literal number 13 to produce a sum at Z (Z is also a variable data value, generated as a consequence of program execution).

To explain the contents of machine language instructions more fully, a very simple program for the 8080 microprocessor is shown in Figure 3.1. In this example the design provides for retrieving two numbers from memory, adding them together, and storing the results in memory. The actual coded values, as they are stored in program memory, are shown in *binary* form in the figure.

In summarizing this discussion of machine languages, we take note of the general orientation of the thought processes necessary for writing programs. Once clearly

Step	Command	Bit Pattern	Remarks
1	LOAD A	00 111 010 10 000 000 00 000 000	Load Accumulator with contents of Memory address 128. (Two bytes are required for the address code.)
2	MOVE AB	01 000 111	Move Accumulator to Register B.
3	LOAD A	00 000 010 10 000 001 00 000 000	Load Accumulator with contents of Memory address 129.
4	ADD BA	10 000 000	Add Register B to Accumulator.
5	STORE A	00 110 010 10 000 010 00 000 000	Store the result at Memory address 130. (Sum is in the Accumulator.)
6	HALT	01 110 110	End of problem, stop processing.

Figure 3.1 A 2-byte addition problem in 8080 machine code.

defined, a processing problem must be thoroughly reduced to elementary sequential steps. Each of these steps must agree with a particular command capability of the computer. The remaining task is to prepare a list of the machine-recognizable codes that represent each of the commands to be executed. When loaded into the memory of the computer, each of these coded commands is serially fetched, decoded, and executed, on a one-at-a-time basis per machine cycle.

3.2 Assemblers

A glance at the machine-language program in Figure 3.1 shows the potential for extreme tedium when writing programs of more than a very few instructions. Because of the primitive command set of microprocessors (as in this example of an 8080), a great number of instructions must be encoded to accomplish even rudimentary processing problems. Few useful programs will contain less than several hundred programmer-supplied instructions, and large processing jobs may require as many as several thousand.

There are three major difficulties associated with writing programs in machine language:

• Lengthy binary-coded strings are difficult to remember.

- The programmer must maintain exact knowledge of all memory locations used, and for what purposes.
- The exactitude necessary in writing long strings of binary sequences is fraught with opportunity for errors.

Assemblers overcome these difficulties to a very great extent. By providing for substitution of a textlike form of command, the burden of remembering the binary

Step	Command	Mnemonic	Comment
1	LOAD A	LDA	The word LOAD is abbreviated as LD, and the Register Identity is added.
2	MOVE AB	MVB	MOVE is abbreviated as MV, and only Register B is specified, since in this example the Accumulator (A) is implied by design convention.
3	LOAD A	LDA	Same as step 1.
4	ADD BA	ADB	The second D of ADD is dropped, and Register B is identified. The Accumulator is assumed.
5	STORE A	STA	STORE is abbreviated as ST, and A is the Accumulator register.
6	HALT	HLT	The vowel is unnecessary.

Figure 3.2 Mnemonics: memory-aided forms of abbreviation.

equivalent of each machine instruction is considerably lessened. At the same time, the opportunities for errors are significantly reduced. A programmer is less likely to misspell a word than to make transposition errors in numeric code strings. The words used as language commands with most assemblers are really abbreviations rather than standard English.

The abbreviated forms of command are referred to as *mnemonics*. By careful selection of the various abbreviations used to represent machine instructions, the entire list of commands for a given language can readily be committed to memory. Through practice and repetitive use of these mnemonics, many programmers are able to recall the entire command set for several languages.

Compare the list of mnemonics in Figure 3.2 with the commands in Figure 3.1.

The letters (and any other characters) used to abbreviate machine commands are a function of design of the assembler program used to translate the programmer-supplied commands to their machine-code equivalents. A list of the mnemonic commands and the rules for their use constitute an *assembly language*.

Another difficulty of machine-language programming, mentioned earlier, is overcome with assemblers by permitting the use of symbolic names for memory address locations. In the earlier example, memory address locations, numbered 128, 129, and 130, are actual (absolute) addresses. The *symbolic* facility of assembler (and compiler) languages equates a programmer-supplied name with an absolute machine address during the assembly translation process. In the previous example, the programmer could have chosen the following symbols:

QUANTA   for the value to be located at address # 128

QUANTB   for the value to be located at address # 129

TOTAL   for the address at which the sum would be stored (130)

During the assembly process, the programmer-supplied symbolic names are assigned address values according to the design of the assembler program. The conventions for the use of symbolics are relatively few. The most important rules are simple: (1) duplicate symbolic names may not exist and, (2) any repeated references to a given memory location must use the same name.

Other rules for the use of symbols, common to many assemblers, call for a fixed character-length limit and restrictions as to which characters may be used in forming symbolic names. Some examples are

- No symbolic name may be greater than six characters.
- Imbeded spaces are not permitted.
- The first character must be a letter of the alphabet.
- Other characters permitted include the numbers 0–9.

The exact rules that must be adhered to are dictated by the design of the assembler program for a given language. These conventions are necessary to ensure proper translation of the symbols to machine addresses.

Thus far we have discussed abbreviated commands and symbolic names used to denote memory storage locations. An assembly language has an additional form of expression that a programmer uses.

During processing with the assembler, the programmer must be able to supply certain instructions to the assembler to allow it to translate the programming statements to machine-language instructions. This assembler commanding function is accomplished through the use of programming instructions that, when encountered in the source program, direct the assembler to perform certain actions.

These assembler-directing instructions are called pseudo-operation commands. Some typical examples of psuedo-ops are as follows:

ORG*nnnn*   ORG, an abbreviation of ORIGIN, directs the assembler to establish a beginning memory (absolute) address at the location designated by *nnnn*. In using this command, the programmer would actually insert the address desired in place of *nnnn*.

END   This command, the last source statement of the program, enables the assembler to recognize when it has encountered the end of the program.

PAG   As the assembler processes the source program and during printing of the program listing, this command causes the printer to slew the paper to the top of the next *page.*

RES*nn*   This command instructs the assembler to RESERVE a specified (*nn*) number of bytes or words of memory to be used by the program for data storage areas.

Step	Symbol	Mnemonic	Address	Remarks
01	BEGIN	ORG 203		Originate Begin at location 203.
02	QUANTA	RES 1		Reserve 1-byte storage areas.
03	QUANTB	RES 1		
04	TOTAL	RES 1		
05	START	LDA	QUANTA	Load Accumulator with byte 203.
06		MVB		Move Accumulator to Register B.
07		LDA	QUANTB	Load Accumulator with byte 204.
08		ADB		Add Register B to Accumulator.
09		STA	TOTAL	Store Accumulator at byte 205.
10		HLT		End, stop run.

Figure 3.3 Program source statements prepared for assembly. During translation the assembler program allocates 3 bytes of memory for data storage. Machine-language commands, coded as binary bytes, begin at memory address 206. Program execution begins at address 206 (step 5). Steps 1–4 furnish advice to the assembler program.

In Figure 3.3 the previous programming example is shown as it would appear in an assembly language.

Before we progress to the actual translation processes and how assemblers work, it is important to recall that the command mnemonics, rules of composition of symbolics, and pseudo-commands for directing the assembler are all dictated by the design of the *assembler program.*

Assembly languages are artificial languages, at least in the sense that words, spellings, and forms of expression are sensitive to a programmer-designed assembly program. The output of translation for machine-language assemblers is dictated by the machine-language rules of the intended computer.

First we shall examine what assemblers do and how they work, then we shall explore the subject of totally artificial assembler languages whose pseudo-code object instructions are designed to benefit interpreters.

The process of assembly consists of reading each programmer-supplied statement, analyzing it for form and content, and translating the intended meaning to an

31

equivalent machine-language command fully encoded in binary form, ready to load into the computer and execute.

The data processing problem of translating assembler-language programs into computer-executable form can be reduced to individually defined subprocessing tasks. Not unlike other program design problems, the assembler design can be broken down into successively smaller discrete tasks.

The functions of an assembler can be subdivided into the following major tasks.

1   Parsing: Scan and edit the input statements.

2   Translation: Equate the command, pseudo-op etc., with a code form.

3   Symbol management: Store symbolic names for cross reference; match comparisons; preclude duplicates.

4   Syntaxing: If a command, symbolic name, or parameter is invalid, provide syntactical notation to the programmer.

5   Address allocation: Allocate and maintain counters that denote memory utilization: resolve symbols to actual addresses.

6   Generate machine code: Construct complete machine-language commands using the translated op codes and actual addresses; store object code.

7   Listing: Produce a printed program listing: source statements, object code, syntax comments, and memory addresses.

Figure 3.4 is a simplified diagram of the logical relationships of the major components of an assembler. In actual design, most assemblers are either *double-pass* or *single-pass* designs. Generally, assemblers designed to operate on systems with only serial file devices employ a *double-* pass architecture. High-capacity random-access file capability makes possible the design of efficient single-pass assemblers.

The major tasks may be variously divided in the two-pass design, but the first phase consists essentially of tasks related to input, and the second phase does the processing and the output. The one major task that must be split between phases is that of symbol managing. During the first pass, a table is created of all of the symbolic names the programmer used. This pass reads and edits each source program statement and analyzes all symbols for the benefit of phase-two processes.

Upon detection of an incoming symbol, the assembler first determines if this symbol has already been encountered. If no match exists in the symbol table, this input is considered to be a new name, and it is added to the table. When a match occurs, nothing further is required in the first pass. After the entire source program has been read and analyzed for symbolic names, the table is complete, and the second pass may begin.

During the second pass, whenever the intent of a programming statement is to reference a memory location by use of a symbolic name, the symbol table is searched for a matching name. When found, the location counter for the symbol is substituted for the name, and the *object code generator* routine assigns the same machine address

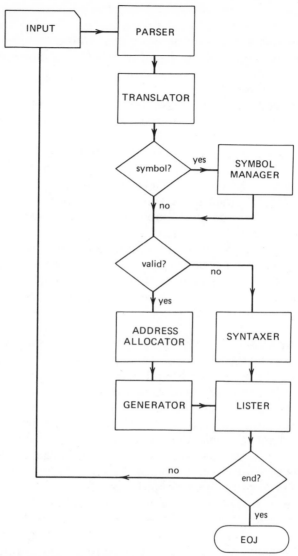

Figure 3.4 The workings of an assembler program.

value for all matching names. If, during the second pass, programming statement attempts to reference a symbolic name that was not detected as an address indentifier during the first pass, a syntax error notation is provided to the programmer. No machine address can be established for unindentified symbols, but many assemblers arbitrarily substitute a special code or *null address* to provide assistance to the programmer. By making such default decisions, the process of assembly can be allowed to complete the translation of the entire source program, *although correct performance is unlikely.*

Symbol table managment is more complex in the single-pass assembler. The major complexity surrounds the problem of what to do when a referencing attempt to a symbolic address is returned as a *no-match* after searching the symbol table. The solution to this predicament can be of two types. Where the statements are being accepted serially, the mismatch can be saved until a later statement defines the symbol, reserving syntactical notation until the entire source program has been processed (if the name is *never* encountered).

On higher-capacity systems, the single-pass assembler may use *look-ahead* a technique to resolve unidentified references: A high-speed scan is made of the subsequent statements looking for the equivalent symbolic name. Normal assembly is suspended during this scan, to be resumed when a match is located *or* the end of the file is encountered. Translation proceeds from the point where the look-ahead scan was initiated, and successive statements must still be fully processed. In either type of assembly process the end product remains the same: machine-intelligible object code, and a concise printout of the programmer-supplied statements, error comments if any, and the assembler-provided translation values.

Thus far in our discussion of assembly languages we have determined their significant advantages: easier programming because of their English-like forms of expression, and the much simplified addressing methods of using symbolic names. Noted also were the artificial qualities of such languages, attributed to the fact that it is the assembler program's design that dictates the grammar and semantic rules of assembly languages.

In the design of machine-language assemblers, the programmer can enjoy wide latitude in choosing conventions to be associated with the format of the input source statements. The output requirements for the machine-language object code are rigidly prescribed by the architecture of the destination computer.

Assembler languages and their associated assembler programs can be totally artificial in an interpretive software system. The output form and content in this instance is a translated pseudo-object notation that is dictated not by hardware but by the software interpreter. This insensitiveness to machine characteristics can be fully appreciated by recalling our earlier discussion of the advantages in being able to extend or expand primitive microprocessor command sets.

In essence, where warranted, new commands can be added to an assembly language by providing for their respective input and output translation by the assembler program. The necessary interpretive routine that recognizes this new command and causes actual machine functions must be created in the native language of the using processor. There is a significant correlation between assembly language forms of expression, their respective assembler program, and the machine language of the computer. For an interpretive software environment, the specific attributes of the native processor is one step further removed from dictating language facilities.

3.3 High-Level Languages

The high-level programming languages are frequently referred to as *compiler languages* (as opposed to assembly languages). As was discussed in the preceding section, the assembly languages offer many advantages. The lengthy process of writing computer programs is considerably easier in an assembly language than in machine-language code. Similarly, the compiler languages offer certain advantages. As a general statement of fact, high-level programming languages offer a quantum increase in ease of use over the assembler types.

There are several schools of thought within the computer industry as to the exact extent of increased efficiencies when using compiler languages. Although it may be arguable as to how much credit should be ascribed to the following advantage points, there is usually a consensus at least as to their merit.

1   **Increased programmer production.** Various studies tend to prove that the net production of programming efforts, in terms of numbers of lines of program statements, is approximately equal regardless of the language used. Net production in this context includes the written source program statements, any debugging efforts required, and any recoding necessary to finally produce a correctly working routine. The basis of this advantage argument lies in the theoretic ratio of 10 to 1 for compiler statements versus assembly-language source lines. An exact comparison of any two languages may give a different ratio, but compiler languages are considerably more expressive than are assemblers, and thus require fewer total lines of programming.

2   **Programmer training.** Computers are very sophisticated and highly complex machines. Since high-level languages are oriented toward processing problem definition rather than machine-sensitive tasks, the emphasis in training is on learning the language rather than the internal workings of the computer. The processes of learning and teaching compiler programming languages is in many ways not very different from foreign language instruction. Essentially the same types of instruction are necessary for assembly languages, but with the added requirement that the intricacies of the computer itself must be understood.

3   **Personnel posture.** A programmer who is thoroughly versed in high-level languages may program for many different computers. A high level of proficiency in any language requires considerable training and practice. Programmers who have spent years developing proficiency in specific assembler languages may be restricted in their job opportunities. Conversely, the owner of a system who employs high-level language programmers also has advantages: (1) a greater labor pool from which to select personnel, and (2) reduced in-house training because of the use of industry-common languages.

4   **Superior documentation.** For several reasons it may be necessary to review periodically the internal design of a computer program. Programming statements written in a language such as COBOL are significantly easier to read and comprehend than listings of machine instructions. The textual format of COBOL procedural statements is so nearly like written English phrases that

35

the program listing tends to serve as a narrative description of the program's design.

Countering arguments often result in discussions concerning which is better, assembler or compiler languages. The first argument of the assembler advocate is usually that assembly languages offer greater machine efficiency than do compilers. A finite comparison of any two language implementations will usually prove that an experienced machine-language programmer can produce more efficient code than a compiler. In some circumstances, these economies in memory usage or processor speed can be as high as 2 to 1. Resolution of such arguments is often difficult because it is difficult to establish if such savings are sufficient to compensate for all the advantages listed above.

Additionally, these controversies must be tempered by an appreciation that, in day-to-day practice few programmers can achieve consistently optimum programming routines. A particular programmer may be able to program faster in assembler than a compiler language, but a compiler language program will execute properly, *sooner,* since in the latter case the programmer's efforts are directed more toward problem content than toward the serial sequences of the computer.

Selection criteria of programming languages also prove controversial. A brief review of the various arguments suggests the following approximate rules (for general-purpose data processing systems):

1   High-level languages should prevail.

2   The choice of an assembly language should be subject to restricted usage, and then only to those instances requiring maximum performance.

3   All applications should be written in compiler languages, but system software and utility programs may use machine assemblers.

Microcomputer-based systems may have to compromise these rules further because of a lack of sufficient resources to implement properly the higher forms of sophisticated software available in their larger counterparts. There is admittedly a considerable burden associated with high-level language capabilities. Compiler programs are often many times larger than assemblers, and a more sophisticated operating system is usually dictated.

The overhead required to support high-level language compilation is not constant for all systems, nor is it necessarily common for all languages. An analysis of some of the standard languages and their respective compiler designs suggests certain practical choices for relatively small computing systems. The following is not intended to criticize the many commercially available languages, but rather to appreciate the various types possible and some of the more typical implementation methods.

A global-level categorization of compiler language types can be developed from the programmer's view of their descriptive capabilities. From this perspective, two types of languages may be recognized: (1) those that are problem-oriented (such as

RPG RPG II), and (2) those that are procedure-oriented, such as COBOL, FORTRAN, and BASIC.

The design emphasis of the RPG (Report Program Generator) language is to facilitate easy definition of a processing problem. As an assumption, RPG anticipates that most data processing problems concern the repetitive functions of data *input,* computational *processes,* and *output* of the results. Further, a basic premise of RPG is that the programming efforts necessary to describe these three functions (input, process, output) is not, on average, in equal proportions. An analysis of the program library for many business and accounting data processing system applications will reveal imbalances between input-output and processes. Such an analysis will show three norms: (1) Input and output descriptions require approximately equal programming effort. (2) Comparatively, the procedural processes required are simplistic and/or highly repetitive, and in total, less than for either input or output. (3) Most jobs are serially cyclic, consisting of one-record input, computation sequences, one-record output; and deviations to this can be handled as exceptions.

Although the basic assumptions on which the RPG language is founded are valid for many installations, greater flexibility is often required to describe computational processes. Such is the forte of the *procedure-oriented* languages. These high-level language types may be further classified according to their respective expression methods. COBOL can be said to be capable of expression of functional procedures. Other compiler languages such as FORTRAN (and its simplified cousin, BASIC) provide for describing computational problems in the form of mathematical expressions.

As a brief form of review of the different programming language types and their relationships, see Figure 3.5. It is immediately apparent that the first distinct categorization is between the assembler and the compiler types of languages. The higher-level language implementations are further subdivided into groups, with still another dimension possible for the procedural languages.

To clarify further the syntactical differences among the various languages, consider the following examples of programming statements, each constructed to solve a simple addition problem.

1 In COBOL: ADD FIELD-A TO FIELD-B, GIVING FIELD-C.

2 In BASIC: LET C = A + B

3 In an assembler:
```
LOAD A    FIELD-A
MOVE AB
LOAD A    FIELD-B
ADD BA
STORE A   FIELD-C
```

The orientational differences can be appreciated for each of these examples, as well as the ratio differences in the number of statements required to solve a problem. The functional expression form of COBOL (1) is more narrative than the arithmetic form of BASIC (2). The example of an assembler (3) requires five statements to accomplish

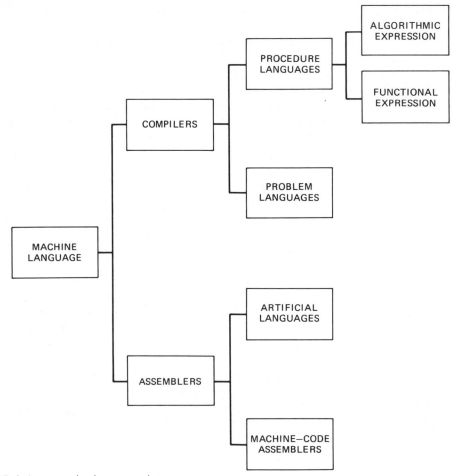

Figure 3.5 A programming languages tree.

the same process that is possible with a single line of programming by the compiler languages.

Notwithstanding the considerable variety in forms of expression for the different languages, the internal design of compiler programs is in many ways common to assemblers. A reason for at least partial similarity is the need to produce, as a final product of compilation, machine-intelligent object program code. In fact, several commercially available compilers are designed in two distinct parts, *the second of which is actually an assembler program.* The first program is a translator that converts the high-level language statements to an assembler-language form preparatory to the assembly phase of compilation.

One of the more complex functions of processing by a compiler is *parsing* of the source statements—that is, the discrete scanning of a line of source code to detect the various symbols, operators, and delimiters. Once distinct values are obtained, before translation can occur, the *semiotic* and *pragmatic intent* of the programming expression must be analyzed to determine an appropriate machine command capability. Typically, compilers read an entire source program, creating various tables of the parsed values. In a succeeding phase, different algorithms are invoked to accomplish the necessary translations, obtaining both operators and operands from these tables.

Compilers tend to be more complex than assemblers, and greater system resources are frequently necessary to support the compilation processes. Although certain processing inefficiencies can be attributed to compiler languages, the degree and extent of these inefficiencies is difficult to quantify. Most of the advantages ascribed to high-level languages concern ease of use and lower training burdens. To summarize: Compiler languages tend to be more cost-effective in the business world of data processing, and where their selection adequately considers system resources they are favorable for use with microcomputers.

PART

2 Interpreter Architectures

Architecture... a method *or style* of structure.

To design software systems requires knowledge, discipline, and artistic talent, much the same as that of other fields of engineering. No pretence can be made here of treating discipline or artistic talent, but a contribution to knowledge is made by providing some of the basic composition aspects of software interpreters.

The first chapter of this part is divided into three sections to facilitate a discussion of possible forms of stored program code used to drive interpreters. The design of an interpreter must consider the intended use of the system. The manner in which a system is to be used tends to dictate the structure of internally stored programs. It is from these requirements that the major functional components of an interpreter can be established.

The practical order of progression is from design to implementation. In Chapter 5, various implementing methods are examined. Once the major functions required of an interpreter are identified, it remains only to decide where and how each may be satisfied. The three sections in this chapter identify certain aspects that must be considered in the internal design of interpreter routines and their storage allocation. Although the discussion is not exhaustive, it is hoped that ample food for thought is provided.

Chapter

Interpreter Types

The basic role of an interpreter is to accept as input segments of code that represent programmer-supplied instructions, analyze that code for content and intent, and cause machine processes to fulfill that intent.

The first examined here assumes that no preprocessing has been applied to the source-language statements, and that the interpreter must act on full lines of programming. The syntactical forms of construction for most languages contain many semiotics intended to benefit graphic representation. These elements, although meaningful to the programmer, are unnecessary to the functioning of the program and actually constitute wasted space when internally stored. An alternative is offered to the full source processor that operates on programmer instructions that have been condensed to eliminate nonessentials.

The greatest economies of internal storage may be accomplished by borrowing from assembler or compiler technologies. Through preprocess translations, programmer-supplied source can be reduced to a codified form for better memory efficiency. A considerable reduction in the complexities of the interpreter itself is also possible with this form of architecture, but it does require a greater amount of supportive software and processing time for the translation processes.

Each of the following sections addresses the system user's view, since it is the application of a system that is most important.

4.1   Expanded Source

A *source code* interpretive system is one that operates directly from *programmer-supplied* language statements. Traditional data processing methodologies require librarying and maintenance of two forms of computer programs. The source program, a

42

machine-readable data file, consists of all of the records (individual statement lines) for a given program. During processing by an assembler or compiler, a second program called the *object file* is created. It is the object program that is loaded into the computer's main storage to accomplish processing. The original source program file must be retained to facilitate program maintenance. Whenever it is necessary to make additions, deletions, or modifications to the design of an applicational program, because of changed requirements or deficiencies in the original design, these changes are made to the source program. A new object program is then generated to replace the previous version in the object program library.

The most significant attribute of a source code interpreter system is that only *one* program file exists. It is the programmer-supplied, *source code program file* that is loaded into the computer to accomplish a data processing job. Since the assembly or compile process is thus circumvented, the functional responsibilities normally attributed to those programs are passed on to the interpreter. Before examining the extent of this impact on the interpreter, the advantages to the operator of this type of system must be noted.

1 *Program maintenance.* As in the more traditional software systems, program modifications are still made to the source program file. Once a change is encoded on the file storage medium, no further processing operations are necessary, save perhaps test running of the new version of the program to ensure the correctness of any changes. Of course, testing of changes is required in any system type, but it is not as lengthy a process here, since preparatory translation tasks are omitted. In cases of extensive changes, where the modify-and-test process requires several repetitions to achieve satisfactory results, this time saving can be considerable.

2 *Simplified library.* In the first instance, two programs are catalogued in the program library for each applicational task. As a minimum, the user of a small system may have several dozen programs; and a few hundred libraried programs is not an uncommon number. The processes of maintenance of such as extensive library, such as maintaining indexes, copying of backup files, and periodically listing program files, can consume considerable time and effort. In a source interpretive system this librarying activity is simplified since the object twin (of source and object) is eliminated.

3 *Reduced media requirements.* Although this advantage is tertiary, it must still be recognized. Actual saving is sensitive to a variety of factors, but an approximate ratio of 50 to 1 can be assumed as an average difference in storage requirements between source programs and object programs. More credence can be allowed this argument where the particular storage medium (such as magnetic tape cassettes) is most suitably managed by dedicating individual units for each program copy.

4 *Simplified operations.* Since no requirements exist for compiling or assem-

bling programs, no documentation or training for their use is necessary, thus imposing fewer burdens on the operator.

The aspects thus far enumerated are considered common to any source code interpretive system. Two different implementations of source interpreters are possible, however, each with its own arguments, both pro and con. The more simplistic of these assumes that all programming tasks, such as source program entry and modification, are accomplished as individual job steps, separate form any activities associated with the running of applications. A design of this type provides separate programs for program creation and maintenance.

The *batch-mode* source interpretive system is especially advantageous when programming activities can be done external to the system. An example of such a system is one with unit record capabilities. Because program source statements may be captured in punched cards with an off-line keypunch, no processor resources are committed during this activity. Similarly, program maintenance is an off-line function, because manual file manipulation is done with discrete records in the form of cards. Individual cards may be added to, removed from, or replaced within a source program file, none of which requires use of the computing system.

An alternative to the batch-process interpreter system is an *interactive* one. This implementation provides for accepting source statement input and modifications as an integral function of the interpreter software. The increased complexities forced on the designer of such a system may be adequately compensated by the advantages afforded certain users. As examples, consider the following systems environments most benefited by an interactive source program interpreter.

1   *Students.* The process of learning to program can be significantly enhanced by the ability to see immediately the cause-and-effect consequences of program entry or modification made possible by rapid switching from entry to execution mode.

2   *Operations research.* Real-time accessability to the source program file permits easy changing of not only variables, but coded algorithms as well.

3   *Software development.* Both professionals and hobbiests can appreciate the facility to experiment and test programs during development, with no lost time experienced while awaiting compilation of prototype programs.

4   *Unstable applications.* Where an especially high frequency of changing requirements prevails (that is, in some process control applications), minor changes are easily accomplished each time an application is loaded to run, with an updated version immediately available for capture.

An impression can be formed as to the differences imposed by either the batch or interactive software designs. Essentially, all of the requirements of the former are common to the latter. One additional functional component is required in a system using an

44

interactive design. This routine performs the tasks associated with keyboard entry of program source statements.

Other interpreter routines have the same requirements, but their internal structures may be slightly different to accommodate the nuances of dynamic program modification. The first of these we shall consider is the *program loader.*

When copying program code from a program source file to memory in a batch mode of operation, the processing flow is serial and in ascending sequential order. As each successive program statement is read it is placed into memory; the process continues until the physical end of the file is encountered. Program execution is delayed until the entire program has been allocated to a storage location in memory; or, in the more sophisticated systems, some program segements may be placed in temporary storage on disk media to facilitate in-run overlaying on demand.

The loader routine for an interactive source interpreter must be capable of being invoked at any time, in addition to the exclusive use time attributed to initial program loading. The simple loader of the batch interpreter is enhanced to accept program source record input from not only a serial files medium, *but from the system console as well.*

The syntaxing activity of the command translation process must be sufficiently extensive to preclude erroneous source program entry attempts that may, as a consequence of invalid interpretation, cause loss of data program memory. This need to check the validity of program source is also inherent to the batch-oriented interpreter, but it is often simpler since it doesn't have to contend with changes occurring *while a program is operating.* The logical placement of the syntaxing function in either system may be at various points, as long as each line of source program is intercepted and qualified prior to execution.

One feature of a software system provides for check-pointing of system status to facilitate recovery from run-fatalities. Suspension of processing operations can be caused by several types of failure during data processing operations. In addition to the possibilities of mechanical or software failure, the interactive interpreter involves another risk factor. Since the operator may suspend operation of the application program, enter modifications to the stored program, and resume program execution, unpredictable (by the interpreter) results can occur that necessitate an enforced abortion.

The magnitude of this risk potential should be fully appreciated before deciding on the overall software architecture for a given system installation. The advantages of an interactive source program interpreter are attributable to the extremely flexible program modification capability. It is possible that in certain applications the extent of this flexibility may impose intractable operation problems.

Consider these points of contention. When designing programs for operation in a traditional environment, the programmer assumes that he is in complete command. His assumption is that he is responsible for whatever occurs, either internally within the computer or with the data file contents accessed by his program. The basic premise of fault analysis is founded on this assumption. When errors occur, it is the program that is usually first suspected. If the operator of a program is different than the programmer, and the design of an interactive source program interpreter permits changing programs

45

in-run, the potential exists for the programmer to be falsely accused of errors. No inference is intended that source interpreters are disadvantageous, but rather, carefully designed safeguards are required in the design of systems for installation circumstances such as these.

By way of review we note the advantages of source program interpreters as being chiefly concerned with the absence of prepass program translation requirements. The simpler forms of implementation assume that program entry and maintenance operations are accomplished as individual batch jobs. The flexibilities of interactive source input, with immediate execution capability, are often desirous, but additional design burdens are imposed on the architects of these systems.

4.2 Condensed Source

The previous section made passing reference to the storage inefficiencies that occur when full source program statements are used as input to an interpreter. In this section a more complete examination is made of the contents of programming-language statements, and some of the ways by which the advantages of source interpreters can be retained in a more memory-economical form than as complete images of the input records.

Certain techniques of condensing source statements into compressed forms have indirect user implications, so we shall first view source program entry from that perspective. To show source code formatting conventions, the syntactical form of the *BASIC* language will be used hereafter, unless otherwise noted. Other languages will be more or less different, but BASIC is sufficiently representative for our purposes.

Consider the following two examples of source program lines:

```
00103 LET A = 5, B = 10
00104LETC=33,D=27
```

Many commercially available software systems permit either form of source line formatting. The graphic quality of line 103 is obviously better than the next line. The spaces between the elements of the source line have no value other than to improve readability by the human eye. Given certain conventions and presentation sequence rules, processing algorithms can be designed to interpret either type of line with equal facility. An immediate space savings is obvious in the second example by the simple omission of the spaces. Counting each of the spaces as character positions, the total storage requirement for line 103 is 23, and for line 104, only 17—a savings of nearly one-fourth. Of course, the crudest implementation convention can exploit this single space-saving trick by imposing on the programmer the responsibility to economize on the use of spaces.

There is another opportunity for the programmer to influence the amount of actual storage required. Note the following program lines:

```
00100 LET A=5
00200 LET B=17
```

00300 LET C=33

Assuming that the logical structure of a programming routine would permit it, these same instructions could have been written as a *compound expression,*

00100 LET A=5, B=17, C=33

An internal space saving would be realized by avoiding unnecessary replication of the keyword LET (two times), and the two additional line numbers (00200 and 00300). In both examples, the run-time execution affect would be identical; that is, the literal values 5, 17, and 33 would be placed in locations A, B, and C, respectively.

Notice also the difference between these examples and the preceeding ones about the use of spaces for graphic purposes. By retaining the spaces between elements on the line and by omitting them adjacent to the equals character, readability is maintained but a savings of *six space characters* is realized.

Only a minimal software effort is required to support an expanded format for graphic purposes and a space-free format for storage. Where the expanded form exists in the source statments as stored on the file medium, *concatenation* (and space removal) can occur during program loading. The program routine that manages this task could be relocated so as to cause a similar savings on the file medium at the time the source lines are captured. To provide for the expanded format in program listings, an inverse process, or *deconcatenation* routine, would be needed to replace the previously omitted spaces.

This concept can be further applied to the line numbers. The first two zeroes (*00*100) have no real value, and serve only to provide vertical alignment of succeeding lines on the printed page. By suppression of these insignificant digits, a savings of two characters per source line (for the range 00100 to 00999) will occur. In a manner similar to the space-suppression algorithm, both an obverse and an inverse routine would be required to suppress the zeros for storage and replace them for documentation purposes.

The concepts thus far enumerated have centered on *omission of insignificant characters* to benefit storage savings. Another practical method of savings for both media and memory space is *character substitution.* In the previous examples, the keyword LET was used. It is not necessary to store the three individual characters (L, E, and T) if a single character code is substituted. The total permutations possible of the 8 bits of a byte character structure are 256 (00000000 to 11111111). By assigning a unique binary code (1 byte) for each of the keywords of a language, a *single character* can identify each possible word or command.

Care must be exercised, however, in the formulation of character-to-word substitution tables. In designing a statement parsing routine for BASIC source lines, a usual convention is to assume that the keyword begins in the first position (scanning left to right) that is *non-numeric,* that is, immediately after the line number digits. Again, a two-way conversion process is necessary where the media-stored source lines contain substituted codes for keywords, to facilitate printing of keywords instead of perhaps unprintable code configurations.

Another popular technique for conserving storage space is *numeric packing.* All of the printable characters of the ASCII code set (American Standard Code for Information Interchange) require 6 bits. In byte-oriented systems, usually a full byte is allocated for storage of each character. As we noted above, a total of 256 unique code configurations is possible within 1 byte of 8 bits. Consider the following representations of numeric values from the ASCII character set.

GRAPHIC VALUE	INTERNAL CODE (HEXADECIMAL)	ACTUAL BIT VALUES
0	30	0011 0000
1	31	0011 0001
2	32	0011 0010
3	33	0011 0011
4	34	0011 0100
5	35	0011 0101
6	36	0011 0110
7	37	0011 0111
8	38	0011 1000
9	39	0011 1001

It is immediately apparent that only *half of a byte* is required to represent the full number range of 0 through 9 (actually, one-half of a byte can range from 0 through 15). If, because of design conventions, we can anticipate that a given byte is supposed to contain numeric values, the leftmost binary value of 0011 is superfluous, hence there is an opportunity to store two decimal numbers in one byte. By dividing the 8-bit byte into two 4-bit halves, *each half may store any of the numbers, 0 through 9.*

The different techniques described so far for condensing source program lines are applicable to varying degrees for any language. There are other possibilities, but they tend to be restricted to specific language-formatting conventions. A term generally used to denote the type of formatting of the preceeding examples is *free-form.* Free-form formatting is characterized by the continuity of data characters on a line, each element following in close succession. Syntactical meaning of program lines formatted in this way is derived by adherence to the following rules.

1 The presentation sequence of different elements is constant, that is, the line number is always first, followed by a keyword, followed by expressions or arithmetic functions.

2 Multiple expressions are separated by delimiters (such as commas).

3 Arithmetic functions use operators between respective operands. (The plus sign is an operator in the expression $a + b = c$.

Free-form formatting is a usual implementation characteristic of languages such as BASIC, FORTRAN, and, in a slightly stilted fashion, COBOL. An alternative formatting scheme is employed with some languages, quite frequently with assembly languages.

48

Columnar formatting is characterized by *fixed placement* of source-language elements along the input line.

In columnar formatting conventions, presentation sequence is fixed, just as with free-form, but additionally, the *relative positional placement* of fields has significance. Since each discrete value begins at a fixed location on a line of code, *no field delimiters are required.* The parsing algorithms for processing columnar formatted source lines are less complex than for free-formatting. Probably the most elaborate example of columnar formatting language conventions is that of RPG. Since RPG, by definition, is a problem-oriented language, the columnarized input of source lines is used to denote *problem specifications.*

It is possible, at least theoretically, to design software systems that provide for either type of formatting (free-form or columnar) for any language. Notwithstanding the nuances of each, and their potential impact on processing routines, selection of one or the other should be based on the mechancial characteristics of the input device and their attendant *human factor considerations.*

Columnar formatting implementations have strong genetic ties to punched card equipment. The mechanical design of keypunches permits programmatic control of field registration and automatic skipping from one field to the next. Because of this, relative spacing of data elements along the length of each card is highly automatic, or at least very easy for the operator to invoke. This facility for easy input, coupled with relatively simple parsing algorithms for processing this format, has made columnar formatting popular for many years.

The advent of modern data capture devices has caused free-form formatting to become more prevalent than in the past. Since most of the commercially available languages predate the CRT (cathode ray tube)-based input devices, many systems still employ columnar formatting conventions. In certain system configurations columnar formatting tends to impinge not only on operator ease, but on software design as well. Where it is desirable to maintain compatability with standards of implementation, or with preexisting supportive software, it is necessary to design so as to use VDU (visual display units) devices as if they are keypunches.

When columnar formatting conventions prevail, methods for condensing source program statements must provide for concatenation of the fields along the data input line without losing their respective identity. A usual solution to this problem is to insert unique delimiting characters between fields. This is a columnar example:

(positions 1–6) LINE NUMBER	(7–12) LABEL	(13–18) OP CODE	(19–24) OPERAND A	(25–30) OPERAND B	(31–36) OPERAND C
—	—	—	—	—	—
001100	START	LOAD	A	25	
001200		LOAD	B	0	
001300		MOVE	B	TOTAL1	TOTAL2
001400	LOOP	ADD	1	TOTAL1	
001500		MULT	2	TOTAL1	TOTAL2
001600		SUB	1	A	
001700		BRL	B	A	LOOP

In designing a parsing routine for this example, assuming that the source lines are stored relatively spaced as in the example, each of the elements (fields) can be detected on the basis of its *relative displacement from position 1.* Two qualifiers are established for each field, *the starting point,* and *the maximum possible number of characters permitted per field.* An arbitrary omission of unused spaces in this instance would eliminate recognition. The implementing technique shown here uses the slash as a delimeter:

```
001100/START/LOAD/A/25/
001200//LOAD/B/0/
001300//MOVE/B/TOTAL1/TOTAL2
001400/LOOP/ADD/1/TOTAL1/
001500//MULT/2/TOTAL1/TOTAL2
001600//SUB/1/A/
001700//BRL/B/A/LOOP
```

The *slash character* used in this example serves to separate the individual values and permits eliminating unnecessary spaces; of course, the presentation sequence is maintained, even to the extent of using adjacent slashes to denote empty data fields. It is possible to produce traditional program listings with the fields columnarized by formatting the print line using the slashes as delimiters (and suppressing the printing of the slash character).

For the convenience of the operator, the *space character* is a more desirable delimiter than the unhandy *slash* on some keyboards. Whichever character is chosen, care must be taken to ensure that it is used as a delimiter only, and has no semiotic value within the source-language statements.

In summary, then, it is advantageous to condense source program statement lines to better economize on the use of memory (and file storage media). Two practical techniques for creating condensed input records are (1) suppression of unessential characters, and (2) code substitution for keywords and similar constants. Whether free-form or columnar formatting conventions apply, presentation sequence of elements of a line must be maintained, and delimiters are required to denote field identities. If it is desired to economize media storage by condensing source lines at the time of capture, inverse or expansion routines are necessary to reestablish graphic quality documentation.

4.3   Object Code

The internally stored program code can be of two forms. The first two sections of this chapter discussed using *programmer source* line notations for the purpose of system resident storage. An alternative form of internal representation is *program object code.* The distinguishing characteristics of each are as follows.

1   Source program code (both expanded and condensed) preserve the sequence of entry of lines of code and respective elements within each line.

2 Programs internally stored in object form do not necessarily retain any commonality with original source statements, at least with regard to presentation sequences, either successive lines or fields within individual lines.

With the possible exception of machine-language assemblers, sequence presentation conventions of programming languages have no particular relationship to either memory organization or machine command structures. The assembly languages maintain execution sequence alignment between source and object for procedural instructions, but not necessarily for fields within statements.

It may be recognized, then, that regardless of the software system chosen, at some point in the translation processes, *transformation* may take place. In language implementations using assembler or compiler processes, this transformation is accomplished concurrently with translation from source code expressions to object code format.

In a software interpretive system a variety of methodologies is possible as to when and where translation and reformatting of source code lines occurs. A scheme similar to assemblers and compilers would use a preprocess translator. This translator (either assembler or compiler, depending on the language) would accept each of the source lines as input, analyze it for content, and generate as output a *pseudo-object program* file. It is this object program that is internally loaded into main memory to be further interpreted at execution time.

The significant advantage of a system that operates on a pseudo-object code format is removal of the burdens for translation from the run-time interpreter. Since pseudo-object instructions can be constructed to the maximum benefit of the interpretive processes, significant speed and storage advantages can accrue. Not only is the object form more conservative in its use of memory, the interpretive routines themselves are shorter. The transliterations accomplished by the preprocessor enable less complex routines to support the simpler code forms.

Before discussion of the practicalities of pseudo-object composition, their use should be reviewed from an operations perspective. The same pro and con considerations apply to pseudo-object systems as to the machine objects discussed in Section 4.1. In addition, from the analyst's point of view another level of complexity exists.

In a software interpretive system using as its driving force a pseudo-code instruction form, three languages are involved: (1) the source programming language, (2) the pseudo-object, or interim language, and (3) the machine language of the processor. Although the operator may not be aware of this multiplicity of languages, the system analyst most assuredly is. In the event of software failure, fault diagnosis may require detailed analysis of all three levels of software. Depending on the maturity of each portion of the software system, the usual priority in debugging efforts is (1) the application program, (2) the assembler (or compiler), and (3) the machine-language interpretives.

The potential for increased software maintenance complexities should not be overlooked. The normal consequence of locating an error or deficiency of design in a compiler, assembler, or interpretive routine is a follow-on effort to patch or otherwise modify the faulty component. The very close interdependencies among a programming

51

language, its translation processes, and the interpretive software system can frequently cause a domino effect when changes are necessary. Also, the impact ratios for the different software components requiring modification are not necessarily proportional. As an example, a relatively nominal language change can cause extensive overhaul to an interpreter.

One of the prime considerations, in the formulation of pseudo-object code structures, then, is to facilitate maintenance of both the interpreter and the object code generator routines and any supporting programs.

A practical approach to formulating a pseudo-object architecture is to allow an approximately equal influence by each, the source language format and the processor command set. In effect, the pseudo-object code occupies an intermediate position between these two extremes. This philosophy has a tendency to distribute the processes of translation and interpretation among the respective software components.

Here, too, as in the case of machine languages (Section 3.1), the common denominator of all pseudo-object instructions is an *operation code.* Since each command sequence is to be acted upon by a software routine, the designer enjoys complete latitude in choosing the content and form not only for the operation code but for each of the elements comprising a particular instruction as well.

The first step in the process of designing a pseudo-object operation code set is to analyze thoroughly all of the *lexical* possibilities of the source language. This process can be facilitated by logically grouping the commands and other keywords according to *type of function.* A possible group categorization follows. These will vary for certain languages, but they are representative.

1 *Data movement.* MOVE, COPY, LOAD, STORE, FILL, etc.

2 *Arithmetic.* ADD, SUBTRACT, MULTIPLY, DIVIDE, etc.

3 *Logic.* BRANCH (on conditions: greater, less, equal, etc.), COMPARE, JUMP (conditional), TEST, IF, GOTO (conditional), etc.

4 *Input/output.* INPUT, OUTPUT, GET, PUT, READ, WRITE, PRINT, etc.

5 *Macro calling.* SQUARE ROOT, LOG, SINE, COSINE, RANDOM, CALL, etc.

6 *Data defining.* ALPHA, NUMERIC, BINARY, BOOLEAN, MASK, HEX, etc.

7 *Pseudo-commands.* RESERVE, ORIGIN, DIMENSION, ARRAY, PAGE, END, etc.

Whether or not data-defining (group 6) language constructs require any recognition within the interpreter environment is sensitive to data structuring concepts, and we reserve exploring these possibilities until later. The pseudo-commands (group 7) generally do not require any provisions within the program object code composition, since they are decoded and acted upon by the language-translation process.

The following example describes how the process of design can proceed from this point. Although this example may actually be used, other implementations are possible, subject to the vagaries of specific languages and microprocessors.

After categorization of the commands and keywords of a language, a tally of the elements within each group is done. Assume the following conditions.

1 The total number of groups is not more than 16.

2 The total number of commands per group is not more than 16.

3 The processor command set is oriented to 8-bit bytes.

The above factors lend themselves to a scheme of using 1-byte codes as object program operation codes. One-half of a byte (4 bits) can be used to denote the command group, and the second half of the same byte can identify a specific command within a group. The command decode process for an operation code of this convention is relatively simple and straightforward. An example of the logic required for decoding and transfering control to the appropriate interpretive routine is shown in Figure 4.1.

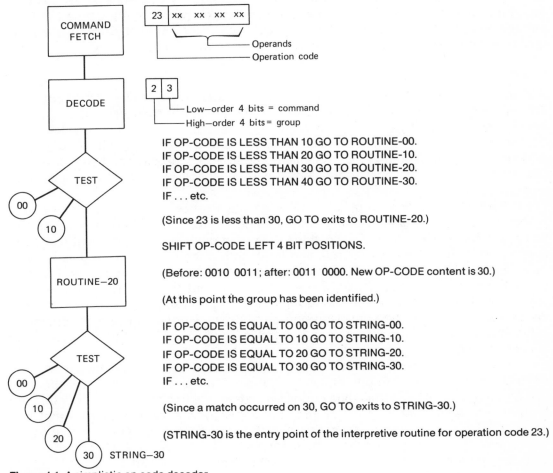

Figure 4.1 A simplistic op code decoder.

To reiterate, the intent of this example is to describe decode logic, and the necessary machine-language commands to accomplish this function are sensitive to a specific computer. Once a tentative design has been established for operation code structures, consideration must be given as to how to address data values stored in memory, and what their respective organizational structure should be.

Three characteristics of a source programming language must be considered in deciding on a data-memory organization plan. They are as follows:

1 Are definition statements required to be grouped together? or

2 May data discriptors occur interspersed with procedural code? and

3 Are both symbolic names and literals permitted as operands?

The relevance of these considerations can be gleaned from the following discussion. Although the logical significance of data content may vary considerably, essentially only two types of data storage occur: (1) data that is normally left-justified within a storage area, that is, alphabetic data; and (2) data that is normally right-justified to facilitate alignment for arithmetic processes, that is, numeric data.

The Fixed Word Concept.

Assume that all numeric storage areas consist of a fixed number of bytes (frequently 8). The address of a numeric field of data stored in memory then coincides with the leftmost byte of an 8-byte group, and the data contained therein is right-justified. This convention may also assume that unused positions to the left of significant digits are automatically zero-filled and that decimal numbers are packed, each byte containing two digits. Typically this convention uses the leftmost half-byte (high-order 4 bits) for algebraic sign values ($+$ or $-$).

Further conventions apply with the fixed word concept for alphabetic or alphanumeric data types. Again, memory contents addressing is based on increments of 8 bytes. The beginning address of an alpha data item coincides with the first character (alpha data is normally left-justified), and the length of an alphanumeric data value is delimited by a final null byte (00 in hexadecimal notation). Alpha character strings may exceed the artificial memory word length of 8 bytes, but the beginning address of a string is a multiple of 8. Note that alpha values less than seven characters in length may cause wasted space in the right-hand portion of 8-byte words, and an eight-character value may waste an entire 8-byte word (the trailing null will occupy the first byte of the succeeding word).

Certain inefficiencies do occur with the fixed word concept, but they tend to be nominal when compared to other implementations. This concept is often practical for use with languages that permit data definition statements to occur anywhere within the program coding sequence. Most programming instruction courses suggest that it is good practice to arrange all data definitions and working storage areas as a group at the beginning of a program. Where the language permits, however, there is no assurance that data definition statements will not occur interspersed with procedural code.

Data headers.

During translation of the source program, a definition statement will cause generation of a code to be placed in memory at the respective address for each constant or working storage area. In a byte-oriented system this code may be 1 byte wide, and the bit permutations possible are sufficient to describe the adjacent data field. A possible implementation of this concept might employ the following conventions.

1 Data headers are placed in the first position of all constants areas, or working storage reserved areas; each header occupies 1 byte.

2 The effective address of any data storage area is the address of the stored header, *plus 1*; data values are immediately contiguous to their respective headers.

3 The two most significant bits of the header (leftmost/high-order) are used to designate field type, that is, alpha, numeric, binary, etc.

4 The remaining 6 bits of the header byte denote the length of the associated field, each bit representing 1 byte (limit 64 bytes).

Whether the additional byte per header in this instance is more or less efficient than the previously discussed fixed word concept is debatable. Specific languages and processors have an influence, as do average program size and numbers of data-defining statements per program. The data header concept provides for byte-level addressing, and no unused areas occur since all constants and storage areas are contiguous, separated only by their respective headers.

The data header concept is suitable for language implementations that require segregating data-defining statements from procedural programming areas. Conversely, the technique of placing header codes in memory at the respective storage locations is more complex for those languages that permit data definitions in-line with procedural codes. Before describing the practical exceptions to these conventions it is important to describe more fully an interpretive aspect of data headers.

During the program instruction fetch process, when instruction operands constitute addresses to be associated with an operation code, a preexecution subroutine is accessed before transferring control to the appropriate interpreter sequence. This routine fetches the data header code for the respective address, and either transfers the data to a work area or preconditions dedicated software registers with the header qualifiers for the benefit of the interpreter routine that must process the associated data. For implementations using variable-length object instructions, or when the numbers and types of operands permitted is an associative function of the operation code, the data header preprocessing routine must be accessed subsequent to the command decoder, but prior to transfer of control to the interpretive sequences.

It was previously implied that exceptions exist as to the applicability of data header architectures. The following selection criteria are not absolute, but they do typify successful commercial software systems.

1   Assembly languages that permit data-defining statements in-line with procedural code: *Use fixed word data storage concepts.*

2   Compiler languages that require grouping data definitions apart from procedural statements: *Use data header methods.*

3   Assembler or compiler languages that use no preprocess translator (that is, the interactive interpreter systems): *Use data descriptor tables or data header chaining techniques.*

With regard to item 3 above, the data descriptor table technique is a variation of the basic concept of data headers. A table area is allocated in memory during program initialization. Each table entry contains two elements. The first value is the data header code (as in the previous example), and the second value is the effective address where the data is actually stored. Of course the header occurs only as a table entry, and is not needed in main storage. All data values, constants, and working storage allocations are then adjacent to each other, fully dependent on identification by their respective headers in the descriptor table. The data value qualification technique described for preprocessing headers applies equally here. The significant difference is in the *command operand address.* The operand value in this instance is the *table entry address.* (The actual data address is the second of the two elements contained in the descriptor table entry.)

Another variation of the data header concept is that of header chaining. This architecture is especially applicable to languages such as BASIC and FORTRAN. Notice two distinguishing implementation characteristics: (1) high-level procedural language, and (2) data-defining source program statements permitted anywhere within the program. The following implementation methodology is viable.

1   When a data-defining statement is encountered, construct an appropriate header code.

2   Allocate sufficient memory storage (apart from the procedural object code storage area) and establish the effective address.

3   Append the effective address value to the data header code.

4   Insert the combined header entry in-line with the procedural object program in its respective location as dictated by the presentation sequence of the programming statements.

5   During program execution, any statement referencing a program line containing a data header will indirectly access the associated data by chaining from the address value contained in the header.

6   During interpretation the descriptor portion of the data header is used to qualify the type and length of the referenced data.

Pseudo-operation codes and data storage qualification have been discussed thus far. A complete object code instruction may comprise other elements as well. Operand values (either data-definition addresses or actual storage addresses) may be appended to the operation code. In the event a programming statement specifies a *literal value* (as opposed to a symbolic storage address), two techniques are available to the software designer: (1) Imbed the literal value within the object code in lieu of an address; or (2) store the literal as a data constant, as if it had been defined by the programmer with a data-definition statement. In this case, then, an address value would be generated and appended to the operation code, similar to other operands.

A usual choice between these two methods considers literal types. For unsigned numeric integers, the literal is imbeded in the object code as an immediate data operand. An indicator code within the object code instruction is used to denote this as an actual data value (not an address), and depending on other conventions, the type of data intended may be indicated (decimal integer, hexadecimal, binary, etc.). Since alpha literals may involve lengthy strings, they are best treated as though they were introduced by a definition statement.

Figure 4.2 shows a pseudo-object code instruction for a prototype interpretive software architecture. This example is intended for illustrative purposes only and does not indicate all of the variations possible, nor should it be inferred that this is the most efficient or optimum design.

In summary of this section on pseudo-object code structures for interpretive

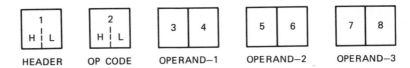

1. **INSTRUCTION HEADER:** 1 byte.
   (H) Number of operands (0, 1, 2, or 3).
   (L) Literal operands code (0 - none, 1 - first, 2 - second, 3 - third).

2. **OPERATION CODE:** 1 byte.
   (H Command group (0–15).
   (L) Instruction number (0–15).

3–4. **FIRST OPERAND:** 2 bytes.

5–6. **SECOND OPERAND:** 2 bytes.

7–8. **THIRD OPERAND:** 2 bytes.
   - Number of operands is variable.
   - Address range is 0000–FFFF (hexadecimal).
   - Alphanumeric literals: 2 ASCII characters.
   - Decimal literals: 0–65,535 (if converted to binary).
   - Literal and address operands may be intermixed.

NOTES: The *minimum* pseudo-object code instruction is 2 bytes (*header* and *operation code*). The *maximum* command width is 8 bytes.

Figure 4.2 A prototype pseudo-object code format.

software systems, the following points are reiterated. The intended application of a system (operation, language, and the processor) suggests certain requirements. From these requirements, major interpretive functions can be established. The functional, internal processing routines of the interpreter tend to dictate object code forms. To the extent practical, the design philosophy should allow equal influence by language characteristics and machine-language structures. The role of the pseudo-object program is to function as an intermediate language between the programmer and the computer. Object structure selections should attempt to balance the translation and transformation processes between the assembler or compiler and the interpreter software routines.

Chapter

5

Interpreter Storage

Because interpreter programs represent overhead, their designers must be continually aware of potential impacts on storage requirements. In the design of interpretive software systems for microcomputers, virtually all planning decisions must be tempered by the need to economize.

The first section of this chapter explains *macro* and *micro* software concepts, which are often contenders in memory-economizing debates. Most high-level languages provide macrocommand capabilities. In an interpretive system, the pseudo-object program is, in reality, a form of language. Just as a programmer may employ macros, intermediate object commands may also invoke macro routines. How this is possible and the effects of doing so are important considerations when designing interpreters.

In the second section architectural considerations are addressed: the appropriate placement in memory of the functional components of interpreters and their cohabitants, the application programs. Effective memory allocation can have considerable influence on the applicational viability of a system.

The final section considers *firmware.* Interpreter systems do not necessarily require that all processing be accomplished by software routines. How these processes may be apportioned and some factors to be considered in the design of hybrid interpreters are noted.

5.1 Macro and Micro Instructions

As the terms macro and micro imply, their difference is relative. A micro instruction is the smallest nondivisable unit of code that can denote an imperative function. Macro instructions are symbolic identifiers for series of instructions that collectively accomplish a specified task.

For the purposes of this discussion, the term *micro* refers to machine-language instructions of the microprocesser's native command set. Macrocommand has two connotations. A language macro, a verb or keyword of a programming language, may on the surface appear no different than any other language command. The difference is one of *internal implementation* by the language-translation process.

The second meaning inferred by the use of the term macrocommand is for a subroutine that is a preprogrammed module, symbolically named by the programmer to be called by programmatic reference.

In traditional software systems, where source programming statements are translated to machine-level object code, the usual distinction between language macros and program macros is determined by their code types. An example of a macrocommand within a language is SQUARE ROOT. Because the calculation of a square root requires many iterative arithmetic steps, a machine-language routine is provided to optimize execution speed. The requirement to compute square root can then be satisfied by a single source statement that calls the square root routine.

Some application processing requirements are repetitive in nature and, when it is practical to do so, canned functional routines can be preprogrammed to be used repeatedly. Notice also that a subtle distinction between language macro and program macro can be made on the basis of their utility. As a general rule, language macrocommands are provided to facilitate *recurring computational processes*. Program macroroutines are designed to preclude redundancies of *application programming*.

During source program translation processes there are two ways by which macrocommands may be embraced. As source statements are being read and converted to object code, when a macrocommand is encountered, the following method can apply. Using the macrocommand name as an identifier, locate the associated string of instructions. Assuming that the routine being called is already in machine-language format, insert the entire string of instructions at this point in the object program being generated; source program translation then continues with the next program statement. This methodology is referred to as *in-line macrobinding*.

The other technique for macro translation is *external binding*. In this case, the storage address for the macroroutine is ascertained using the macrocommand name for identification, *and only this address is inserted* in the object program being generated. During execution of the translated program, when the macrocommand is encountered, a subroutine jump is executed to the addressed routine. Upon completion of the macroroutine, program control is returned to the next command in sequence immediately following the macrocommand.

An apparent disadvantage of the in-line macrobinding technique is *code replication*. For each occurrence of a statement referring to a given macroroutine, the object code string is repeatedly copied into the object program then being generated. The programmer can avoid this redundancy by employing subroutine programming techniques. The source statement that invokes a macroroutine can be contained within a program subroutine that calls the desired macro. The control transfer returning sequence is then from the macroroutine back to the subroutine that called it, and upon exit from there, back to the program sequence that performed the initial program jump.

Either of these macrobinding techniques (*in-line* or *external*) has certain design implications. Of special significance are these: Where is the macroroutine object code? During translation? During program execution?

To answer the last question first, the macroroutine must either be *internally resident* in program memory, or at least be *immediately available as an overlay.* In the case of in-line binding implementations, the macroroutine object code is assumed to be imbeded within the user's application code. Which brings us back to the question of where the macroroutine was during translation.

Allowing the copying of macro subroutines in-line into programs during source code translation implies that they are *continuously and randomly available,* in their entirety, *during program translation.* Depending on the number of libraried macros, and their collective size, a random files device may be necessary on the compiling system (assuming that memory resources are inadequate to contain both the translator program and the macroroutines).

A serial-files-only system configuration tends to indicate a preference for the external binding technique. All that need be available during the translation process in this case is a table of the valid macrocommand names and the preestablished address where each will be stored during program execution. Of course, this address value does not have to be an absolute memory address, but could instead be a relative address value that represents an offset from some common point.

The function of binding external macroroutines with the application object program can be accomplished as a postprocessing routine by the translator. An alternative that tends to conserve file medium storage is to impose a binding requirement on the program loader routine. In this instance, applications and macroroutines are variously dispersed in the software library and the components of a run unit are located and linked together *during program loading.* Although the loader is more complex, macro object code occurs only as single copies on the file medium, rather than being repeatedly contained within each using application.

The subject of language macrocommands is one of *intraprogram* communications. The facility for one program to call another (program macrocommands) is referred to as *interprogram* communication. The significance to be noted here concerns communicating, or passing parameters between a mainline process and a macroroutine.

Computational processes generally involve input and output data (This is not necessarily true of machine steps such as HALT, but such functions are not usually macrocommands.) The structural methods and conventions associated with the passing of data parameters between software routines is referred to as software *interfacing.*

The problem of interfacing language macrocommands with their calling sequences for intraprogram transfer of parameters is accomplished in a controlled, disciplined environment by the translation program. For proper interfacing of interprogram communications between applicational programs, the responsibility remains vested with the programmer. This requirement has a tendency to be compounded by various factors. What was originally designed to be a universal programming routine may not be appropriate for, or necessarily be compatible with, different programs within a system. The scope of problems associated with interprogram communication by program macrocommands has a tendency to increase with larger programming staffs, especially those with high attrition rates. Notwithstanding these complexities, program macrocommand facilities within a software system can preclude many redundant programming efforts.

The internal design of interpreter programs can also take advantage of macrocommand concepts. In the strictest sense, the individual interpreter routines constitute microcoded macroroutines. The interpreter routine for a pseudo-object program command may consist of either a sequence of macrocommands, or an individual microcoded routine unique to a specific operation code.

Consider these examples. Assume that ADD is a permitted programming language command and it is internally represented as a pseudo-object operation code. The interpreter decoder, upon proper identification, transfers program control to a series of machine-language instructions (the interpretive routine) to carry out the intended addition calculation. Since addition is a primitive arithmetic function, common to the microcomputer machine-language capability, a discrete adder routine is warranted. Some microprocessors however, do not have a machine instruction to do multiplication. The interpretive process for satisfying a programmer specified MULTIPLY operation could be a macroroutine, MULTIPLY interpreter.

Instead of a completely microcoded routine for interpretive execution of the multiply operation, an iterative loop structure would call the ADD interpretive until the loop count matched the multiplier. In this case, then, the adder routine is effectively a macroroutine. This example also points up one of the most effective techniques by which the overall size of a software interpreter can be constrained.

Macro software concepts have, then, several implications for the designer of an interpreter. There are the language macrocommands, which are imbeded within the programming language, and their comparative difference to other commands is transparent to the user. And there are program macrocommands, the language facility by which the application programmer can employ macro techniques in the design of libraries of applications.

In-line binding and *external binding* are the two methods by which source program translation processes can affect program-to-macro linking. The alignment of input and output arguments *within a program run unit* is a function of intraprogram communication interfacing. Programmer-defined symbolic macroroutine names also require interfacing rules to allow the transfer of data parameters between programs. Although certain language provisions may be available to facilitate this, the details of interprogram communications must be resolved by the programmer.

The most literal definition of macro concepts views each of the pseudo-object instructions as macrocommands. There is no unique difference in the intermediate object program that distinguishes between language macros and other commands.

As a final note on the subject of macro instructions, an additional terrace within software layering is a suggested methodology for using macrocommands to minimize the overhead of interpreters.

5.2   Software Interpretives

This section is devoted to memory allocation of the various components of the software system. An overall software topography must include memory mapping for the data areas and procedural code storage for both the interpreter and the application program.

Priority consideration must be allowed for the storage of data that needs to be directly addressable by microprocessor machine commands. The extent to which machine commands may range in their addressing is dictated by processor architecture. Actual restrictions vary for the different microcomputers available, and many impose differing limits for the various commands of their respective machine language.

Next in our list of design priorities are considerations for the protection of systems software from any "cannibalistic" tendencies of an application program. The need to maintain software integrity is a prime responsibility of the software architect. The most comprehensive syntaxing algorithms cannot completely safeguard memory content, but judicious allocation of storage can ensure that the only thing subject to loss due to application errors is the application program. On the surface this attitude may seem vindictive, but actually it is quite practical and the reason this is so will be examined shortly.

The last part of this section concerns working storage areas and software buffers that must enjoy global usage by both the interpreter software and the application program. A typical example of global data storage is input and output data buffers. After an interpretive process establishes data record contents in a memory area, it is necessary that other software routines have access to that data. Efficient memory mapping conventions can preclude unnecessary movement of data between remote locations for the benefit of disjointed software routines.

A prototype memory map is shown in Figure 5.1 for illustrative purposes. The basic theme of this topography is to locate all machine-language programming in low-order memory and all pseudo-object program code in high-order memory. One of the more obvious reasons for this basic premise is the assumption that interpreter software is relatively static in design (in terms of memory requirement), and application programs vary in size from one job to the next.

The general flow of interpretive processing is *command fetch, parse, syntax, decode, syntax,* and *interpret* (in the diagram, the number sequence is 6–1–2–3–2–4). The primary task of the *command fetch* routine is to maintain a program counter and retrieve application program instructions. After the fetch routine places a pseudo-object command in working storage, and respective processes of parsing, syntaxing, and decoding can access it.

One aim of this topography is to keep the most comprehensive routines as close to work-data addresses as possible. The purpose is to facilitate use of machine commands that have range limitations for addressing. Compromises are necessary, however, in trying to keep working storage in proximity to the command interpreter routines.

63

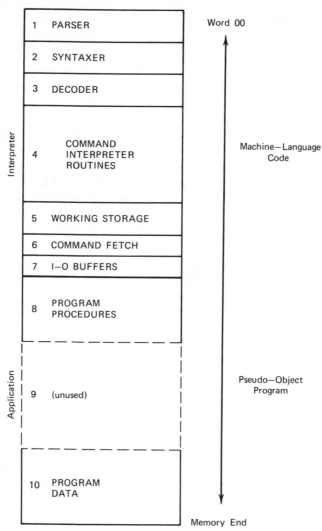

Figure 5.1 A prototype memory map.

The chosen arrangement of the functional routines of the interpreter program is to benefit relative addressing of procedure or data addresses. *Immediate-relative* addressing is a common machine-language capability. (*Plus* or *minus*, incremental addressing from the immediate instruction point.) This form of addressing is usually restricted as to the permitted range. In a byte-oriented processor, for example, the restriction is usually 128 bytes forward or 127 bytes back. (An 8-bit byte can represent decimal 256, thus a 1/2-byte limit for either direction).

This attempt to maximize the use of immediate-relative addressing stems from the need to constrain the overall size of the interpreter program. Wider address operands are necessary to range to the higher addresses, so the intent here is to limit the number of routines that must access throughout memory.

This is also the motivation for locating the command fetch routine near the upper boundary of the interpreter program area. A subfunction of this routine can be assigned to process all data movement activity for the application program data area. Thus, the number of machine commands that must range to the extremeties of memory is wholly contained within one functional module of the interpreter. All other interpreter processes need access only data that is contained within the boundaries of the interpreter program area.

Further clarification is needed as to the nature of the working storage area. This space is allocated for storage of user program data that must be processed by the command interpretives. Special software registers, counters, accumulators, and so on, that are required for individual interpreter routines are located immediately adjacent to their respective routines. This method of allocation further enhances the use of immediate-relative addressing techniques.

The reason for splitting the application program code is twofold. The location of procedural code contiguous to the interpreter boundary permits the addition of procedures, in ascending sequence, beyond the initially loaded program. By *inverted loading* of data constants and allocated work space from the upper boundary of memory, additional data space can be assigned as necessary. This method of assigning memory, from either end toward the middle, precludes assignment contentions that could otherwise occur if the two groups were contiguous. If these two portions of program were loaded as adjacent blocks, additions to one or the other (depending on which is sequentially first) would either cause *fragmentation* or a *relocation* exercise.

The second reason for splitting the application program, and the reason the data portion is in high-order memory, concerns memory security. Any application program attempt to write data to memory at an address beyond logical data storage will encounter the physical limit of memory before any serious (to the interpreter) corruption can occur.

The rationale for containing out-of-bounds addressing attempts within program data areas concerns software failure analysis. It is a wholly false assumption that programs will always work correctly. In recognition of the many trial attempts sometimes necessary to achieve a logically correct program, proper emphasis must be applied to the potential risks.

To explain more fully, allow the following inverse reasoning. If an out-of-bounds, write-to-memory attempt caused corruption of any of the procedural contents of the interpreter, the results would be totally unpredictable. Debugging efforts would be confused, probably because of difficulty in establishing which software component failed. Since the potential exists that errors may be inherent with the interpreter, it is at least initially difficult to ascertain whether a problem is attributable to the interpreter or the application.

Less probable, but still highly possible, are chain-reaction problems. A single displaced or inadvertently modified code within the boundaries of the interpreter may have momentarily transparent effects. A single byte (or even a bit) alteration may be extremely difficult to isolate, yet continued processing experiences compounding errors. As an example, consider a one-character displacement error when accessing an alphabetic string. If the corrupted code happens to be a counter within the interpreter that is suffering extraneous incrementing, by the time program processing finally reaches a fatal error, several thousand instructions may have been executed. A doubly demanding debugging difficulty!

Second on our list of security priorities is the application procedures area. During the analysis of corrupted data values, the ability to ascertain the exact memory contents of procedural object code is a big plus for the programmer. Conversely, if a memory dump reveals corrupted object code within the procedures area of a program, the very instructions that are causing the problem may have been overwritten. Again, a circumstance such as this further complicates debugging efforts.

Without the benefit of clarification, it may appear that contradictory theories have been suggested. One of the primary functions of the syntaxing routine is to qualify both the content and the intent of programmer-supplied statements. In theory, it is possible to construct algorithms that would preclude any illogical instruction ranging attempts. Practicality usually dictates constraining actual design philosophies to a point that is far short of proving this theory.

A reasonable approach to designing syntaxing routines limits their functional criteria to examination of single lines of programming. The risk, though, is failing to detect structural inaccuracies for series of statements. A well-remembered experience of even novice programmers is the infamous program that is syntactically clean but blows up during execution.

A brief example of this type of programming error will tell the tale. Envision a routine that is intended to clear 100 work storage fields in memory. A commonly used programming technique would provide for moving blanks to each field separately with a program loop. On each successive iteration of the loop sequence, a successively higher addressed field is cleared. The series of instructions that comprise the loop contain a test function to determine when 100 iterations have occurred. Even if all of the programming statements for this routine are syntactically correct individually, any error of design that allows the looping process to continue beyound a count of 100 will cause clearing of memory beyond the intended area. If procedural code is located just beyond the designated area, the program will blow up. Much better to let runaways run into the end of memory!

The astute will raise the point of addressing wraparounds. This phenomenon is the consequence of carrying when doing addition. Typically, with machine-language programming, a carry attempt beyond the leftmost boundary of a counter field or register will result in the register being reset to zero—hence the potential to wipe out word zero in the event of an address wraparound by a runaway loop. Register overflows are possible of software detection with some microprocessors, and interpreter addressing routines can be designed to error-trap these conditions. Where software registers are being used, or if the microprocessor does not support overflow detection, more sophisticated algorithms are necessary to preclude overwrite attempts beyond the end of physical memory.

One further point about safeguarding memory contents: As a suggestion to the programmer writing applications for a topography such as the one illustrated, place data-defining statements for the most important data last (in relation to other data statements). Due to the inverted loading method, the last-named data storage is the closest to the center of memory, and is therefore the most secure.

Further use can be made of the center (uncommitted) storage space in memory. As a process of program loading, the extremity addresses should be known. Assuming that the size of program overlays can be ascertained, a halving algorithm can be used effectively to center overlays, thereby maintaining an equal distribution of unused space for additions to either procedures or application data. There are also certain utilities (usually software diagnostics) that can be centered in otherwise uncommitted memory when it is desired that these utilities be coresident with an application program.

In reviewing the guidelines for developing a software topography, the following considerations should be noted.

1 *Software security.* Memory mapping should provide for safeguarding the contents of memory, and the order of priority is first for the interpreter, then application procedure code, and last for application data.

2 *Low-order memory.* The interpreter program should be placed so as to begin loading from address zero.

3 *High-order memory.* User application programs (pseudo-code) are placed beginning with the upper boundary of the interpreter. Splitting program procedures and data has certain advantages, primarily in permitting additions of either type without conflicts.

4 The internal arrangement of the functional routines should allow for maximum use of immediate-relative addressing within the command interpreters.

5 Global work storage should be situated to the mutual benefit of the interpreter and the application program. Special work areas for command interpreters should be adjacent to the interpretives to facilitate immediate- relative access.

5.3 Firmware Interpretives

Firmware is software that is no longer soft (an oversimplified definition perhaps, but true nonetheless). That firmware is considered firm is because the area of storage of firmware cannot be written into by normal programming processes—normal in this context meaning through the use of software routines within a system that can read or copy from a firmware storage area.

Initial commercial applications of firmware concepts were motivated primarily by the vendor's desire to protect system software from accidental (or intentional) alteration or overwriting by user programs. In modern microcomputers this same basic motivation persists, but at least three more valid reasons have been added to the why-list for firmware. These additional reasons have genetic ties to integrated circuit technology.

67

MOS (metal oxide semiconductor) memory chips are volatile—when electric power quits, so do the bits. ROM (read only memory) integrated circuits are nonvolatile —they don't lose their bits, even when power is removed. The use of ROM for at least certain types of software is especially advantageous. The architectural trends of modern computers makes them totally software-dependent. Most computers today are incapable of beginning operations from a power-off state without some type of cold-start initialization program.

In a computer with volatile main memory, in the event of power failure (or even a normal shutdown), some means must be provided to load a program to restart operations. In the simplest implementations of firmware, a rudimentary bootstrap loader program allows copying of more sophisticated programming from a system-resident external media device at power-up time. Storage of this loader program as firmware in a ROM circuit is additionally advantageous because ROM is memory. That is, it is addressable by software routines, is actually a machine-language program, and therefore may be invoked as if it were a software routine.

Another reason firmware ROM programs have gained in popularity is execution speeds. Comparisons of some low-cost RAM (random access) and their ROM counterparts reveals a substantial speed advantage for ROM-based software. DMA (direct memory access) electronic techniques allow memory-to-memory (or peripheral-to-memory) block transfers of data synchronously with CPU activity, affording another reason for ROM firmware preference.

Where software is stored as firmware in ROM, it may be rapidly copied to main memory (where it is then soft) and may then be altered as desired during processing. This implies that virtually any software routine could be captured as firmware for the benefit of solid state storage, but it would otherwise be the same as any software at run time. While this is certainly true enough, the fallacy of a hasty conclusion is in assuming that firmware is firm, but not rigid.

There are two ways by which software may be made firmware. The ROM implementation is an electronically enforced firm storage. In core memory systems (nonvolatile) firmware may also be protected by electronic circuits to preclude any write function accessing that area of storage. And it is possible to employ firmware methodology using software routines to protect firmware storage. It is somewhat debatable as to whether or not programming that is resident in main memory is properly called firmware, but the connotation intended here is for ROM-based firmware that is rolled into soft memory, but is maintained firm through the use of software techniques.

These two different methodologies have different implications for the designer of an interpreter. Figure 5.2 shows graphically the differences for a software topography. The discussion of the previous section of this chapter concerning software topography remains valid for method 2 as illustrated, but not completely for method 1. Specifically, the previous suggestion to place interpretive-dependent working storage adjacent to each command interpreter will not work where the interpretives are executed from within firmware storage. Again, firmware, by definition, implies that storage areas cannot be written into, therefore no work areas may be contained therein. There are also restraints on particular machine-language programming techniques. (These specific limitations are discussed as a separate topic later.) The rationale for the physical place-

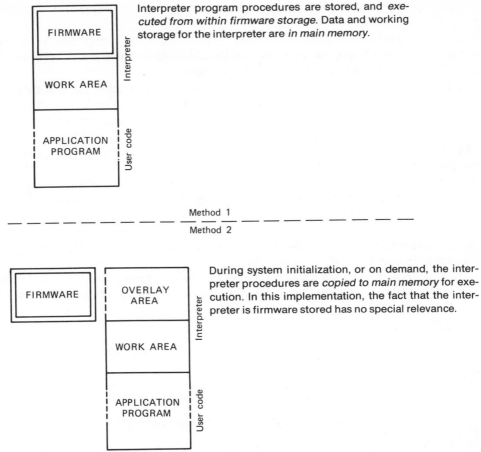

Interpreter program procedures are stored, and *executed from within firmware storage.* Data and working storage for the interpreter are *in main memory.*

Method 1

Method 2

During system initialization, or on demand, the interpreter procedures are *copied to main memory* for execution. In this implementation, the fact that the interpreter is firmware stored has no special relevance.

Figure 5.2 Two methods of storing an interpreter in firmware.

ment of the interpreter program beginning in word zero, is not valid for this architecture either. The characteristic of self-protection of firmware that is electronically protected relieves software designers of the responsibility for safeguarding those areas.

As for the restrictions on programming techniques, a not uncommon programming technique with machine languages is to modify programming commands during execution. As an example, consider the following process. Assume that a program branch instruction is located at memory word 100. In anticipation of later encountering this command during sequential execution through this memory address, if based on a certain conditon no branch should occur, the conditioning algorithm will overwrite the branch instruction with a NO-OP (no operation). Naturally, commands changed in this manner must be programmatically restored (if that is a logical requirement).

As a general statement, the restriction on the use of this type of programming technique may be considered a nominal limitation. There are usually alternative design techniques that are equally viable, and in fact, some schools of thought contend that these tricks are not good practices anyway. In any event, firmware cannot accommo-

69

date these techniques because of the inability to change anything that is firmware stored.

Interpreter design considerations thus far discussed are concerned with explicit differences of using soft versus firm storage for interpreter software. There are, however, some implicit factors that must be reckoned with.

First, during development, firmware is software. The significance of this simple statement should not be overlooked. Designs that are initially intended to employ firmware storage begin test development in a soft environment, but the planners will be cognizant of the requirements of firmware-based software. The risk of assuming that an originally totally soft system will remain soft portends the possibility of a complete redesign if requirements change.

When software should become firm in the development process is a matter of ratios of the accuracy of design and the effort (or cost) involved if changes become necessary. There are several types of ROM circuits that are commercially available today, many of which have provisions for erasing and reuse. Decisions regarding how much, what, and when software should become firm are based on numerous judgment factors specific to each system design.

Some general guidelines can be offered for the what-software considerations. A tentative priority list for what should be attempted first in firmware storage is as follows:

1   Code sets, constants tables, etc.

2   Discrete algorithms for tasks such as SQUARE ROOT, etc.

3   Executive functions: command fetch, parsing, etc.

4   Command interpretive routines (except I-O associated).

5   Data manipulation such as buffer-to-buffer exchanges.

6   Command decoders

7   I-O associated interpretives.

8   Syntaxing routines.

9   Error trapping and memory management routines.

This list should be considered only a guide, and actual implementations will necessitate compromise. The basic philosphy for the ordering of this list concerns delaying as long as possible firmware casting of the more comprehensive routines, or those most likely to suffer changes during development of the total system.

In summary, the primary differences between firmware storage of interpreters and totally soft systems concerns the fact that firmware storage areas cannot be written into. Early-on memory topography plans must reconcile these differences during basic design efforts. Any possibility that an intended soft system might eventually go to firmware should anticipate that eventuality during initial design. Actual conversion from soft to firmware storage involves judgments that are sensitive to specific system architectures and implementation methods.

70

PART

3

Interpreters—
A Design
Approach

Problem: To design a software interpreter for a microcomputer.

A logical approach to solving any problem must begin with an accurate definition of the problem. Development of a solution to a problem can be an orderly process when the definition has an orderly structure. It is the aim of this part to suggest a methodology by which software interpreter problems may be defined.

A top-down approach begins by dividing the scope of the problem into more easily defined subdivisions. Each of these subdivisions may then in turn be further subdivided. A twofold advantage accrues to this approach. Not only may each portion of the problem be analyzed separately, but a proper perspective can be maintained as to the relationships of the parts to the whole.

The first subdivision of an interpreter design problem is the identification of three factors: (1) the software environment, (2) applicable software architectural considerations, and (3) interfacing requirements dictated by the components of the system. Each of the chapters that follow is devoted to one of these respective areas, and each is sectioned into further subdivisions.

Figure 6.1 provides a graphic representation of topical breakdowns suggested for defining interpreter design problems.

Chapter 6 describes a software taxonomy by which a classification can be made of the system attributes, language characteristics, and application requirements. It is these three variables that make up the environment in which a software interpreter must operate.

It is from the detailed analysis of the software environment that

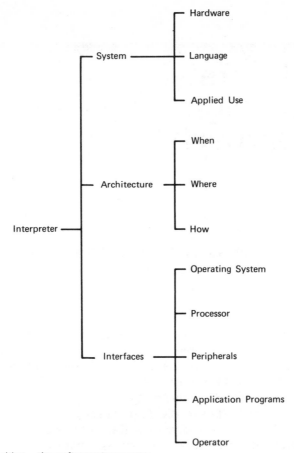

Hardware

System ——————— Language

Applied Use

When

Architecture ——— Where

Interpreter ——— How

Operating System

Processor

Interfaces ——— Peripherals

Application Programs

Operator

Figure 6.1 Problem definition—the software taxonomy.

we may ascertain major architectural considerations. The process of defining requirements to be satisfied by the interpreter involves the basic questions of when to interpret, where to interpret, and how to interpret. It is not intended that implementation techniques be decided during problem definition, but rather, a description is sought for the structural implications of when, where, and how as imperatives.

Since the interpreter commands a central role, it is essential that it effectively interface to the other components of the system environment. The operating software, the computer, and its adjuncts represent relatively static elements that have interfacing requirements. Application programs and operator functions also have conditions and peculiarities that must be satisfied. A thorough identification of each of these is necessary because each represents an aspect of the total problem of designing an interpreter.

After the detailed description and analysis effort the process of design entails functional planning. Chapter 9 describes a charting technique for mapping functional components of a software interpreter. The template method suggested facilitates not only component identification in a hierarchical manner, but the interfacing relationships between components as well. The software template is also subjected to a subdivision process, showing major, minor, and subfunctional decomposition.

To reiterate briefly, a structured problem definition provides for a structured solution approach. A nearly one-to-one relationship can be developed between discrete elements of the problem and functional component solutions. In essence, definition is problem decomposition and design is solution composition.

73

Chapter

6 A Software Taxonomy

When an architect sets out to design a house for someone, he must compose a structured list of all the factors to be considered. He might use as a major subdivision of the total problem the various topics of climate, building materials, and number of occupants. Each topical list might then be further extended to include temperature extremes, humidity, terrain, foundation requirements, age and sex of family members, infirmities, and so on. The architect of a software interpreter system must also subdivide the problem definition, and an analogy to residential architecture is possible.

The software environmental considerations must include the computer, base operating software (if any), peripheral devices, and the operator communications console. Material requirements are dictated by the composition and features of the programming language. And, just as houses are built for human use, so too are computers. Comfort and usability are the primary inputs to human factors engineering, and as such they should enjoy due regard from the designer.

Each of the following sections of this chapter is devoted to describing one of the taxons that influence interpreter planning.

6.1 System Attributes

Foremost on a systems description list is the computer. Adjuncts that are attached to the computer for data storage purposes, and the communications disciplines for the movement of data to and from, enforce certain things on interpreter designs. The console or control panel by which the operator effects guidance or detects operating status requires specific support provisions within an interpretive system.

An examination of processor architecture begins with a study of its machine-

74

language structure. Analysis commences by listing the full instruction set in groups according to usage.

Primitive arithmetic command capabilities require extensive routines to support high-level mathematical computations. The basic functions of addition and subtraction are inherent to all computers. Subtraction is accomplished internally within most microcomputers by inverse addition. Multiplication and division are performed by repetitive addition and subtraction, respectively. Since digital electronics depends on binary arithmetic capabilities, whether both binary and decimal is possible with individual command provisions is significant. Register shift commands can facilitate arithmetic processes. Interpreter routines for multiplication and division that use shifting logic for binary values are often shorter and faster than repetitive decimal methods. Mathematic interpreter routines also depend on working *registers.*

Registers

The number and size of registers must be considered. The most important of these is usually an *accumulator,* the register into which the results of many operations are eventually loaded. In addition to acting as a primary storage location for intermediate results, arithmetic and logical operations depend on the accumulator and specified work registers or memory locations.

The other working registers are for scratchpad purposes and may be used individually or in pairs. Provisions (and limitations) for using registers in pairs are important; most memory addressing algorithms need two registers to contain a complete address value. A *status bit register* may be associated with the accumulator. This special-purpose register is used for storage of conditions that result from internal data operations. Individual bit patterns within the status register provide for programmatic detection of carrying operations from addition, rotation, and so on. It is this register that may also be used for storage of algebraic signs to be identified with accumulator contents. Logical comparison operators use the status register (or some other special register) to identify test results for conditions such as odd, even, or zero content.

Program Counter

A special-purpose register is required to contain the address of the next machine-language instruction to be executed. It is also required that this register be of sufficient width to accommodate the largest permitted memory address. The machine instructions that have access to this register determine the sequence-altering capability of programming routines. Branching operations involve changing the contents of the *program counter,* thereby designating which instruction is next executed. Subroutine jump and return processes depend on a specially dedicated register to store a pointer to indicate interim branching addresses. Whether this register holds actual addresses or memory storage address pointers will determine the need for memory stack allocations, and whether there are absolute or artificial limitations on the nesting of subroutines.

The interrelationships of the different registers, their numbers and sizes, and different machine-language commands have a bearing on interpreter architectures. The operational capabilities of instructions and registers determine the flexibility and versatility of a central processing unit, and the most optimum use can be made of these features by judiciously allocating memory storage and efficiently designing software routines.

Memory

Although the various registers have a memory function, the CPU does not contain memory as it is normally defined in computer terms. The primary memory is external to the CPU and is interconnected by electronic pathways called *buses.* The numbers and sizes of data buses are an essential descriptive quality of a microcomputer. Address bus capacities must be sufficient to permit binary values that denote all possible memory cell locations. The data bus width equates to the machine word size. For a byte-oriented system, an eight-channel bus can accommodate 8-bit word parrallel transfers between the CPU and memory locations.

Normally, data movement in and out of computer main memory is controlled by the CPU. To copy the contents of one memory location to another requires that the data be moved through the CPU on a word-at-a-time basis. An exception to this is possible for those systems having DMA (direct memory access) capability. DMA takes control of the address and data paths from the CPU for direct transfers of blocks of data. These transfers can take place internally (from one memory location to another), or externally (from memory to a peripheral, or vice versa).

The importance of word size, memory capacity, and accessing methods cannot be overemphasized. Overall memory storage allocation of the software system is sensitive to these considerations, and procedural logic must contend with the manner and methods by which memory contents may be established or altered.

Peripherals

Rudimentary computing systems have only a minimum of switches and indicators for inputting data and outputting results. Most systems, however, have greater capabilities, and some attain extremes of sophistication. In all system configurations, regardless of scope, the purpose of the adjuncts attached to the computer is for data movement into and out of the computer memory. The ability for the computer to READ data (accepting input) or to WRITE data (generating output) requires representation of the data in binary form. The meaning of binary notations, in the sense of what unique bit patterns are intended to represent, is a function of code tables.

The majority of data processing systems that employ microcomputers use one of the industry-common, standardized code sets for storage of data. The function of digitizing electronic signals into binary codes is accomplished by data input devices. Encoded data in memory is transferred in digital form to output devices. The special significance of code set conventions to the software designer is whether or not the same code sets are used by all input-output devices and internal computer processing.

As an example of the type of problem that often occurs, and that must be early recognized during design planning, consider the following. The electronic design of a microcomputer keyboard is ASCII encoded. That is, when a key is depressed, the ASCII binary code that is transferred to the computer is unique for each character, as depicted by the key cap. In ASCII, the letter A is represented in binary form as 01000001. The meaning of this bit string is a function of internal recognition. It is the responsibility of processing algorithms to denote the intended meaning of the letter A for this bit pattern.

Because of the variety of peripheral devices that may be configured into a computing system, and the potential for one of several standard code sets (or even a unique, custom one), it would be a false assumption that all will be compatable. In the event (as an example) that a keyboard generates ASCII character codes, but a file storage device (that is, a flexible disk) uses EBCDIC data encoding, the responsibility for reciprocal code conversions may rest with the software.

Another aspect of peripheral processing is computer control and access. Interrupt signals are used to invoke data transfers between peripherals and the computer memory. The timing and control section of the CPU recognizes interrupt requests and suspends command execution while data transfers take place (again excepting DMA transfers, where program execution may be permitted to continue concurrently). In most microprocessor implementations, a machine-language instruction is provided to ENABLE or DISABLE interrupt recognition by the CPU.

Any time subsequent to execution of an ENABLE interrupt command, an externally generated signal will cause the CPU to trap-out for device servicing. The nature of this trap-out function is a subroutine jump to a programmer-supplied address, where the instruction sequence will accomplish the necessary data movement between the input-output data lines and a memory location. Once the required data transfer requirements are satisfied, a RESET instruction will nullify the interrupt request and the servicing subroutine will exit back to the processing sequence that was in control at the time of I/O interruption. When set, the DISABLE causes the CPU to ignore device stimuli, providing the programmer exclusive control of the processor. When logically practical to do so, a programmed ENABLE will cancel the CPU exclusive status, and program execution will continue, and will again trap-out on interrupt requests.

Depending on microprocessor type, at least three different interrupt technologies are commercially available. The simple interrupt is, as the name implies, the most primitive (and the most common), and works essentially as described above. Recognition of a simple interrupt places the burden for peripheral identification on the servicing routine. A data value is placed on the transfer bus by the peripheral concurrent with interrupt signaling. Machine-language programming logic is necessary to decode the first character transferred to determine from what peripheral the data is coming. The converse is necessary for data output. The servicing routine places a peripheral code on the bus prior to generating a peripheral interrupt condition.

Vectored interrupt techniques are slightly more complex. Microprocessors that provide *vectored interrupt* capabilities permit device designation as an operand value to be associated with ENABLE, DISABLE, and RESET instructions. By specific designation, these instructions are active only for the designated device, and all other interrupt requests are ignored by the CPU. The greater flexibilities offered by vectored interrupts are highly advantageous to the software designer, but they do impose greater burdens and responsibilities for effective use.

Priority interrupt capability is now being offered on some of the latest microcomputers. This technology is borrowed from the traditionally larger computers. Prioritization codes are appended to the vectoring operands to denote which devices should have preferential access to the system. The complexity of utilization of priority interrupts enforces programming logic considerations in the design of servicing routines. While in the process of servicing an ENABLED low-level prioritized device, a higher-level preferred interrupt may cause a trap-out to another routine. Ensuring that all servicing routines are completely accomplished and the return calling sequences are maintained suggests several implications for the software architect.

Device control and data formatting requirements also have significance for the interpreter planner. Tape and unit record peripheral types are referred to as *serial files* devices. Paper tape readers and punches generally provide for serial recording of words (commonly word = byte) along the length of the medium. Sequential processing is a function of reading (or punching) one character at a time, using interrupt servicing algoritms. DMA implementations can provide the capability to transfer complete strings of characters, but data bus transfers between memory and the peripheral are still in a character serial mode. In most microprocesser implementations, the burden for advancing the tape (and detecting device availability status, etc.) rests with the software system.

Punchcard processing equipment has much in common with paper tape devices, with additional requirements for initiating card movement cycles. Columnar scanning of card data is on a character-by-character basis, with serial transfer of data between the peripheral and memory. Although both tape and card media are capable of variable-length data records, card records are usually formatted so that one card constitutes one data record. Paper tape implementations may denote record (and field) lengths by establishing character count parameters, or by using unique codes to signal the beginning and ending breakpoints between logical records.

Again, code set conversions may be required of the servicing routines, and memory buffer storage areas must be allocated by the software system. These considerations (device control and formatting) also apply to magnetic media devices, but additional burdens are imposed, depending on type.

Magnetic tape media, whether reel-to-reel, cassette, or cartridge, offer at least two significant advantages over their mechanical forerunners. Bit densities (character to media space ratios) are higher by several magnitudes, and *the medium is reusable.* New data may be overwritten on the same tape, thereby replacing old or no longer useful records. Greater buffer storage areas may be required of the software system due to the higher character densities and read-write speeds attainable with magnetic media. Software driver routines for magnetic devices suffer interrupt timing problems that are not experienced with the slower mechanical devices. The data transfer rates attainable with some high-speed peripherals is greater than the speed of the microprocesser—a principal reason for DMA technologies.

Typically, record data stored on serial media devices is accessed in a *sequential* manner, the order of processing being dictated by the physical placement of records along the length of the media. Specific records may be located by advancing or rewinding tape media to locate data that matches key identifiers, or according to a physical count from a given point. Although physically possible, *random* accessing of data records on serial media is not usually practical (because of search and rewind times), and the software designer should not allow any undue influence for these capabilities.

Rotating mass storage devices on the other hand, are especially advantageous for *random access* applications, and their effective use is a special concern of the software designer. Whether disk cartridges, drum devices, or the newer, more economical, flexible disks are employed, the software impacts are essentially the same. Additional storage space is necessary in memory to contain index tables to permit storage of record and file vectoring parameters. Device control is simpler, since they continue to operate without any start-stop cycles common to the serial devices. Moving-head (read-write unit) peripherals do impose *control* and *timing* responsibilities on their software drivers. Data is recorded on disks along circumferential tracks, and head movement is in and out along the radius of the continually spinning disk. Directional control of the read-write unit may be required of the software.

Multiple media devices impose additional responsibilities on software systems. Applicational requirements frequently expect the software to maintain logical advice as to which files are physically located on the respective drives, as well as continuity of data bases spread across multiple media. Because disks and drums are magnetic media, *destruct updating* (overwriting) is usual, and it is frequently a burden of the software system to know what areas are allocated, unused, and any gaps between contiguous records and files.

Many of the device control, data accessing, and other software driver burdens thus far discussed are servicing functions normally allocated to an *operating system.* In defining the systems environment in which a software interpreter must reside, where provided, the operating system is worthy of separate analysis. It is important to note, however, that in the absence of an operating system the peripheral servicing routines of the interpreter must suffer the brunt of I/O management. To reiterate: I/O management is dictated by system configuration and application requirements; whether these are provided by the interpreter or the operating system is academic—*they must be programmed for somewhere.*

Another role that is traditionally assigned to the operating system is program loading. In an interpreter-alone software system, program loading is a discrete routine, requiring access to I/O management and memory management supporting routines. Command access to the program loading function may be invoked from within the interpreter (program command), or from the operator console. The operating system executive routine is generally responsible for resource management, and program loading impacts three classes of resources: (1) CPU, (2) memory, and (3) an I/O device.

An *executive routine* is required (in the operating system, or as a discrete interpreter routine) for operator communications devices. Three types of console devices provide operator control and monitoring.

- *Direct access.* Hard-wired switches and lights connected to CPU.
- *Interactive.* Keyswitch activates display directly, and communicates with the software (usually in a character mode).
- *Conversational.* Operator input is intercepted by software and display response is output by software, facilitating dialogue exchange (usually in a message mode).

The *direct access* console switches generate interrupt signals, and some cause loading of encoded data into CPU registers or dedicated memory locations, depending on the microcomputer's architecture. It is important for the software designer to qualify these aspects early in the planning stage. Of significance may be the need to specially dedicate registers or memory areas. Adequate software integrity provisions are sensitive to the degree and extent the operator is permitted to forcibly interrupt the processing.

Interactive or *conversational* console devices consist of keyboards and either serial printers or solid state character displays. Cathode ray tubes (CRTs), liquid plasma, and light-emitting diodes (LEDs) are the solid state technologies presently in vogue for computer console displays. The difference between *interactive* and *conversational* devices for the software system is one of controlled output. For the conversational devices, all displayed data is generated under software control. Specific programming sequences are necessary to output data to the display, including mirrored reflection of operator input when necessary. For the interactive devices, the displayed data may occur as the result of either the operator's input or programming routines. Additional software commands are required for the interactive devices to preclude accidental loss of displayed data due to overwriting of operator input.

CRT page management entails a host of software burdens. Some of the major requirements that must be accounted for include message formatting, vertical line and page scrolling, and cursor control. The cursor is a positioning indicator that enables an operator to know on what line and at what position the next character input will be inserted. There is such an extreme variety among commercially available microcomputers that it would be futile to attempt to list all of the possibilities here. The software designer will have to identify specific requirements for the targetted system. Some generalizations are offered to show the types of consideration necessary in the design of software systems.

Formatting

Printable characters are formed by dot matrix techniques; characters occupy rectangular cells of fixed dimensions, each cell having defined rows and columns within which contrasting colors of dots appear. Some of the typical matrix ratioes are 5×7, 7×9, and 9×9. Most CRT-based display devices automatically generate alphanumeric characters from standard binary codes electronically, imposing no special software burdens.

There are, however, special display implementations that permit software-defined character representations, and these require discrete output driver routines. Sophisticated graphics capability is available on the more advanced displays, posing the need for special software functions. Depending on electronic design provisions, programmed control is possible for features such as blinking of characters, halftone intensity control of fields of data, and special effects with different colors.

Vertical scrolling of displayed lines, groups of lines, or an entire display page is possible under software control with some devices. End-of-line wraparound with automatic line advance is a similar feature. Random cursor control (arbitrary repositioning) is usually possible by one means or another. Any or all of these features is potential on commercially available systems. Whether these features are under the absolute control of electronics or software routines, and whether the operator is provided keyboard manipulation capability, must be accurately ascertained and analyzed for software impact.

The number of characters per line and the number of lines per page can dictate buffer storage requirements in main memory. Many CRT devices employ *internal memories* (necessary for screen refresh purposes), but a few depend entirely on the computer's memory. Certain application requirements may be best satisfied by replicated storage of screen data in both types of memories. Again, these factors are sensitive to exact system designs, but software planning must encompass these aspects to whatever extent necessary.

Operator consoles, or more frequently, data input work stations, may be interfaced to the computing system using data communications protocols and techniques. Modern data communications technologies have advanced to an extent that this topic is nearly a separate speciality field within the industry. As a consequence, no detailed explanation will be attempted here. Essentially, however, the software requirements for providing for remote communications between computers and computer devices is closely akin to peripheral-to-computer interrelationships. Software driver routines and data buffer areas are required, and CPU interruption may be internally or externally invoked.

Additional procedural logic is imposed for formatting blocks of data for remote transmission, involving the insertion of special character groups at the beginning and end of messages. Line disciplines and message protocols are dictated by the sending and receiving appliances and the type of transmission facilities used. Each of these aspects tend to impact software routine designs, and in the absence of an operating system, specific functional routines are required within the interpreter software architecture.

In summary form, the software environmental analysis must include the microcomputer, peripheral devices configured with it, operator console devices, and any resident operating software.

6.2 Language Considerations

"There is no such thing as a free lunch" is an often quoted axiom. Just as some price must eventually be exacted for sustenance, so too there is a fiscal reckoning for the conveniences of programming languages. And the connoisseur's price is not necessarily a linear progression from that which is tolerably palatable. While dietary law (or language selection) may be dictated from on high, affordable menus are attainable by adroit chefs.

The language discussion in Part I centered on the characteristic types of languages; the orientation here is toward specific features and their impacts on software systems. While this section is not intended to be a complete semiotic treatise of programming languages, each of the related areas of semantics, syntactics, and pragmatics must be explored sufficiently to arbitrate interpreter design decisions.

Similarly, lexical elements and the grammar of a language is subject to design considerations to accommodate programming dialects. And finally, specific rules of calculi are considered, to portray the importance of conventions and their consequent influence on parsing algorithms.

Since a programming language is a communication vehicle between man and machine, and is solely a written language at that, the entree subject deals with composition and formatting. Basically there are two choices: free-form and columnar, each with attendant advantages and burdens.

For either, a parsing routine is necessary to process programming language statements preparatory to other phases of translation. Software systems that depend on assembler or compiler programs relegate source parsing responsibility to the translator. Interactive source entry systems must accomplish parsing at time of entry. Notice that for either system the requirement prevails and only the *when* and *where* aspects differ.

The operational conviencences of free-form formatting for modern source entry devices were cited earlier, as were the reasons for the advent of columnar conventions. Attempts to modernize traditionally columnar-formatted programming languages must reconcile both the cost burdens for memory and speed impacts. The reasons for these increases can be appreciated by identifying the respective processing tasks for each type of parsing routine.

A programming routine for discrete examination of a columnar-formatted language statement is based on certain assumptions regarding source input.

- Lexical elements are arranged serially in a predefined sequence.
- Grammatical significance is determined by relative field positioning.
- Semantic determinations are made by the absence or presence of values within fields.
- Syntactical composition is qualified on a field-by-field basis and by field-associative algorithms.
- Maximum field sizes are predefined, precluding any need for character-level scanning.

In essence, then, text editing of columnar-formatted source is oriented toward field-level (whole words) examination. The alternative of free-form formatting necessitates character-level qualification of input statements. A two-tiered design approach is implied in this case. A phase-one parsing routine scans a programming statement on a character basis, restructuring the input into a columnarized format. Phase two then consists of the same processes required had the programmer provided columnarized input.

The complexity and extensiveness of character parsing routines is subject to several vagaries. Rigid syntactical rules can serve to limit the variety of permitted forms of composition, and unique delimiters can simplify identification of lexical elements.

The liberal rules for phraseology permitted by some languages pose specific complexities for the translation processes. Consider the following COBOL expressions:

```
000100      ADD FIELD-A TO FIELD-B.
000200      ADD FIELD-A FIELD-B.
```

The semantical intent of these examples is identical. Program execution will result in summation of the specified fields, and the result will be contained in FIELD-B. The statement parsing routine must contend with the insigificance of the connective "TO." Notice, however, the potential for ambiguity in the example presented next.

```
000300      ADD FIELD-A, FIELD-B TO FIELD-C.
000400      ADD FIELD-A FIELD-B FIELD-C.
```

Some compilers would process these statements differently. Commonly, for line 000300, FIELD-A and FIELD-B are independently added to the contents of FIELD-C. For line 000400, however, chain addition may take place; FIELD-A may first be added to FIELD-B, and the resulting sum then added to FIELD-C. In these cases the contents of FIELD-C would be identical, but the value of FIELD-B following execution of either of these statements would be different. A COBOL compiler offered by another vendor might generate yet a third result for line 000400 by adding FIELD-A to each succeeding field only (FIELD-A to FIELD-C and FIELD-B to FIELD-C).

Even language standards impose unnecessary levels of duress. The ANSI COBOL standard would accommodate the earlier example for line 000200, but would not permit that of line 000400. It can be appreciated that a parsing routine could permit either of these statements and the responsibility for discrimination would be delegated to the syntaxing routine.

Compound statement expressability is inherent to some programming languages. This provision frequently imposes overhead because of the potential for multiple-line statements. Traditional columnnarized languages enforce a single imperative construct per source line. Again citing COBOL as an example, the semantical intent of a program expression may not be ascertainable until scanning encounters a sentence terminator (a period). Parsing activity may have to embrace 10 or 15 (or more) lines of programming until the end of an expression is determined. While only slightly more complex, the real significance is in the amount of storage that may be required to contain long strings of source data temporarily. The potential exists that excessive allocation of work areas is in effect wasted for a high percentage of the time. Compare this with the fixed storage required for regimented languages that limit single statements to a maximum of one expression per input record.

The linguistic relationship between the programmer and the computer involves pragmatics as well as semantics. Columnarized languages (traditionally the assemblers) provide for only single discriptive or imperative expressions per source line. During translation processing, the number of lexical elements that must be examined to derive semantical intent is constrained by physical (and logical) record lengths. In virtually all such languages, only a single verb (command) can occur per line of programming. Even though several subjects (operands) may be specified, their grammatic classification can be deduced by their relative positions. Ambiguity is avoided because there is no doubting to which verb the nouns pertain.

The higher-level languages permit compound constructions, hence another dimension of complexity. The following example will serve to exemplify the software designer's problem:

```
001100   IF ABC IS GREATER THAN 5 AND XYZ IS LESS
001200       THAN 25 GO TO INPUT-ERROR-ROUTINE.
```

While the parsing and syntactical checkout of these lines of programming is fairly straightforward, the word "AND" poses a special implication for proper translation. Procedurally, the logical comparison of ABC and 5 must be established, also for XYZ and 25, and then the truths of these tests must be compared. An explicit requirement for an additional machine sequence can only be implicity deduced ("AND" is the clue).

Second, there is a syntactic relationship between the combinatorial comparison and the imperative "GO TO INPUT-ERROR-ROUTINE." Where the individual lexical elements, their grammatic arrangement, and semantic intent qualify, the absence of an imperative function should evince a syntax error because of illogical construction. In analyzing languages that permit compound expressions, the potential complexities for syntaxing routines must be thoroughly appreciated.

Token parsing is a requirement posed by languages such as FORTRAN and BASIC. Mathematical expressions may contain symbolic identifiers, literals, precedence delimiters, and operators. It is a function of the parsing routine to scan all of the characters in an expression string and identify and categorize each *token*. The algorithm for parsing mathematical expression strings is based on conventions. For standard programming languages the usage conventions are well established and are generally common to all. Two sets of rules apply, one to facilitate the scanning function and the other to establish arithmetic operations precedence. The following example is written in the BASIC language:

```
00100 LET A=(B+5)*(C-4)+1
```

Formatting Conventions

Serial scanning operations proceed from left to right, and the first two fields are quickly determined. The line number must be first, and may contain only numeric integers. Character testing then encounters a space, three letters, and a space. The keyword (in this case "LET") is expected to be the second value in the statement and it must begin with an alphabetic character and contain no spaces. The leading space is ignored (looking for a letter), the "L" denotes the start of a keyword, and the following letters are appended with scanning temporarily suspended when the space following the "T" is encountered.

The word LET can now be compared against a lookup table for valid keyword possibilities. A possible imposition for the software designer should be noted at this point. If you must permit the programmer optionally to omit the space between the word LET and the following symbolic identifier ("A" in this case), isolation of the keyword will require a more comprehensive algorithm.

The diagrams in Figures 6.2.1 through 6.2.7 are provided for your study in the mechanics of parsing BASIC statements. The first illustration (Figure 6.2.1, p. 86) functions as the praser mainline—each of those following (Figures 6.2.2—6.2.7, pp. 87-94) are subroutines to the mainline. These diagrams are only representative of parsing logic, and for the sake of brevity, the detail tasks for the subroutines are not shown.

The symbolic memory *address tag* is anticipated to be next, and it must be followed by the *equals* separator. The succeeding characters are denoted by individually comparing them with permitted types. The parentheses is a special token to benefit precedence of arithmetic sequences. The *plus* and *minus* signs serve to denote their usual function of addition and subtraction. The *asterisk* is a special token to represent multiplication, and a common symbol for division is the slash (/). By convention, any *alphabetic* character appearing after the *equals* separater must be considered as a symbolic memory address tag, and all numeric characters are decimal literals.

Additional formatting options can have various impacts on the size of parsing routines. Compound expressions may be permitted in conjunction with certain keywords, and are usually of the form of using *commas* to separate individual expressions. Higher-level mathematics capabilities require a more extensive set of *operator tokens* that must be recognizable to the parsing routine.

Functional Precedence

Once the semantical meaning has been derived for all of the tokens and groups of characters contained in the total expression, the *procedural intent* is qualified next. The sequence in which arithmetic operations are performed usually follows normal algebraic rules. Unless perentheses dictate otherwise, *involutions* are performed first, then *multiplications* and *divisions*, and finally *additions* and *subtractions*. In the absence of parentheses, and where it matters mathematically, operations of the same precedence are associated to the left; that is, A-B-C is interpreted as (A-B)-C, A/B/C as (A/B)/C, and so on. Pairs of parentheses (left and right) serve to delimit portions of operations for an expression string. Each function contained within a set of parentheses is *first* performed (according to the same rules of precedence), and the results of parenthetical operations are saved as interim values. These temporary values are then operated upon

85

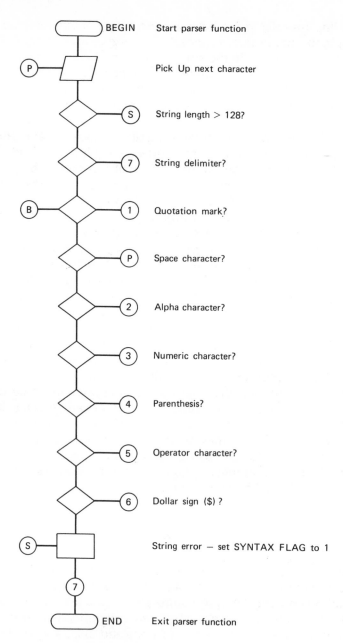

Figure 6.2.1 A parsing routine for BASIC expressions.

by the rest of the functions as if they were substituted for the parenthetic expression, again using the same precedence rules.

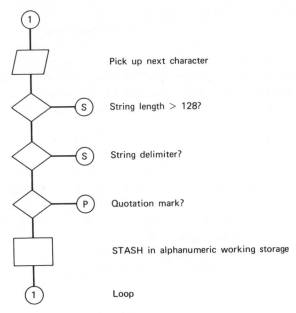

Pick up next character

String length > 128?

String delimiter?

Quotation mark?

STASH in alphanumeric working storage

Loop

Figure 6.2.2 (Figure 6.2 cont.) Delimit quoted strings.

In analyzing language requirements, the systems software programmar must quantify the number of different arithmetic operators possible and the degree of sophistication permitted for nesting of parenthetical expressions.

In summarizing language consideration significance, it is first noteworthy that the *when* and *where* aspects are dictatorial. The characteristics of a given language become nearly transparent to an interpreter, assuming the results of translation by an assembler or compiler is a pseudo-language. For the interactive source interpretive system, however, the software must suffer the same burdens as an assembler or compiler program.

Based on language-implementation choice, formatting conventions impinge significantly on the parsing and syntaxing burdens required during source statement translation. Individual languages may also suffer unique requirements. The extensiveness of commands provided, the sophistication of symbolic possibilities, and the portent of compound logical equations must be collectively evaluated by the software designer.

Where limited resources prevail, many opportunities are possible for language feature negotiations between the user and the interpreter designer. By constraining formatting conventions and some of the more liberal options for expressiveness, a subsetted dialect can substantially reduce the size of source processing routines.

6.3 Application Requirements

The degree to which a user is satisfied with the performance of a computing system is subject to many influences. In actual experience, many horror stories associated with unhappy computerization attempts are the direct consequence of poor selection of a product. Although the system designer may have no control over the ultimate selection of his product, it is critical that the intended user profile be anticipated.

By the same token, an especially fine hardware product may be devalued by inefficient or inappropriate system software. As an absolute minimum, the user of a computing system expects accurate, reliable operation. Other evaluators, such as convenience and flexibility, suffer mixed priorities depending on usage posture. Hardware features, operating system provisions, and application program options are all subject to a variety of criteria.

Interpreter software is also subject to the same appraisals as are the other system components, but one trait that is predominantly required is transparency. In fact, the more ethereal the interpreter is, the more successful the system is likely to be. For those software interpreters that coexist with an operating system, and where all language-translation processes require preprogram operation, it is relatively easy to camouflage the interpreter. In the absence of an operating system, however, or for the interactive processes, system, application, and operator interfacing impose many responsibilities.

Application

Application is intended here to include the entire realm of what a system is used for, by whom it is used, and the nature of the workload for which the system is acquired. Some of the more common uses for which microcomputers are used include:

- Business data processing (accounting tasks).
- Word processing (language text entry and editing).
- Educational, explicitly as computer science tools, and implicitly to assist in instruction of math or logic courses.
- Scientific processes, including engineering, quantitative analysis, and operations research.
- Process control (to manage and sequence machines and devices in operations such as manufacturing, communication, transportation and other mechanical processes).
- Software development, as both a test bed and a laboratory.

The human factors study must include an analysis of the prototype users. The relative educational level of operators, their experience and familiarity with computing systems, the extent and frequency of use, and their reasons for using the computer must all be taken into account.

Comfort, ease, and convenience, and the degree of interactivity to be expected, can all contribute to a positive attitude on the part of the user and, therefore, on the success of the system installation. Operator psychology is especially important in the design of any software tasks that require dialogue or interactivity during use of the system. Any unnecessary complexity may irritate a scientist, frustrate a bookkeeper, or infuriate a fellow programmer. Some of the many types of persons that may be encouraged to use a microcomputer system include:

- Engineers, electrical, mechanical, structural, etc.
- Mathematicians, actuaries, estimators, etc.
- Students, both of computer science subjects and others.
- Programmers of systems software and user programs.
- Bookkeepers, data entry operators, controllers, etc.
- Managers, executives, supervisors, etc.

The types of processing, frequency of use, and volumes of data to be processed dictate performance criteria. Whether only a few data items are to be subjected to thousands of iterative computations, or only a few calculations are necessary but they must be made repeatedly for thousands of entries is an important design consideration. In some instances only a few hours of computer operation per day (or less) may be required. In others, the system is in continuous use around the clock, and in still others, actual use is spurious—the system is constantly ready, but only intermittently accessed. Each of these application circumstances has its own requirements to be addressed by the systems designers. The following list includes some of the job-related characteristics to be considered.

- Short jobs, high frequency (6 hours or more per day).
- Few different jobs, long runs (half-dozen programs, each running in a dedicated mode for hours at a time).
- Dedicated systems, infrequent use but high-speed execution required whenever invoked.
- Occasional usage, speed and throughput requirements a function of convenience only.
- Small quantities of data subject to continuous or recursive computations.
- Large volumes of data, balanced, or excessively of input or output derivation; low or disproportionally mixed as to the number of calculations.
- Single user, or multiple users in a single or multiprogramming mode; dedicated devices and files or shared together.
- Relative volatility of requirements for programmed tasks (basically static, or frequent program changes necessary).

Assuming that the hardware configuration and the programming language is a given, the first design decision for the interpreter must be whether or not interactive source input capability should be provided. Next it is necessary to identify whether more than one language is to be accommodated. Occasionally a mixed requirement prevails, where one language must be interactively processed and others may be batch-translated with assemblers or compilers. Another type of option may permit interactive programming operations for development purposes, but facilitate streamlined operation for normal processing runs.

89

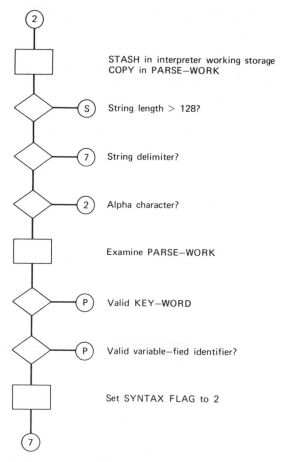

Figure 6.2.3 (Figure 6.2 cont.) Argue alpha tokens.

If the entire software scheme is to use batch pretranslation processes for the user source programs, the design emphasis should be on optimal pseudo-code interpretation with the only requirement for operator interfacing in the event of run time error conditions. There is naturally a strong interdependence between the assembler (or compiler) and the interpreter, concentrated on the pseudo-code involved. Second, in systems such as these, it is usual to put as many of the translation processes as possible in the translator program. The more amenable the compiler, and the more beneficial the pseudo-code form is to the interpreter, the less the overhead of the resident software during program execution.

Since in the interactive software system the program routines for managing source program entry, semantical translation, and syntactical qualification are employed only occasionally, many of these software routines are viable candidates for overlaying.

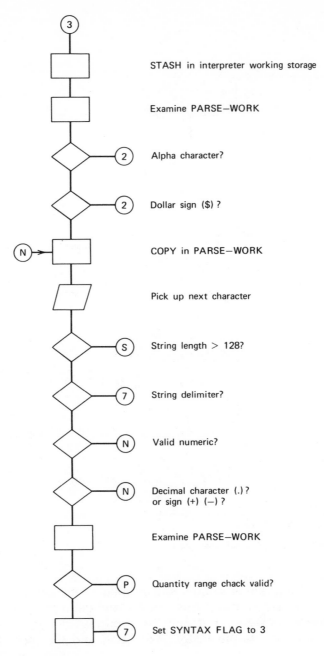

Figure 6.2.4 (Figure 6.2 cont.) Isolate literals.

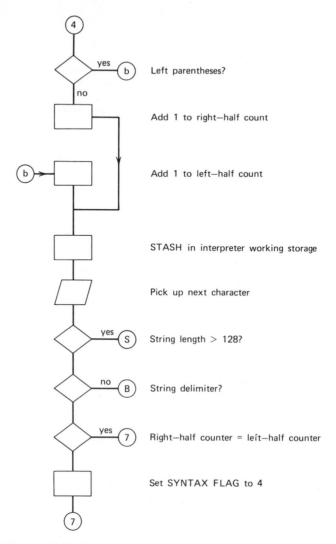

Left parentheses?

Add 1 to right—half count

Add 1 to left—half count

STASH in interpreter working storage

Pick up next character

String length > 128?

String delimiter?

Right—half counter = left—half counter

Set SYNTAX FLAG to 4

Figure 6.2.5 (Figure 6.2 cont.) Delimit parenthetical values.

Occasional programming attempts by mildly interested or novice operators requires greater assistance during source entry and debugging operations. The experienced programmer, however, not only requires less dialogue and coaching by the system, he in fact expects the fastest execution and the most stringent syntactical assistance.

High-volume I-O systems, such as for general business accounting, necessitate comprehensive peripheral management and files maintenance and protection provisions. The possibility of a poorly designed application program sequence destroying a

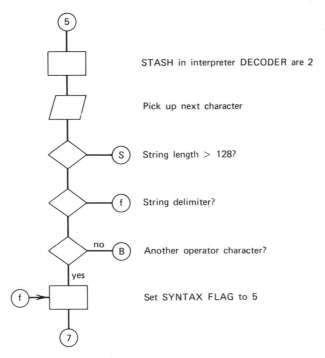

STASH in interpreter DECODER are 2

Pick up next character

String length > 128?

String delimiter?

Another operator character?

Set SYNTAX FLAG to 5

Figure 6.2.6 (Figure 6.2 cont.) Isolate operators for decoding.

sizable data file suggests that the greatest care should be employed in syntaxing all I/O functions.

Number crunching applications, such as for operations research problems, require the most efficient computational support routines. A logarithmic reiterative sequence may have to continue for several million loops, and start-to-stop time can range from minutes to days, depending on whether the loop time is in nano- or milliseconds. The degree, frequence, and extent that tables and arrays are required to support application processes is also a subject of design study. Table accessing, searching, and string manipulations are common to many jobs, and where these tasks are frequent or lengthy, efficient command interpretives are required.

Multifaceted requirements, such as for dual modes of operation, or multiprogramming or multilingual tasking, suggest a high degree of modularity in the software system. Discrete interpretive string processes can commonally be shared between two different source languages, more so if a high degree of common pseudo-commands and formats is possible. Multiprogramming systems dictate reentrant coding conventions in the design of interpreter routines. Since CPU operations must fluctuate between user programs, exclusive use of processor registers is never assured, requiring main memory duplicates in many cases.

The overall size of user programs, especially in relationship to system and memory resources, may require extensive support of program segmentation and overlay

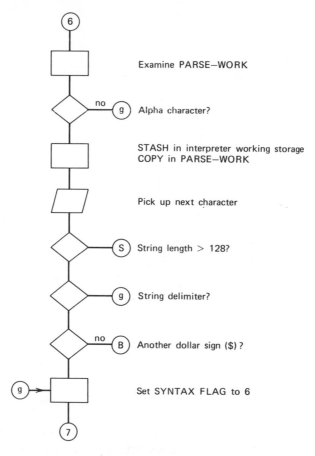

Figure 6.2.7 (Figure 6.2 cont.) The string variable marker ($).

capabilities. Whether, and to what extent, these provisions are automated can impose varying burdens on the interpreter. Similarly, rapidly changing job mixes may necessitate efficient program loading and housekeeping routines, sometimes even more so than for in-run processes. By the same token, where the usual posture is to load and run a given program for several hours at a time, relatively slow loading and initializing operations may well be justified since they have minimal influence on overall processing throughput.

Application programs that are primarily operator-paced do not require especially fast execution, so balancing judgments tend to favor memory optimization over efficient processing. An extension of this same theory concerns slow-speed devices. CRT displays are quite frequently slow (compared to CPU cycle times) and may not justify the most optimum coding techniques. An actual timed test of one such system showed that the processor was hampered to the extent it was only operating at one one-hundredth of its rated speed.

94

Overall, it is the user's requirements that must enjoy the highest priorities during systems design planning—including the design of the software interpreter. Owners and users of microcomputers acquire systems to accomplish specific tasks, and the nature of these tasks must be fully analyzed to establish design criteria. Subtle requirements are not easily identified, but yet may make the difference between success and disaster. A positive attitude on the part of an operator can do much to assure success, and every consideration for ease and convenience will be rewarded. Conversely, a frustrated operator can adversly affect the most brilliantly designed system. Usability is a relative quality, subject to qualification by the experience level of the operators, their motivation for use of the system, and the degree to which they expect the system to aid and coach them.

Chapter

Architecture Selection

Thus far we have assumed that the software designer has little or no choice in the selection of the hardware components, the programming language to be used, or the intended application. Where this assumption is invalid, the architectural aspects of software interpreters may influence the system planning process.

Once the analysis of the hardware system, the programming language, and the application requirements is complete, the basic architecture of the software interpreter is selected. At this point the when, where, and how relates to the functional processes, their placement, and the plan of access. The chart in Figure 7.1 shows how each of these factors may be broken down for consideration.

This chapter is devoted to the questions of when, where, and how to use interpreters. The aim is to show the cause-and-effect relationship between the system environment and software architectural selection factors.

7.1 When to Interpret

The matter of *when* to interpret includes the entire range of processes to be accomplished, from programming to operation. The key element of this subject is *source statement translation*. The two most basic solutions to translation are prepass compiling (or assembling), or delaying translation until program execution. Hybrid solutions, varying the amount and degree of preexecute tasks, are also possible, but this is more a matter of specifics than generality. The following four categories are chosen to facilitate further discussion:

- Prepass translation.
- Translation during program loading.
- Translation at time of source program entry.
- Execution time translation.

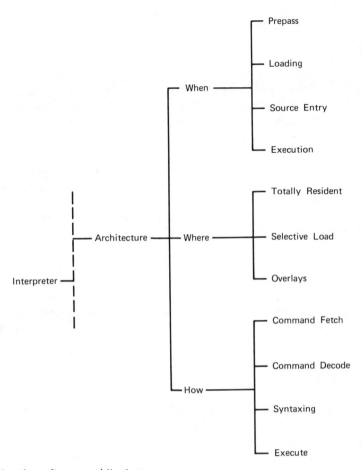

Figure 7.1 Selecting the software architecture.

The traditional software schemes for programming computers use the prepass translation concept. The order of activities then includes program preparation, source statement encoding and capture, program compilation, object code generation, and program execution. This methodology is still viable for many systems requirements, including microcomputer systems that are fully based on software interpreter concepts.

The two factors that can enforce selection of a prepass translation system are *memory* and *language*. Virtually all alternatives to prepass translation require more system resources. Some languages (such as COBOL) are especially demanding as to the scope and complexity required for source translation, often requiring use of the entire system.

Where circumstances permit, by omission of the more extensive features of a language, translation burdens may be reduced sufficiently to negate the need for separate batching of the compilation process. For many microcomputer systems, limitations on memory and peripheral availability may require honing of the higher-level languages, even when prepass compilers are employed.

The delta point for these compromises is usually where subsetting leaves off and syntactical deviation begins. Subsetting by omission is subject to user programming requirements and the degree of dependency placed on certain language features. Deviations in the syntax area will result in a *language dialect,* and whether or not this is acceptable depends on requirements for commonality. These arguments tend to hold true regardless of the architectural placement of the translation processes.

Prepass processing of the source file can be attempted with only a single pass, or may require several batches of read and write operations to accomplish complete translation. Generally, where prepass compilers are used, the philosophy should be to allocate as many of the functional responsibilities as possible to the compiler program. The reason for this suggestion is to minimize the burdens of the software interpreter during program execution. Once the decision is made to use a prepass scheme, every effort should be made to accomplish there everything that does not have to be delayed until actual runtime.

Where program loading time is not critical, another possibility (actually a derivation of prepass compiling) is to translate source during program-to-memory loading. This methodology tends to be restricted to circumstances where program segmentation and overlays are not involved. Obviously, not all languages lend themselves well to this architecture, and the degree and extent to which full source to pseudo-object transformation is possible may be curtailed.

A relative mix of systems attributes that tends to warrant this concept includes:

- Low-speed I/O devices (especially serial only).
- A subsetted alogorithmic language such as minimal BASIC.
- Sufficient memory to house the loader-translator.
- Slightly less than optimum execution speed is tolerable.

Implementation of this scheme is oriented toward reading the source statement file, condensing the source to conserve memory, stashing, the result in program memory, and building data reference tables. Some restrictions that may be imposed on the usual language conventions may be as follows:

- No multiline expressions are permitted.
- No compound expressions are permitted.
- Data definitions may be required to be separate from procedural instructions.
- Rigid formatting rules must apply.
- In-run linkage with other programs is not permitted.

While the cumulative effect of this possible list of restrictions may seem excessive, not necessarily all of them need apply to a particular design. An interesting possibility for this design is to share the loader space with the data storage area required by the user's program. Upon completion of the load function, the portion of memory that contained the loader program is reallocated for user program use. Techniques such as this, combined with restrictions as above, can permit the use of software interpreters in many rudimentary computing systems.

A popular system configuration for microcomputers uses a CRT display and keyboard for both programming and operation purposes. The factors with which the software designer must contend for this architecture include the requirements for syntactical assistance, frequency of source entry, and the ratio of program size to available memory.

At the time of acceptance of a source line statement, the programmed functions to be accomplished are as follows:

1 *Parsing.* Scanning of the line to determine lexical elements and semantical intent.

2 Syntaxing. Qualifying order of presentation and key word validation.

3 *Translation* of keywords and operators to pseudo-codes.

4 *Symbol table entry.* Cross-match for validity and repeated usage. Update table with any new symbols.

5 Loop to accept another statement.

Factors that influence the actual overhead requirements include keyword tables (for lookup qualification), reserved memory space for the symbol tables, and the number and size of the interpretive routines necessary to support the language commands.

Most of the conservation techniques described earlier can be applied to this type of architecture as well. By reducing the variety of language features and constraining the formatting and construction options, the system-resident software requirements may be held to a reasonable level. A balance must be reached between user-dictated requirements with regard to the convenience aspects of source translation in an interactive mode and the overall anticipated size of user programs, as well as the need to change or modify programs frequently. A possible compromise that may be acceptable is to permit interactive source statement entry prior to program execution, but with no further modifications after a run has been attempted.

The significance of this restriction is that it will require reloading of the entire software system to accomplish a change after testing runs. The advantage to software designers is that they can use the area of memory that contains the interactive translation routines for multiple purposes. When the operator invokes execution of the stored program, a housekeeping function can clear and reallocate all areas of memory that previously contained the keyboard input, display, line parsing, and all other translation routines.

Full exploitation of this concept would use a single area of memory for the following purposes:

• Program loading—assuming that no further load requirement exists for a particular run once initial loading is accomplished.

99

- Source entry routine, including parsing, syntaxing, and translation; may also include keyword constants, etc.

- User program working storage—cleared prepatory to running.

- Program copying—ability to capture the user program to off-line storage media could be executed from this area.

- Program listing—again, a storage area.

The final possibility for when to accomplish the translation phase of the interpretive process is to delay all processes until actual execution time. Naturally this method will result in the most severe speed degradation at run time, but the least delay is experienced otherwise. Applicationally this may be the most suitable design architecture for software development work. Where source statements are captured off-line, and the predominant need is to run-test and debug repeatedly, speed degradation is not really important. Major emphasis for this type of implementation is for run-time software integrity. Thorough syntaxing is necessary, especially of write-to-memory instruction sequences, to preclude erroneous overwriting of program memory or system software storage.

As we have seen, the *when* factor of architectural selection is more concerned with the source translation process than with pseudo-code interpretation. Regardless of the transformations that must take place, actual stored program code interpretation can occur only as each interim object command is fetched and decoded. The decoder routine establishes the address of the interpreter sequence necessary to fulfill the intended function and transfers control to that string. Successive interactions of this flow dictate pseudo-code interpretation when the program is actually being executed.

7.2   Where to Interpret

The *where* aspect of software architecture selection concerns the placement of the *data, program code, interpreter routines,* and all the sundry *related parts* of the total system. The contributing influences to be carefully planned include the peripheral and media availabilities, main memory mapping constraints, and the logical accessing requirements for the various components.

To be detailed in this section are the arguments pro and con of totally resident software schemes, alternatives that employ selective loading methods, and the relative differences between overlaying and roll-in, roll-out techniques.

The *totally resident* concept, as the term implies, assumes that the entire interpreter program and all necessary supportive routines are contained within main memory during all phases of system operation. Some of the more obvious disadvantages of this architecture include the high overhead and the ineffective use of areas of memory that contain program data and instructions that are infrequently needed—in fact, that may not be needed at all during some runs.

Consider, for example, the entire spectrum of software that deals exclusively with

100

interactive source input and translation. In a user environment where only occasional use is made of these functions, either to create a new program or to modify an existing one, the overhead involved may not be cost-effective when compared to other possible uses of this space.

Since only a fixed amount of main memory is available for the storage of both application programs and system software, the allocation of this important system resource should be carefully considered.

The obvious advantage of the totally resident software system is simplicity. To add another dimension of complexity to the overall design to accommodate reuse or selective use of memory costs in terms of development effort and additional programming. Care must also be applied in the selection of alternatives to ensure that the savings in memory are fully justified when compared to the complexities involved and the net extent of additional programming required.

The first candidate technique for conserving memory as a function of the software architecture is selective software loading. The basic idea of this concept is to load to memory only those routines necessary to support a particular application. Several techniques are appropriate for consideration in evaluating the appropriateness of selective loading.

During systems initialization, and while the software is being loaded, the opportunity for the operator to influence *what* is loaded may be provided. Actual implementing techniques for this can vary considerably. Different components of the interpreter are stored on separate media, and whether or not they are presented for loading is left to the operator to decide. A variation of this method provides the operator the ability to enter a series of parameters to be used during the loading process. As each segment of the software is encountered in a continuous-run sequence, the parameter table is checked to ascertain which sections to bypass.

The second method assumes that the necessary identification for each software segment is programmatically argued, and that the loader program contains the necessary logic to accept the parameters, qualify their accuracy, and apply them during loading.

The inherent weakness of both of these schemes is in the level of responsibility imposed on the operator. Under the assumption that the operator knows (or has been told) what software segments are necessary at a given point in time, whether or not all of the software is in fact loaded, may not be learned until much later.

Several implementing techniques can be used to cause the loader routine automatically to copy to memory the necessary interpreter modules to support a given program. One is to cause the compiler to generate a parameter table (similar to the operator-provided table); this table permits the loader to distinguish which software is to be loaded. It is also possible to cause the loader itself to identify which interpreters are necessary by closely scrutinizing the object program during the read and load process.

Typically there are numerous interpreter modules that are necessary in all cases, as well as others that can be estimated to be nearly always needed. By this assumption, only a relative number of modules are subject to discriminatory loading, thus lessening the complexity of the loader routine.

101

Overlaying is another technique for effectively managing the use of a limited memory. Assume for the moment that a half-dozen or so modules can be identified that are used relatively infrequently. By setting aside a memory space sufficiently large to accommodate the largest of these modules, they may all share the space on an *as needed* basis. In actual practice, when required, a chosen overlay is loaded, then executed. This module remains in residence until such time as another is required, it then being overlayed by the currently needed routine. This methodology is of course dependent on *random access storage media,* and assumes that no status or interim values need be retained to benefit the module that is being overwritten.

A more sophisticated overlaying concept is one that does provide for saving of intermediate values. Instead of arbitrarily overwriting a previously called module when the need for the overlay space is encountered, the existing contents are first written out to random access files storage. The incoming routine then overlays into the shared space; it too is subject to being rolled out to facilitate another module being rolled in.

Some of the complexities involved in implementing this level of overlay capability may not prove worthwhile, depending on the space savings possible in comparison to the additional programming required. Acceptable performance can also be a factor. The simple overlaying scheme does require time to fetch and load a called overlay. Whether the time-out is viable is a function of frequency of occurrence and the cumulative effect of repeated overlaying. The roll-in, roll-out type of implementation also suffers speed degradations; theoretically these are twice as severe, since an unload function must precede any overlay loading.

According to relative complexity, then, the selective loader concept is the simplest to implement, followed by destruct overlay and roll-in, roll-out techniques. Overlaying also dictates the availability of random access files devices; further, that the media is available in-run and already contains the necessary software routines. Balancing judgments in either case must compare the possible memory savings with the number of candidate modules and their anticipated frequency of use. The resident program size necessary to support the overlaying operations must also be considered (it is quite possible in some instances that the management routines may be larger than the selected callable interpreter modules). Second, indiscriminate choices in design can result in a thrashing mode where an unacceptable amount of time is consumed loading (and unloading) overlays, giving a disproportional processing allocation to the user program.

7.3   How to Interpret

Having previously discussed the when and where aspects of software architectures, we now consider the *how-to* factors. It is not intended to list implementation techniques here, but rather to identify the factors that can result from hardware or application requirements.

Since the functional requirements of parsing routines have been covered elsewhere, this section is limited to the basic functions of command fetch, decode, and syntax; and the individual interpreter strings are covered last because of their unique relation with programming language commands. Fetching, decoding, and syntaxing are all considered to be common to the entire interpreter, and because of their highly repetitive use they should enjoy the optimums of operation efficiency.

The Fetch Routine

Assuming that all mechanical devices are ready, and the required software and program have been properly loaded to memory, an operator RUN signal will cause the computer to begin operation. In virtually all computers, from an initial start-up state, the first stored software command to be executed is in memory location zero. Beyond that point the next instruction to be executed is a function of program sequence. Typically the first task to be accomplished from the zero point is to establish any counters, work registers, and so on, that are necessary to support succeeding logic requirements. In an interpreter software system, one of these counters is the user program instruction address pointer.

This pointer (program counter) is required to contain the address of the next program command to be executed. The initial value to be contained in this counter is the address of the first user program command, possibly initialized as a task of the program loader.

During the operational cycle of fetch-decode-syntax-execute-loop, it is necessary to update the program counter with the address of the next instruction to be executed; this update must take place prior to entering the beginning of another program cycle. There are two ways by which this counter can be updated: (1) automatically, or (2) as a result of interpreting a user program control instruction.

Automatic updating is an incremental process, effectively causing sequential execution of the application program. The number of words (or bytes, etc.) to be added to the program counter is dictated by the length of the current instruction to be executed. If the command that is about to be executed is 3 bytes long, 4 is added to the program counter—that is, the current command length, plus 1.

At the beginning of the fetch process the program counter determines which instruction is to be executed next. The example of a prototype pseudo-object code format described in Chapter 4 (see Figure 4.2) contained a header code in the first byte position of each command. Implementation of this type of format would cause the fetch process to examine this header (addressed by the program counter) to determine the number of bytes to follow that comprise the complete command, that is, the operation code and the associated operands.

The fetch process may then move the entire command to be executed to a working storage area in anticipation of transferring control to an interpreter processing string. Although the program counter could be updated at this point, with the incremental factor denoted by the current command length, it may not be the most logical time to do so. Should a syntax error, an operator interrupt, or any other cause for incompletion of a full operational cycle occur, a logic recovery may be required to attempt reexecution of this same command. If the program counter was arbitrarily updated prior to successful execution of the current command, the address from which this command was fetched would no longer be known.

Where hardware or applicational facilities permit processing interruption at any finite time, it is usually necessary to know the address of the last user program command attempted. One possible implementing technique to satisfy this requirement is to cause all interpreter strings to exit through a common end-of-loop routine that accomplishes the update of the program counter immediately prior to beginning the next operational cycle.

The other possible updating influence on the program counter is the result of interpretation of a program control command. As an example, if a program BRANCH command is encountered, the effect of interpretation of this command is to load the program counter with the address referenced by the BRANCH. This results in a branching function because the next program command to be fetched will be the one addressed by the program counter.

It is also required that the control command interpretives not exit through the end-of-loop update routine, but they should instead go directly to the beginning of the fetch routine.

The command fetch process is essentially no more than a data field moving function that uses the program counter value to address main memory to accomplish transfer of a command to working storage. The length of the memory field to be moved is dictated by the format of the pseudo-object code structure. Once all tasks are complete, the fetch routine then transfers control to the instruction decoder.

The Decoder

The primary function of the decoder is to establish the entry address for the appropriate interpreter string. Whether the algorithm employed is dependent on a lookup table or an address calculation scheme is a matter of design choice. A source code interpreter (or condensed source) generally requires a comparison table of valid keyword possibilities. In a system using true pseudo-object codes, the artificial command set can be constructed so as to benefit an address calculation algorithm.

In either case, any invalid code combination should cause a direct exit from the decoder to the syntaxing routine. To enable the syntax routine to ascertain the reason for this *out-of-sequence accesss,* a special code is generated by the decoder to indicate trap-out of an invalid command. An optional technique is to enter the syntax routine via a different entry point than would normally occur with a valid command.

Another task of the decoder is to qualify operand values. It is at this point that memory boundary violations should be syntaxed. The operations code (or the command header code) is examined to determine the category of each operand. All operands denoted as memory addresses are compared to upper and lower range limits. Any address detected to be illegal should cause the decoder to pass the *error condition* to the syntaxing routine.

The remaining function for the decoder is to initialize any software registers that are used for memory-to-memory data movement. The exact nature of this task is sensitive to the type of data formatting convention used. The different data structuring methods were described in Chapter 4, as were their associated usage rationales. Other possible tasks of the decoder can include code conversions, such as binary-to-decimal for literals, and presetting of any flags or indicators used by interpreter strings.

The Syntaxer

The chief role of the syntax routine is to error-trap illegal conditions and effect communication with the operator. The most simplistic implementation is merely to signal a PE (program error) and enter a WAIT state. Additional possibilities include providing advice as to the address of the invalid command and providing error recovery management. Operator interfacing conventions are discussed in the next chapter, including error status and recovery considerations.

Before proceeding to interpreter string considerations, this is an appropriate point to review efficiency topics. Since the command fetch, decode, and syntax processes must be cycled through for every program instruction, it is these routines that have the greatest effect on overall interpreter performance. The design rule is to do majority-common tasks here, and to delay unique functions until the appropriate interpreter routine is entered. In deciding which tasks should be performed where, it is important to recognize that all preinterpretive operations will be encountered and executed for every programmer-supplied instruction. Any task thus accomplished that is *not necessary for a given interpreter string* only serves to degrade total systems performance.

Interpreter Strings

In general, the design philosophy for the major functions of fetch, decode, and (less emphatically) syntaxing should be to optimize execution speed, with only minor emphasis on the memory usage required. The converse of this rule of thumb is applicable to the design of the interpreter strings, however, with certain exceptions.

The total number of different interpreter strings necessary is dictated by the programming language instruction set. An overall design theme should be to make maximum use of subroutine techniques and macrocommand concepts. As many as 50 or 60 separate routines is not an uncommon requirement, and some languages may require even more. Primarily for this reason, the design emphasis should be on economizing on *space* requirements, with execution *speed* as a subordinate consideration.

This suggestion should not be considered an absolute axiom, however. In analyzing the nature and types of applications for which the system is to be used, those programming commands that are most likely to occur frequently should be afforded greater emphasis on execution speed. Frequency of use in this context pertains to relative execution frequency and not necessarily to the number of occurrences within the source program. As an example, consider an INCREMENT command.

Within a given source program this command may occur in only a half-dozen places. Typically this instruction is imbeded within a program loop sequence, however, and during execution of the program this instruction may have to be interpreted many thousands of times. A savings of only a few milliseconds by the INCREMENT interpreter string can result in substantially faster throughput. Conversely, in a bookkeeping appli-

105

cation environment, SQUARE ROOT is a rather uncommon task, and slow performance is probably tolerable.

A similar rationale is applicable to decisions regarding which interpreter strings are overlay candidates. Additionally, strings that are implemented as software overlays should not be callable by another overlayed string. Although it may be tolerable to effect one disk access for interpretation of one program instruction, to use several overlay operations to support a given program statement will probably be insufferable.

Careful analysis of the source language command set should identify possibilities for *shared subroutines*—that is, routines to be shared between interpreter strings. The following examples are some suggested candidates.

1   *String moves.* Moves character strings (bytes) from one memory location to another; uses three parameters, (1) sending field position indicator, (2) receiving field position indicator, and (3) field length limiting value.

2   *Data field exchanges.* Moves data from the first-named field to a work area and moves the value in the second-named field to the first. Exchange is completed by moving the work area copy into the second-named field.

3   *Juxtaposition moves.* Places the value of a second-named field immediately to the right of the first-named field using a modifier to identify the starting point for the transfer. The modifier is a relative offset from the first position of the receiving field.

4   *Space filling.* When moving fields of data of unequal length, space fills (with blank character codes) for the remainder of the excess length (if any) of the receiver.

5   *Zone strip.* Replaces the high-order 4 bits of a byte with zeros, regardless of content.

6   *Numeric pack.* Strips zone bits of 8-bit encoded characters and juxtaposes low-order remaining bits (of 2 bytes) into one, maintaining relative sequence. The packed result will contain in the high-order position of even-numbered bytes what was originally in the low-order position. The low-order 4 bits of odd-numbered bytes are then juxtaposed into the low-order position of the even-numbered bytes. The pack operation is then completed by string-moving only the even-numbered bytes together into a receiving field.

7   *Numeric unpack.* This is the converse of the pack function. As an example, the zone portion of the ASCII character set uses the value 0011. The bytes to be unpacked are first split in half, each half being moved to a separate byte. The constant 0011 (decimal 3) is overlayed into the high-order position of odd-numbered bytes. The bits in the even-numbered bytes are first shifted right four positions, then the zone portion is enforced to be 0011.

8   *Graphic notation forms.* Encodes, as characters, binary values to be printed

or otherwise output in hexadecimal notation (or octal, or decimal, etc., depending on code sets).

9 *Clear.* Moves space characters or zeros to any named field; the actual code to be transfered is determined by the type of receiving field (alpha or numeric).

The preceding examples relate to operations that may be required to support certain programming language functions. A similar list of sharable subroutines can be compiled to support peripherals. Determination of possible common subroutines to support I/O tasks requires analysis of language commands, peripheral mechanics, and any services provided by the operating system (if applicable).

In summarizing the *how to interpret* aspect of the software architecture selection process, the three most basic considerations are as follows: (1) Speed optimization is paramount for all tasks that are common to the processing cycle; (2) space optimization is more important for the individual command interpretives; and (3) use of commonally shared subroutines between strings should be maximized. The source language facilities tend to dictate what may be allocated to sharable subroutines, and the hardware configuration delimits what may be common for I/O operations.

Chapter

Interface Requirements

During operation of a software interpreter-based system, the interpreter commands a central role. This lofty position enjoins significant responsibility on the software architect. The operational integrity of the entire systems environment depends on exacting rules and disciplines being established and adhered to.

User program processing by the interpreter requires continuous interchange between the interpreter program and the other components of the system. The intervals at which control may be transferred either to or from the interpreter must be regulated by the overall design of the software system. Second, the state-of-the-system (registers, flags, buffers, etc.) must be prescribed in advance to ensure that the routine receiving control makes no invalid assumptions.

Effective planning of software interface conventions can have significant results on the size and efficiency of the interpreter program. The space savings that can be achieved stem from precluding redundant object code, and execution speed benefits because of having to execute only the minimum instructions necessary.

Each of the major system components is briefly discussed in this chapter to identify those areas worthy of detailed analysis and specific design planning. In order of presentation, these components are the operating system, the processor, the peripherals, application programs, and operator functions. Figure 8.1 is a further extension of the figure at the beginning of this part (Figure 6.1) and shows the relative scope of this analysis to the overall software architecture study.

8.1 Operating System

Whether or not a system has an operating system is a major consideration in the design of a software interpreter. As has been mentioned previously, in the absence of an operating system, the responsibilities normally assigned to it are *imposed on the inter-*

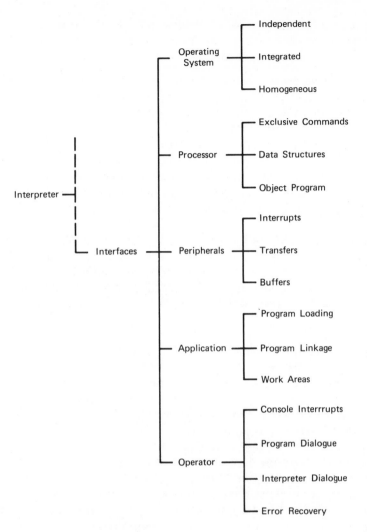

Figure 8.1 Interpreter interfacing considerations.

preter. To facilitate topical discussions, then, three classes of operating systems and interpreters are defined.

1 *Independent.* The operating system is a complete software entity and the interpreter is another, and they are totally independent. The operating system is capable of operation in a traditional manner, whether or not the interpreter is even used. The independence of the interpreter means that it is capable of being used in conjunction with *some* operating system, but is not specifically limited to just one.

109

2 *Integrated.* Where the operating system and the interpreter are still separate identifiable software elements, but they are designed as *mutually interdependent,* this system is classed as an *integrated* software interpreter.

3 *Homogeneous.* Systems that are not operationally oriented to the use of an operating system usually employ a software architecture that is fully homogeneous. An advantage of this type is its smaller size. By eliminating any attempt to maintain separate identities for the *operating system parts* and the *interpreter routines,* commonly shared subroutines are possible.

The nature of software interfacing between the operating system and the interpreter is comparable to that required between individual routines for either. The distinction is that the greater the independence of each, the greater the demands of either upon the other.

In the event that a planned interpreter must interact with a previously existing operating system, a careful analysis is necessary of the precedence factors already established. The designer of an operating system also suffers constraints and is pressured to optimize use of storage and performance. For this reason certain conventions may have been employed, the continuance of which is necessary with any add-on software.

- *Machine-language commands.* Certain machine instructions may have been previously established as exclusive to the operating system. In this case, the exact command restrictions must be identified and obliged.
- *CPU registers.* Similar to machine instructions, certain of the registers (and accumulators, etc.) may have special significance to the operating system, and must therefore remain unaltered by the interpreter.

The above two categories of restrictions are frequently applicable to I/O interrupt servicing functions, and consequently they may not impose serious constraints on the interpreter designer. In fact, the support provided by the operating system relieves a considerable responsibility for the interpreter. Any impositions thus suffered in interfacing to the operating system are adequately compensated.

Other conventions may also apply, and all operating system documentation should be thoroughly reviewed to ascertain their nature and detail. Some possibilities are the following:

1 *Code sets.* Whether ASCII, EBCDIC, or another is predominant, data values to be exchanged between the operating system and the interpreter should be in the same code set.

2 *I/O buffers.* Rules regarding field delimiters may exist. If a peripheral error condition prevails, the consequent buffer content must be anticipated by interpreter READ or WRITE command strings.

3 *Files formatting.* Header and trailer record requirements, if any, and their attendant rules may require special handling. These are usually associated with OPEN and CLOSE operations for serial file devices. For random access files, additional conventions apply to indexes and directories.

4 *Peripheral identification.* Differences between logical and physical designations are usual, and their respective code forms require specifics.

5 *Interprogram communication.* The loader service provided by the operating system is dependent on certain rules—and they must be obeyed.

6 *Operator controls.* The ability to *start, suspend, resume, end,* etc., is dependent on the operating system features. The design specifics provided by these services must be factored into interpreter support routines.

If the application requirement for a microcomputer system involves a homogeneous software design, interfacing rules must be formulated for the various components of the system. The significant difference in this case is the wider scope of the conventions list. Where the independent (and to a lesser degree the integrated) system established a framework for the interpreter design, the software architect must begin from scratch when planning a homogeneous system.

8.2   Central Processing Unit

Software interfacing to the CPU is actually the function of programming in machine language. In this regard, then, the syntax rules and the command code set, by definition, are the interfacing rules. Before embarking on a software design project as comprehensive as an interpreter, however, a machine-language conventions list is recommended. Two topical groupings are suggested for such a list. The first class of rules concerns task structures, and the second prescribes the usage of specific commands, registers, flags, and so on.

A prototype list of conventions for task structures might include the following, subject of course to the micro involved and overall interpreter design requirements.

1 *Nested subroutines.* An artificial limit of four is recommended for a processor that physically provides for seven. Reason: If it is necessary to patch a routine during debugging, subroutine jumping is a handy facility, and up to three more levels of jumps can be inserted without fear of losing the return linkage. Additonally, when enhancing the system, a language-extension feature may best be added by jump-entering an already existing series of nested subroutines.

2 *Loop controls.* A consistent method of counting iterations should be used. (As an example, always decrement to zero from a beginning limit.) Condi-

111

tional exits from within a loop should be placed near the beginning (or the end) of a routine, insofar as possible.

3   *The final instruction* of an identifiable task sequence should be wide enough (3 bytes, etc.) to allow substituting a branch or jump instruction to an add-on area should it be necessary.

4   *Comparison logic.* Consistency is desired—either negative or positive logic. (Always use BRANCH IF LESS, or BRANCH IF GREATER, and not unnecessarily intermingled.)

5   *Recurrent sequences.* Again, consistency; as an example, loading of registers: LOAD A, LOAD B, LOAD H, etc. Unless otherwise specifically necessary, always code in the same sequence.

6   *Do all necessary housekeeping* (register loading, flag setting, etc.) at the beginning of a major routine, then all processes, then all cleanup tasks immediately prior to exiting (subject, of course, to actual requirements to deviate.)

7   *Arithmetic values.* The end computational factor resides in the accumulator: Save it immediately, and any desired interim results. A sequence of instructions between the net calculation point and a subsequent use of the accumulator contents may be sufficient delay to jeopardize that the data therein is still valid.

The preceding suggestions may not be usable exactly as given, but they should provide an insight as to the concepts intended. The following list is also intended to be tutorial in nature, the difference being that this class of conventions applies to specific instructions and processor features.

1   *Register codes.* Truth significance—if 1 means yes and 0 means no, maintain that theme. Where 1 denotes no on occassion and yes on others, debugging is unnecessarily complicated and enhancements are more difficult to interface.

2   *Counters.* If binary suits a majority of requirements, use it consistently, in preference to sometimes decimal, etc.

3   *Flags.* Exception flags such as overflow should be reserved for their intended exception purpose—and reset programmatically immediately upon use detection.

4   *Interrupt instructions.* ENABLE should be restricted to certain routines: (1) READ or WRITE language interpreter strings, (2) the LOADER routine, (3) ACCEPT, DISPLAY, PRINT, etc. DISABLE should always be issued upon entry into any routine where CPU tasks should be exclusive without regard to external stimuli. RESET is the last instruction to be executed upon completion of an I/O service routine.

5 *Shift or rotation commands.* Restrict the use of SHIFT with CARRY to those instances where it is logically necessary to affect the CARRY flag. If the logic at hand does not specifically require altering the CARRY, use a simple SHIFT or ROTATE.

Memory

Although memory is not really a part of the CPU, it is a part of the processing system closely associated with the CPU and is therefore addressed here. A memory mapping plan constitutes a portion of the interfacing rules for use of main memory, at least with regard to structural placement of stored components. Additional conventions are required to accommodate certain implementation features. As an example, consider relocatable software module problems.

The rule: All user program code (procedures) are to be placed in low-order memory immediately contiguous to systems software, and all user data areas are to be stored in high-order locations, descending from the upper physical address limit. Further, all procedural code must be capable of being loaded at various beginning addresses.

The reason: The absolute ending address of the systems software area is subject to change, necessitated by feature additions or modifications to existing routines that require additional space.

The convention: All procedural referencing instructions must use a relocation register value to compute actual addresses. This convention applys only to those instructions that use direct address references. That is, *relative* addressing commands that use the program counter as a base for incremental (plus or minus) referencing are not affected.

Implementation

Two methods are possible to effect relocatability. During program loading the *relocation register* value can be added to all necessary operands, substituting the cumulative result as each pseudo-object command is stored in memory. This process is akin to a filter program. The second method is to compute effective addresses during program execution. This method depends on the decoder routine to retrieve the *relocation register* value and apply it as an add-on to the program counter concurrently with the operand decode task.

Other memory interfacing conventions are possible, but difficult to forecast in an abstract discussion. The formulation of specific rules for a given system design is dependent on the specifics of the targeted microcomputer and applicational usage requirements. Actual rules for *even-numbered byte offsets, modifier constraints,* and *headers* and *delimiters* are usually suggested.

As can be seen from these examples, the motivation for establishing processor and memory interfacing conventions is to simplify design debugging, ease the burdens of adding enhancements, and lessen the possibility of failures in the software system.

113

The actual rules to adopt require analysis of the entire system and usage requirements, and they should be formulated during the *initial planning process.* Although the conventions list may be lengthened or modified during design development, the temptation to ignore the rules should be guarded against. As with other judicial systems, if the law is ineffective, change the law; don't just disobey it.

8.3   Peripherals

Movement of data into and out of main memory is accomplished with input and output peripheral devices. There are two aspects of these processes, each requiring a separate discipline. Peripheral activity may be initiated by a user program instruction to READ (input to memory) or WRITE (output from memory). Second, the intended device must be controlled to effect the transfer of a block of data. The two major interfacing requirements for a typical software system concern the interpretive execution of the READ or WRITE (or similar) commands and the device driver function.

Device Drivers

There are three requirements to be satisfied by software drivers for peripherals: (1) *device control,* (2) *data transfer,* and (3) *status transfers.* Specific interfacing conventions are worthwhile for each of these, and a high-level discipline should apply to all peripheral software structures.

Peripheral devices may be categorized into three classes. *Input* devices such as card readers, paper tape readers, keyboards, and console switches are capable of only one-way data transfer from the device to memory. *Output* devices are also one-way oriented, from memory to the device. Examples of output peripherals are punches, printers, displays (CRTs, etc.), and console status indicator lights. The third class of peripheral devices are commonally called *storage* devices. This class includes those units that are capable of *both input* and *output* activity (two-way data transfers), such as magnetic tape, disks, and drums. Storage devices may be further classified as serial type (magnetic tape), or random access such as disks and drums.

A hierarchical software architecture will typically consist of *manager* and *driver* routines. The class manager routines are major function oriented to provide services common to a class of devices. Examples are the *input manager,* the *output manager,* and the *storage manager.* The interpreter string to accomplish a READ command will pass control to the *input manager* (possibly), from which control is passed to the specific driver that controls the designated input device. This same concept applies to WRITE operations; selection is first to the appropriate class manager, then to the designated driver. The decoder first decides whether the *storage manager* or the *input* or *output manger* is appropriate, based on the operand value of the user command being executed.

The following examples are provided to show the types of conventions that apply to interfacing requirements for peripherals and their attendant software servicing routines.

114

1 Memory buffers

- Two software registers are dedicated to provide I/O buffer arguments. The first register contains the address of a memory storage area to be used as an I/O buffer. The second register contains a character count limit (denotes number of bytes to be transfered).
- Prior to interpretive execution of an I/O command, the software I/O registers are loaded with the required values. If the function is to be an output transfer, the required data is already contained in the buffer area. If the function is to be an input transfer, any values already contained in the buffer area have been saved elsewhere, in anticipation of the buffer being overwritten with incoming data.

2 Command decoder routine

- The operation code (READ or WRITE) indicates direction of the data transfer—to or from memory.
- The operand denotes the specific device and the buffer area to be accessed (by indirect reference to the software buffer registers).
- The class manager can be inferred from the device designation of the instruction operand.

3 Device status syntaxing

- Device driver routines will pass the status of a peripheral to the syntaxer in the event of any incompleted attempt to process input or output.
- Reinitiation of an error-trapped I/O function will be at the discretion of the operator, *when permitted by,* and *as provided for,* by the syntaxer.
- A four-digit status code will be provided by the syntaxer.
  X000: peripheral device unit number (printer, disk, etc.).
  0X00: type of error condition, such as not ready, out of paper, disk not mounted, etc.
  00X0: permitted recovery options. 1 = abort; 2 = abort or continue; 3 = abort, remedy condition, then continue; etc.
  000X: direction of data transfer. 0 = obvious (unidirectional device); 1 = read attempt; 2 = write attempt.

4 Class managers

- Performs *buffer housekeeping.*
- Establishes or validates *buffer register* values.
- Performs any required *code conversions* (data values).
- Initiates the required *interrupt.*
- Passes *control* to the appropriate *driver.*
- *Receives control* back from device drivers, *interacts with the syntaxer,* and *resets interrupts.*

115

Scheduling

Because of the wide disparity in effective execution time for different system components, software design conventions can significantly influence total system performance. The largest differences in timings are those associated with peripherals. To complete a READ function from a magnetic tape cassette device may require a few seconds. During an equivalent period of time the processor (depending on type) can execute several thousand machine-language instructions. Even user program commands (pseudo-object code) can be interpreted at the rate of several hundred per second on the slowest microcomputers.

There are programming techniques that lessen the effects of timing disparities. Whether referred to as multitasking, time sharing, or execution overlap, the purpose is the same: to keep the faster components running at maximum capacity (the fastest often being the processor itself).

The simplified flow chart in Figure 8.2 compares a linear process with a multitasking process. The first example is *linear*: Each task is executed in order of presentation sequence, on a *one-at-a-time* basis. The *multitasking* example takes advantage of the length of time necessary to complete the READ task. Since it can be anticipated that a length of time is required for the READ operation, the ADD task is executed while the mechanics of reading takes place.

Software interfacing rules are required to ensure operational integrity between multitasking routines. The consequence of a breakdown in the subroutine-return linkages is total chaos. A *process controller* routine is usually assigned the responsibility of task scheduling and process-completion management. One method for communicating with the process control module is to pass codes to the controller that identify time-sharable routines. These *task-ID* codes are placed in a queue when a task is initiated, and may be examined by the controller to qualify their active status. When a task is completed its corresponding *ID* is removed from the active queue.

The most significant need for detailed conventions and interfacing rules for peripheral software routines stems from the multiple users of the peripheral devices. Not only does the user's program access these devices, but so do the interpreter, the operator, and utility programs. By planning for the I/O drivers to accommodate all of these users, and by thoroughly defining *before-use* and *after-use conditions* in a uniform manner, overall systems performance is considerably enhanced.

8.4   Application Program

A programming language is a highly formalized set of interfacing conventions—providing the interface mechanism between the programmer (user) and the computer. Not only must these rules be formal, they must be explicit. The programmer uses the language to express processing problems or machine execution sequences. The essence of effective communication is thought transferal with complete understanding from the sender to the receiver. Since the language is the only vehicle available by which the programmer may communicate instructions to the computer, the language must be *precise in definition,* precluding any ambiguity.

116

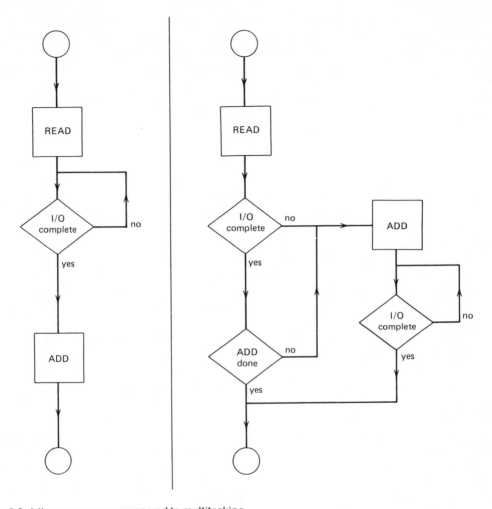

Figure 8.2 A linear sequence compared to multitasking.

The programmer's perspective of a programming language is two-dimensional: (1) the *system's response* to language expressions, and (2) how to describe processing tasks in accordance with the syntactical rules of the language. With the exception of absolute machine-language programming, all programmer-supplied expressions must undergo a translation process to convert source statements to absolute object code. It is required, therefore, that the source processor must also adhere to the language conventions to ensure accurate translation. In an interpreter system the pseudo-object code generated during source translation is subject to a further process of interpreta-

117

tion, hence is another slavish subject of the programming language. Any equivocation permitted by inexact language usage rules suffers numerous opportunities for exposure. Semantical integrity throughout these recursive translation processes can only be maintained by the strictest adherence to all applicable rules.

Program source statement translation was discussed in previous chapters. There are interfacing requirements that have not yet been identified, however, specifically those that can only be inferred by abstract evaluation of language provisions. The following four examples are intended to be suggestive only, recognizing that the exact formulation of a conventions list is dependent on the specific system.

- SWITCHES. Software switches are working storage locations that may be programmatically altered (*on* and *off*) by use of appropriate language commands. The initial state of these switches is usually *off* immediately after program loading. The programmer may then turn them *on* (or *off*) and logically test their status within program sequences. The convention is that all such switches maintain their state, subject only to appropriate program command alteration. The number of unique switches available is determined by the language, and their associated commands are also specified. The need for working storage memory within the systems software area can only be inferred by the provision for SWITCHES in the language.
- FLAGS. Test flags are comparable to switches in all respects except that their setting may be altered by implicit references. A programmed COMPARE instruction may set a FLAG to denote the truth of a logical comparison. Whether or not this flag is arbitrarily reset immediately preceding a COMPARE execution is subject to the language rules.
- INDEX REGISTERS. Working storage is required in the software area for counters that are used by various programming facilities. Again, the need for these counters can only be *inferred by analysis* of the language syntax; the programmer is not responsible for their allocation or definition. An example of a program command that would be dependent on such a register is INCREMENT. Other uses of these registers are to support subscripted addressing techniques—that is, the register contents are used as an address modifier.
- ACCUMULATORS. These are software-allocated working storage areas used to contain the operand values used in programmed arithmetic sequences. A common example is a storage area that contains the REMAINDER following a DIVIDE instruction.

Each of the above requirements is dictated by the conventions of the programming language, and its need can be inferred only by analysis of the language. Explicit rules must be established for their number, individual sizes, and usage, as part of the overall software design plan. Provisions such as these and the complete language syntax list constitute the interfacing conventions for the application program to the software system.

Program loading is another aspect of application program interfacing. Several

118

suggestions have already been offered concerning memory mapping and appropriate placement of software components. How the LOADER operates to effect the required memory allocation is the subject of design interfacing conventions. The program load operation consists of reading the stored program from an input device and copying it to main memory. As each block of program code is read from the device it is stored in an addressed memory location.

The following discussion describes a set of implementing conventions for program loading. Whether these methods are appropriate to a specific system design must be determined according to particular requirements.

Base Address Registers

Two software registers are contained within the working storage area of the interpreter. The first of these is an address constant that denotes the beginning of the procedures area of memory to contain user code. A second register contains the address of the physical limit of main memory (highest possible address).

Load Counters

Each of the base address registers has an associated counter (also located in inter-preter working storage). From a *warm-start status,* each of these counters is initialized at zero. *Warm-start* as used here assumes that the system software has been loaded to memory, but no application program is in residence.

As blocks of program object code are read from the storage device, the com-bined value of the *base register* and its associated *load counter* is used to determine the effective memory address for storage of the incoming block. The length of the block of object code is added to the *load counter* to provide the incremental add-on for the next block of code to be loaded.

Block Headers

The first word of each block of object code has an identification code that denotes whether the object code to follow is *data-type* or *procedures.* Depending on which, the appropriate base address register and load counter are used. The *block header* is used only to identify the respective types of object strings, but the header itself is not copied to memory.

End Sentinel

A final object code block has a unique header that denotes the end of the object program file. Program loading is a cyclic process of the form read-and-store, repeating until the end sentinel is encountered. When this unique header is encountered, the program loading process is complete and control can be transferred to begin interpre-tive execution of the loaded program.

Interprogram Linking

Program overlays (or additional modules) may be called into memory by execution of a programmed instruction for that purpose. When the decoder intercepts a CALL instruction, the command operand (symbolic name of program to be called) is saved in a working storage area and control is transferred to the program loader. The incoming program will be loaded to memory according to the values in the base address registers and their respective load counters. If the incoming program is intended to replace the calling program in its entirety, the registers and counters are set to their initial states. Portions of programs may be overlayed (segmentation) by preloading the base address registers with appropriate values and adjusting the load counters accordingly.

Since the *relative base address* of both procedures and data-type object code is maintained, data values may be passed between programs by manipulation of the base address registers prior to loading a called program. Synchronization of the data descriptors for the preceding program with the one being called is accomplished by a one-to-one replication of the defining statements in each. To facilitate interfacing, the group of statements to be replicated is arranged in the same relative (from the beginning of the data area) position in each of the two programs.

When a program is loaded into memory, it is a convention that all working storage, table areas, and data constants are in their *initial* states, that is, the same as their respective contents were when source program compilation is completed, but before any program execution was attempted. Consider the following example, expressed in COBOL:

```
001100     77 WORK-AREA   PICTURE   X(15)   VALUE IS SPACES.
```

During program compilation when this statement is encountered a string of *15 blank characters* is imbeded in the object code program (preceded by any necessary field header). When program loading occurs, the memory contents of WORK-AREA are initialized by copying into memory the blank character string. The contents of WORK-AREA during execution of the program is dependent on the use of this space by procedural instruction sequences.

Table areas may be defined with single programming statements, and these areas are also initialized as *blank* or *empty* by the same conventions as for single work field defining statements. Again using COBOL, the following example defines a table area:

```
001200     01 WORK-TABLE
001300     02 TABLE-ELEMENTS   PICTURE   X(5)   OCCURS 5 TIMES.
```

The compiler program will cause generation of object code strings that effectively represent a *five-by-five* array in memory when the program is loaded. Each of the TABLE-ELEMENTS fields (5) will contain five blank characters, each preceded by a header. The interpreter implementation convention is that areas thus defined are initialized with blanks during program loading.

Data constants are established in an application program by similar conventions. The following COBOL expression is descriptive:

001400   01 NAME-CONSTANT PICTURE X(11) VALUE IS "ABC COM-PANY."

The object code string generated during compilation will contain the encoded value of "ABC COMPANY" along with an appropriate header value, and the combined string is copied to memory during program loading.

Referring to the previously described memory mapping design, the conventions of this implementation provide for loading of work area allocations, tables, and data constants exactly as they are stored in the program object file, with the exception of their memory sequence. This exception convention is of the form that each incoming definition string is loaded in inverse order beginning with the high-order limit of main memory. As each succeeding data descriptor is encountered, the string length is used as a *negative offset* from the last value contained in the *data* area *load counter.*

In each of the above examples other conventions could be employed, and the determination of rules for a particular implementation is a function of overall software systems designing. Thorough analysis of the programming language provisions, operating systems services, and intended application is necessary to determine applicable interfacing conventions.

In summary, then, two aspects of conventions apply to the interfacing of application programs. The first of these is relative to the *programming language* used. While the language itself defines rules for syntaxing and grammer, semantical interpretation of source program expressions depends on implementation conventions. To enable a programmer to apply language provisions effectively to solve processing problems requires accurate definition of *interpreter implementing rules.* Incomplete description of interpreter mechanics will cause the programmer to suffer trial-and-error experiences until a thorough familiarity is attained. This learning curve can be further compounded by inexact definitions that allow ambiguous meanings to be derived from usage conventions lists.

Formulation of application program interfacing conventions during the software planning stage can ensure consistency of implementation, and accurate documentation of selected rules will facilitate maintenance of the software system.

8.5   Operator

A somewhat paradoxical circumstance prevails when establishing operator interfacing conventions. While it is assumed that the user should enjoy absolute control of the system, certain restrictions are necessary to maintain overall systems integrity. *When* and *whether* to acknowledge a console interrupt attempt characterizes one topic of implementing rules.

Another group of considerations apply to *dialogue interactivity* between the operator and the application program and, separately, between the operator and the systems software. Unless design disciplines are enforced in a logical manner, programmed output messages by the application or the operating software may inadvertently overwrite each other. This aspect must also be studied for *data input by the operator:* an input response passed to the wrong software routine can invoke unpredictable results. Application of specific interfacing conventions during the design of the software system can preclude any such indeterminate circumstances.

In the planning of any system it would be false to assume that all processing will always proceed according to plan. Abnormal circumstances will occur, and it is a function of design conventions to provide for *orderly continuance from abnormal situations.* The separate topics of error recovery and aborted program operations are covered last in this section; and certain suggested conventions are described.

Console Interrupts

Assume for this discussion that the intended system employs a typewriter-style keyboard as an operator input device. Assume further that the keyboard interfaces to the system as a peripheral device and keyed data is accepted into the main memory through the services of an *input device driver* routine. Each key on the keyboard is capable of generating a 1-byte character code, and only one code is possible for each key.

Programmed acceptance of keyboard-generated characters is provided for by machine-language instructions imbedded within the systems software. The normal state of the keyboard interrupt is in an ENABLED mode. This convention permits calling of the device servicing routine in the event of any key depression by the operator. The keyed data is transferred to a software-based *data buffer* area located in *working storage.*

Individual key codes are examined as they are encountered to determine appropriate software sequences. The usual exit of the keyboard interrupt servicing routine is back to the process that was interrupted. Certain specific keys, however, are indentified as requiring *exceptional task management.* As an example, assume that a LOAD key is available on the keyboard. Upon recognition of a LOAD signal, control is transferred to the program loader routine to begin loading of an application program.

As a system security precaution, to prevent inadvertent keyboard errors, the operator may be required by design conventions to use a *multiple sequence* of key depressions to access or invoke any function that results in an irrecoverable condition of the system. The need for this convention is based on the possible destructive overwriting of a new program to main memory, thereby destroying any previously resident program—even though it may not be logically correct to abandon the running program due to the state of I/O devices, files processing states, or working storage values in memory.

Double key selection methods do not exert sufficient safeguards in certain circumstances. Consider potential problems that could occur if an execution sequence were interrupted by keyboard entries that should not be permitted in *any circumstance.* An example of this situation is where the process at hand must be synchronized with

122

mechanical operations, for example, serial reading of data from a paper tape reader. Impromptu recognition of a keyboard interrupt during such a device-servicing function would most probably result in an irrecoverable situation, especially if it is necessary to resume the interrupted process after acknowledgment of the operator input.

The convention that applies to secure the system from untimely requests from the keyboard is to use a DISABLE keyboard interrupt instruction whenever appropriate. Extreme care however, must be employed in the implementation of this convention. The potential is to cause a situation that is totally irrecoverable by logical systems processes.

To describe this risk more completely consider the following theoretic sequence. Upon entry into a tape-read servicing routine a DISABLE-keyboard is issued. During tape reading an error condition is encountered, such as a broken tape. If it is not possible to correct the condition (the tape cannot be mended), reading cannot be resumed, and no keyboard signal can be used to cause a programmed branch to an alternate processing sequence to overcome this difficulty. The consequence of this *stalemate* would necessitate reinitialization of the entire system—probably not the most desirous choice, especially if several hours of processing has to be completely rerun.

Stalemates such as this can be precluded by an additional convention associated with the use of a DISABLE instruction. In any servicing routine that employes DISABLE, the first instruction to be issued upon an error condition is a keyboard ENABLE command. This convention will ensure that operator intervention is possible, but only in the event that an error or exception status is encountered; otherwise the operator is precluded from disrupting system-exclusive tasks.

Once an application program begins execution it is usual that all operator inter-activity with the system is controlled by the then-running application. It is the responsibility of the programmer to maintain operational integrity of the system during program execution. This responsibility includes qualification of any data input by the operator for both *form* and *content.* Inappropriate data entry can jeopardize the validity of data files. More important for this discussion, invalid input can jeopardize the logical continuance of program execution.

Depending on specific microcomputer system requirements, it is not necessarily practical to impose total responsibility on the programmer for all input qualification. Certain conventions of design can provide a greater level of security than can be achieved by merely cautioning the programmer on the risks of careless coding. A suggested principle for the determination of appropriate conventions centers on the distinction between *form* and *content.* Advise the programmer that he or she is responsible for *qualification of content of data entries,* and that the system will provide *syntactical assistance* in qualification of data entry *formats.* The following example (in BASIC) serves to describe the application of this principle:

```
002100 LET A = "bbbbbb"
002200 INPUT A
```

Note: The letter b is used here to show spaces.

123

The interpreter routine that executes the INPUT function will count the characters as they are keyed. If an attempt is made by the operator to enter more than six characters (as defined by the LET statement), an error-status is signalled to the operator by the interpreter. It is also incumbent upon the interpreter to recover to the beginning of execution of statement 002200 to permit another entry attempt. An entry of six or fewer characters will pass qualification by the interpreter and control will be returned to the application for logical validation of the entry content.

The manner in which an error message is output by the interpreter depends on the specific features of the system. The following describes a typical systems capability. Similar conventions may be established to suit a particular system, using this example as a guide.

1   *Hardware characteristics.* The operator's console consists of an alphanumeric typewriter-style keyboard, and an alphanumeric display device for single lines of 32 characters. An audible alarm is provided that can be sounded by software commands.

2   The following programming sequence is in vogue:

    003100   LET A = "ZIP CODE"
    003200   LET B = "*bbbbb*"
    003300   PRINT A
    003400   INPUT B

3   The operator lead-through message ("ZIP CODE") is displayed to advise the nature of the input requested. Program execution is halted on statement 003400 to permit keyboard input.

4   The operator keys the following: 331259. As each character is entered it is counted by the INPUT interpreter routine, and the sixth digit (9) is determined to be in excess of the defined field size.

5   The interpreter routine then sounds the alarm and displays the following message: "ENTRY OVERFLOW." Further execution is precluded by trapping the interpretive on a WAIT command.

6   The operator acknowledges the error condition by depressing the RESUME key. The last message output by the application is redisplayed and the interpreter reinitiates the user command that was in process at the time of the error-trap. In this case, the INPUT command on line 003400 is reentered.

The systems software design convention that provides for the preceding type of example depends on *dual display buffers.* Two 32-character working storage areas are provided in main memory. The first buffer is used to contain application program messages and the second buffer is exclusive to the interpreter. Any interpreter process that needs to communicate with the operator preloads the desired message in the

124

second buffer. The contents of the last output by the application program are saved intact in the first buffer. When the operator signals RESUME, the first task of the interpreter is to move the contents of the applications program buffer to the display device.

As a reminder: The above is only an example. Exact implementing conventions depend on specific requirements and system attributes. The intent of this example is to indicate the degree of planning that must be employed in designing for operator interfacing to the software system.

There is yet another requirement for conventions concerning operator interfacing: *system fault error recovery.* The previous example assumed that the logical recovery process was to force the operator to reenter the requested data. Not all error conditions are so easily recoverable. Consider the problem of equipment malfunction or unavailability. Assume that the following message is output by the interpreter: "PRINTER NOT AVAILABLE." The *printer driver* routine attempted to invoke use of the printer but a status condition was returned that caused processing to be suspended.

It is a function of overall design planning to prescribe the possible recoveries from this type of circumstance. The following conventions are suggested for situations like this.

1 RESUME. The operator can rectify the problem. (Perhaps the printer was turned off—the operator can turn the printer on and depress RESUME).

2 OVERRIDE. The printer is malfunctioning and unusable, but it is logically necessary to return to the application program. For example, the application will access an *end-of-job* routine to close files that were in use. This convention assumes that *device-status* is returned to the program and an alternate processing sequence has been provided for this eventuality.

3 ABORT. The nature of malfunction is such that no further execution of this program is possible and the only choice is to abort the run.

A method of design that provides for these situations is to permit the operator to enter key codes to donote the desired action by the interpreter. As an example, the letter R followed by RESUME signals the operator's desire to attempt to resume program execution (*implying that the condition has been corrected*). Or the operator's entry of the letter O in conjunction with the resume key tells the interpreter to override the user command then in process, transfer the device condition (*a peripheral status code*) to memory, and resume program execution with the next sequential instruction. Similarly, the letter A as an input character is the operator's choice for signalling an ABORT.

Upon recognition of an ABORT command from the operator, the interpreter transfers control to an *end-of-run sequence* that will reinitialize all systems registers and temporary working storage areas in anticipation of next being called upon to load another program. It is especially important to safeguard the operator from hasty or erroneous recovery choices. The conventions for permitting an ABORT should be sufficient to ensure that any such attempt is *emphatic* and *not inadvertent.*

By way of summation, then, operator interfacing conventions must embrace the subject of console-generated system interruption—both *when to* permit, and *when not to.* Interactive dialogue between the application or the interpreter and the operator must be accounted for by design rules that preclude device contention and the delegation of responsibility for operator entry qualification must be decided by design conventions. Overall software planning must also provide for *system* and *device error* recovery situations, and the methods by which the operator may signal recovery choices.

Chapter

9 A Software Design Template

The question now is where to begin. The system attributes have been identified. The user programming language has been analyzed. The types of applications, the general environment, and the experience level of the operator have all been considered. All that remains is to design, code, and test the software system. Planning for an *interpreter* is somewhat different, however, than planning for a *business data processing* application.

A common systems approach to designing an application is to chart *output, input,* and *processing requirements*—and usually in that order. System flow charting may then be used to map the major processing tasks, functional flow, and relationships between major job steps. A detailed process flow chart may also be required to plan the logic of certain computational routines. And finally, careful analysis of the overall system design plan can serve to identify commonality aspects that lend themselves to mutually sharable routines, modules, and so on.

While this methodology is satisfactory for many programming jobs, it is not particularly suitable for designing a software interpreter. In this instance the *input* is known (the program *source file*), the *computational processes* are identifiable (*translation*), and to a degree *output* consists of *interpretive command execution*—at best a crude analogy. And the next step—flow charting—is especially onerous. Perhaps detailed diagramming can be envisioned for particular tasks, but it is difficult to anticipate opportunities for shared subroutines, and more significantly, a perspective for the interfacing of discrete functions is nebulus. Hence the viability of a *software template as a design guide.*

This chapter describes how to compose a template, what it is intended to provide, and how software designing can proceed from it. Whether created as simply a *scratchpad sketch* or as a formal piece of system documentation, a template effort is worthy of the designer's time. And in either case it should not be hastily discarded; it is

127

highly useful during systems debugging. Review it also from the potential of long-range software maintenance; properly drawn it can serve as a design snapshot to a future viewer—yourself, or another.

9.1   Components of an Interpreter

To begin making a template, jot down one-liners of all of the *tasks* that the software must do. This is essentially a brain storming session. Pay no heed to priority, relative significance, or degree of interface dependency. At this point *structure* does not matter, but *requirements* identification does. As the list of notes grows, review earlier analysis of the *system,* of the *language,* and of the probable *application* mix. The more complete this list, the less effort there will be in further planning phases.

The second phase of this process consists of *categorizing* all of the listed items according to function. A practical method of doing this is to prepare an outline, much the same as would be used for a narrative paper or thesis. For most design projects a three-tiered format is useful. The three levels provide for *major, minor,* and *subordinal* ranking. The object of this exercise is to establih a *structure* on which further design planning may be made. The following example describes a pseudo-object interpreter that is integrated with operating system tasks.

I   Monitor

A   Sequencer
1   Program counter (user program)
2   Procedures base address register
3   Working storage base address register

B   Executive
1   Operator to system interface
2   Operator to interpreter interface

C   Class manager
1   Interface to peripherals
2   Interface to processor and memory

II   Program control

A   Command fetch
1   Retrieval of instructions
2   Object string parsing

B   Object program decorder
1   Decoder
2   Syntaxer

C   Operator communications
1   Keyboard input recognition
2   Message output control

III Interpreters

    A I/O group
    1 Discrete routines
    2 Macro routines

    B Procedures group
    1 Discrete routines
    2 Macro routines

    C Data movement group
    1 Discrete routines
    2 Macro routines

IV Resource managers

    A I/O devices
    1 Program loader
    2 Input
    3 Output

    B Processor
    1 Program counter (CPU)
    2 Interrupt stack maintenance
    3 Register initializer

    C Main memory
    1 Space allocation
    2 Working storage management
    3 Housekeeping

"One picture is worth a thousand words." Although the source and accuracy of this quote may be questioned, a degree of credence must certainly be allowed. From the outline a software template may be composed, and its advantage is pictorial. The outline represents structure, but relational perspective is most easily gleaned from a *picture.*

The examples on pages 130, 131, and 133 (Figures 9.1 9.2, and 9.3) show the evolutionary process by which template composition may proceed. Each of these examples equates to a respective level of the outline. There is no special intent to show *size* or *scale* of complexity here; rather it is important to establish *relationships* and *module candidates.* The actual process of drawing the template is reiterative—several sketches and modifications are frequently required. Practiced use of this methodology proves its value: A few hours sketching can save many wasted hours of trial and error programming, and effective module delineation is a positive fallout.

Since the topical names and functional identities in these examples are arbitrary author's choices, the following sections of this chapter are devoted to explanations. The purpose is twofold: (1) a better appreciation of the template method, and (2) examples of some of the many tasks necessary for an interpretive system.

129

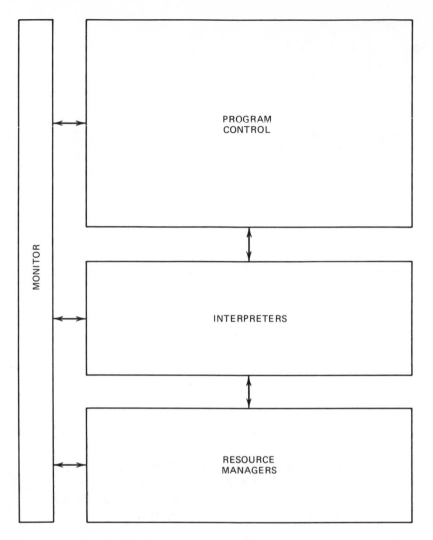

Figure 9.1 Major components template.

The reader is again cautioned that these examples are for illustrative purposes only and that a particular system may require different structures. The template itself and the task descriptions are authentic, however, having been extrapolated from an actual design developed by the author.

9.2 Monitor

The *monitor section* of the software system (see Figure 9.1) serves as a focal point for all that occurs in the software system. Contained within this area are various counters,

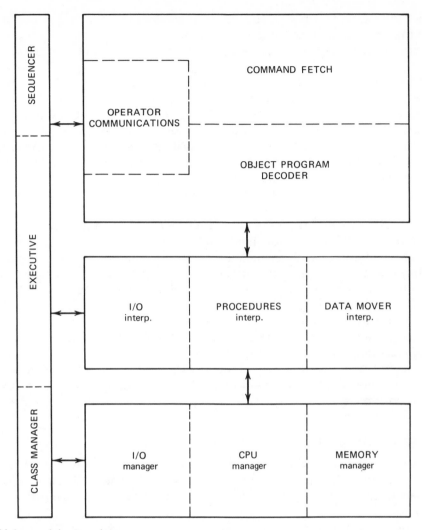

Figure 9.2 Major modules template.

codes, flags and indicators that may be examined to determine the operational status of the hardware, the application program, or the interpreter software modules.

Three separate modules comprise the monitor. The SEQUENCER module reflects the status of the application program. Here a program counter is maintained that indicates the memory address of the user object command that is in process of execution at any given time. The storage requirement is for a data word of sufficient width to contain the encoded address of the highest memory location. A relatively small routine (few instructions) is necessary to update the program counter as each application command is executed. Two static *base address registers* are allocated as storage fields

131

within this module also. The *procedures base address* register is used to indicate the beginning memory location of the procedures section of the application program, and the *working storage base address* register reflects the beginning of the application's data area.

The EXECUTIVE module serves primarily as interface control between the operator and the system. System-level commands, such as LOAD, RUN, HALT, and so on, are invoked through the logic of this module. The primary responsibility of this module is *operations synchronization.* Although a HALT command may be syntactically correct and logically recognized and accepted by the system, it can only be allowed to occur in an orderly sequence. During operation of the system, the EXECUTIVE temporarily stores system commands and releases them for execution only after an examination of all system status codes incidates that all operations by other software modules are complete.

The CLASS MANAGER module contains several code storage words for each of the peripherals and the processor itself, including main memory. The types of status maintained here include which devices are attached, whether they are operational, and whether they are idle or busy. A software equivalent of the CPU interrupt registers and an interrupt priority table is also maintained by this module. Device contention problems (*overlapped attempts by different parts of the software to access I/O*) are resolved here. An attempt by a routine to address an I/O device that is busy or unavailable is checkpointed here and held in abeyance until a BUSY status changes to IDLE, indicating device availability.

The overall design philosophy of the MONITOR section of the software system is to provide an isolated area within memory where overall operation of the system can be *audited* and *controlled.*

9.3   Program Control

The *program control* section of the software system provides for all of the services necessary for programming and operation of the total system. Three sets of modules are assigned to this section, each with its respective tables, constants, and working storage areas.

Console operations, both input (keyboard) and output (CRT), are functionally accomplished by subroutines contained within the program control section. As keyboard data is entered it is stored in a software buffer area of this module. Data that is to be displayed on the CRT must be moved into a similar buffer in this module that is allocated especially for that purpose. Once the application or the interpreter places data to be displayed into this buffer, this module's subroutine for CRT management is invoked to effect the data transfer to the display device.

Three types of data input may be generated from the operator's console. *Systems commands* are those that cause the loading of a program from mass storage, invoke the execution of a loaded program, or suspend or abort program execution. In the programming mode of operation, *program statements* may be entered, changed, or de-

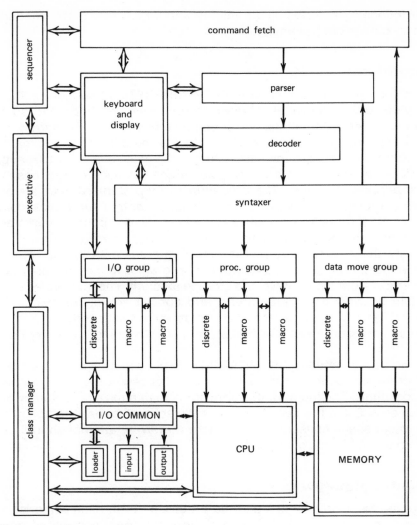

Figure 9.3 Major subroutines template.

leted. In the job mode of operation, the console is used for *data input for applicational processing.*

Two other sets of subroutines are contained within the program control section. One of these sets of subroutines is responsible for *locating* application object commands, movement of the commands from main memory into temporary storage here, and *preparatory setup* of the fetched command prior to attempted execution. The second of these two sets of routines then comes into control to *analyze* and *decode* the user's instructions to ascertain their validity and which interpreter module is to be called to carry out the programmed task.

9.4   Interpreters

The heart of the interpretive system is the INTERPRETERS section of the software. Contained within this section are the individual processing routines that cause machine execution of the intended functions described by the application program. Since there are essentially three major components (*peripherals,* the *processor,* and main *memory*), the interpreter routines are grouped according to the types of activity they support.

The *I/O modules* affect interpretive execution of all user instructions that specify *operation of peripheral devices.* The *procedures group* of interpreters are all oriented toward internal processing tasks such as *arithmetic, control,* and *logical comparisons.* The *data movement group* of subroutines is necessary to accomplish efficient *transfer of strings* of alphanumeric data between various locations in main memory.

The data that is acted upon by the interpreters is data that is supplied by the application, either stored as constants when a program is loaded *or* data that is moved into main memory from the console or a storage medium. The interpreter strings themselves contain no working storage areas, and consist entirely of machine-language instruction sequences. These routines are addressed by the decoder logic, and the data locations to be accessed are established prior to control being transferred to a specific string.

The basic architecture of the INTERPRETERS section is a hierarchical arrangement of discrete subroutines that may be serially accessed by various collective sequencing algorithms. The intent of this concept is to minimize redundancy of common task requirements. Since this section of the software system has the potential of being the largest (most space consuming), it is here that every attempt should be made to economize on the utilization of memory.

9.5   Resource Managers

The peripherals, the main memory, and the processor itself, each comprise separately classified resources. Management of each of these resources consists of identity qualification, physical attributes, and task administration. There is a direct relationship between these module categories and the interpreter string groupings. The *I/O group* of strings relate to the *I/O manager,* the *procedures group* interacts with the *CPU manager,* and the *data movement group* depends on the *memory manager module.*

Each of the resource managers may cross-communicate, and they are all conceptually under the control of the class manager module of the monitor section. The largest and most complex of these three modules is that dealing with input and output devices, but the functional orientation of all managers is similar. The intent is to provide a common point at which resource committment, control, and operation can be carried out.

An additional advantage should be noted for the use of this task isolation philosophy. Should any of these resources be expanded or exchanged, only a restricted area of the software must be modified to accommodate new or expanded features. In theory at least, any hardware change should impose only a nominal software impact.

The *I/O manager* contains the software drivers for the adjunct devices, one driver each, for each of the peripherals. The *memory manager* is responsible for knowing the block assignments of major components of the software system and which areas of memory are not allocated. *Processor management* is the simplest of these modules, but it provides the important service of CPU cold-start initialization. There is also stored here a temporary image of the processor's register contents during I/O interrupt operations.

135

A Design Model—Source Code Interpreter for BASIC

Model . . .an example for imitation or emulation.

Dissect . . .to expose the several parts for scientific examination.

The chapters in this part describe an actual system, certain types of problems common to software design, and a solution approach for similar systems. Before we can begin to dissect the model it is necessary to examine the machine itself. Such is the purpose of Chapter 10. The BASIC programming language implementation described next has been modified somewhat to lend itself to this hardware, the interpreter software, and to benefit the intended user of the system. The word *taxonomy* is again used here as a collective adjective to refer to these combined system and environment attributes.

The remainder of this part consists of three chapters, each of which addresses the overall architecture of the software system, topically divided according to the tasks of *program creation, debug testing,* and *application program operation* in a production mode.

The material dealing with interfaces follows the architecture discussion to show the ground rules by which the *operator,* the *software,* and the *machine* are interrelated. Even the smallest computing systems are highly complex tools, and it is necessary to impose certain rules of operation on the operator. The language by which a system is programmed is itself a rather detailed list of conventions, without which the computer could not perceive the intent of a program. And since the interpreter software system consists of many discrete routines and modules, discipline must be enforced during the design of the individual components to ensure that the sum of the parts equals a whole that will function without fail.

Relying on an understanding of the background material to this point, the final chapter in this part dissects the software system a part at a time. The design template is again used here, this time as an anatomy chart to allow a perspective of the whole while focusing attention on the indiviual parts.

While it may seem that this section reiterates the descriptive material provided in Part III, the aim of the previous part was to understand concepts, and here we describe an actual specimen.

Chapter

10 The Design Taxonomy

In this chapter we discuss the system, the language, and the systems usage scenario. The system is owned by the author and has evolved over a period of time and is comprised of various subsystem components acquired in the hobby computer marketplace. A degree of license has been applied to the implementation of BASIC at the discretion of the author, such modifications occurring as design judgments either to benefit programming ease or to lessen software burdens. The predominant usage requirements were, first, an easy-to-use, quick-to-program facility for general or utility program construction and, second, to provide a teaching tool for the exciting subject of computer programming.

10.1 The System

An Intel 8080A microprocessor is the CPU-heart of this computing system. The internal construction of the mainframe is typical of most such products on the market, consisting primarily of large-scale integrated (LSI) circuits mounted on printed circuit boards arranged in ladder fashion in a rack within the processor cabinet. Also contained in this box are the power supply module, peripheral interface circuit boards, and the computer's main memory module. Rather than reiterate the attributes of the 8080 microprocessor here, the reader is referred to the descriptive data in Section 2.2 which is fully applicable to this instance.

Main memory consists of 32,768 bytes of addressable storage, randomly accessable for both read- and write-to-memory operations. A 1024-byte _read only memory_ (ROM) storage circuit is also accessable to the processor, and contains a boot-up or cold-start routine by which programs are initially loaded into memory on system power-up.

Off-line storage of both software and application data files is on magnetic tape cassettes. A pair of tape cassette transports are interfaced to the processor's data bus and are completely under the control of memory-resident software. The programmed instruction sequence embedded in the ROM circuit is of sufficient scope to control read-to-memory initiation of one block of tape data when the system is first turned on. After loading this small program into memory (starting at absolute address 00), system control is transferred to word zero to begin execution of the program thus loaded, which is a read-and-store routine to bring into memory the software system.

Storage of application program statements or user data files on the cassette tapes may be on either of two tape tracks. Since the transports can only *read* or *write* on tape during operation in the forward direction, the tracks are mutually exclusive, each serving as a flip-side serial extension of the other. Data bytes are recorded on the tape at 800 bits per inch, in records of 128 bytes each. Thus one track (one side) of a cassette can hold upto 1350 such records (on a 300-foot digital tape cassette). The transport moves the tape at 7.5 inches per second when reading or writing, and the reverse rewind time is 90 seconds.

The cassette transport controller contains a 128-byte buffer into which tape data is read prepatory to serial transmission to memory via an 8-bit-wide data bus. Software driver routines are used to initiate head selection, drive motor start-up and directional control, and read or write directional transfers. The processor's interrupt facilities are used in conjunction with data bus port address assignments both to control the transports and to move data into and out of main memory.

Operational status of the peripherals can be software monitored by interrupt-testing certain signal lines of the transport controller. A *write protect flag* can be examined, signaled by the transport, to indicate whether the cassette then mounted has a plastic tab protector inserted or not. Another sensor identifies which of the two sides of the cassette is being used by detection of an off-center notch in the back of the cassette case.

Standard digital tape cassettes common to the data processing industry are used, which contain clear leader sections of tape on either end. A photoelectric cell in the transport detects whether the read head is aligned with the end of the tape (clear leader), and during movement of tape an early warning signal occurs as the end of tape approaches, because there is a small hole in the tape near the leader. Although two cassette transports are attached to the system, only a single controller is used so only one transport can be activated at a given point in time, and data transfers from or to either share a common data bus to the computer.

Operator's Console

All communication between the operator and the system is via a CRT display and a typewriter-style keyboard. The 52 keys provided include the alphabet (A–Z), the numbers (0–9), punctuation characters, and a space bar. In addition to a shift key and a line return, six special keys are used to generate any of the bit permutations possible for 8-bit bytes, that is, 00 to FF in hexadecimal. In a normal typing mode of operation the codes generated by the typewriter keys are encoded according to ASCII conventions.

The keyboard is connected by cable to both the CRT and the CPU, and keyed characters are transmitted to both concurrently. Only the lower 6 bits of keyed codes are accepted at the CRT, but the entire 8-bit code is transmitted to the processor over an I/O data line. The CRT contains a memory module to store the keyed data for the benefit of the screen refresh logic.

The page format for the display provides for 512 characters, arranged as 16 lines of 32 characters each. The character font is achieved by illuminating white dots on an otherwise dark screen, and the dot matrix for any given character is 5 wide by 7 high. The character cells are also grid matrix, 7 wide by 14 high. Two blank verticle rows of dots are used as character separators (the difference between 7-wide cells and 5-wide characters). The bottom row of each cell (five dots) is used as a *character cursor.* During input typing the cursor automatically spaces forward as each key is depressed to indicate the relative input position of the next keyed character.

Data output to the display screen from the central processor is via an I/O port to the CRT controller logic, again on a character-by-character basis. As transmitted characters enter the CRT refresh memory, they appear on the screen according to the location of the cursor character. The cursor position may be dictated by software routines prior to transmission of message data, using a separate I/O port dedicated to this purpose.

Line advancing on the CRT is in effect automatic. It should be appreciated that the 32-character line length is established only within the CRT circuitry, and as such is an artificial boundary to software. For software design purposes, the CRT is in effect a 512-character straight-line data buffer.

Similar in many ways to the CRT architecture is the printer. Character printing is accomplished at the rate of 30 characters per second in a serial fashion, with 80 characters possible to the line. Here, too, the character font is created using dot matrix techniques, and a 5-wide by 7-high grid is used. The character generator logic of the printer decodes incoming ASCII bit patterns to form any of 64 possible printable characters. Transmission from the processor to the printer is character serial using an output data port, and the bus is cabled to the printer controller. Verticle line advancing is in 1/6-inch increments, on a line-at-a-time basis. The specific hexadecimal code OD (carriage return) is decoded by the printer controller logic to cause one line advance and for the print head to return to print column 1. Attempting to print more than 80 characters on a line will also cause an automatic line advance and continuation in the first column on the next line. This facility has special significance from a programming point of view, since it is possible to page space without issuing unique commands to do so.

Recapping the above description, then, we have a microcomputer with 32,768 bytes of memory, a CRT/keyboard console, an 80-column serial matrix printer, and two magnetic tape cassette transports. A pictoral layout of the system components is shown in Figure 10.1, the keyboard key arrangement is depicted in Figure 10.2, and the ASCII character chart for the CRT is given in Figure 10.3.

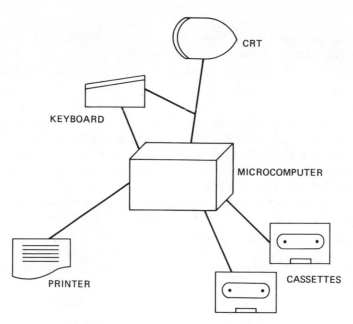

Figure 10.1 Hardware layout of model.

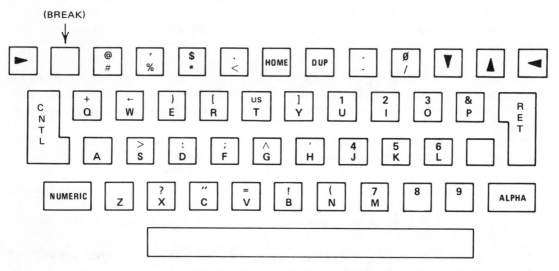

Figure 10.2 Model keyboard layout.

142

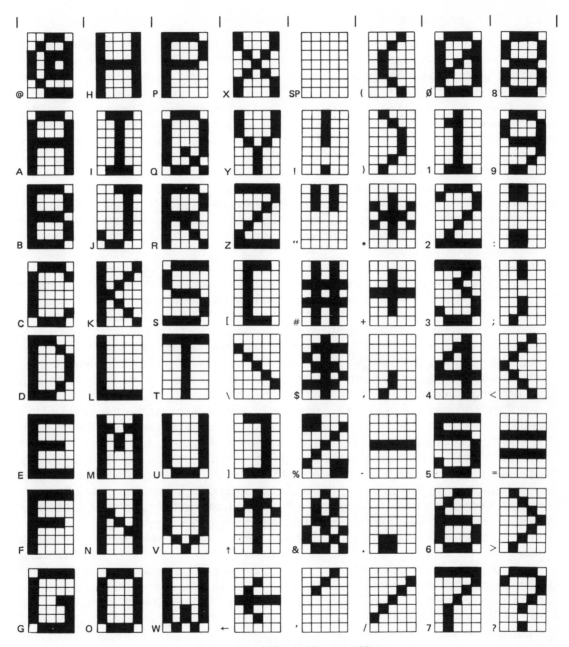

Figure 10.3 CRT graphics capability.

10.2 The Language

The language used in the model is BASIC, Beginner's All-purpose Symbolic Instruction Code or Beginners Algebraic-Symbol Interpreter Compiler. Computer science histories seem confused as to which phrase gave birth to the acronym, but hindsight observation tends to substantiate either.

Beginners: The BASIC language can be learned by the average noncomputer-oriented mathematics or engineering student in a few hours, and the simple conditions and attributes of the language allow it to be mastered with only a few days practice. However, no derogatory connotation should be ascribed to the word *beginners.* Even long-time veterans of the programming profession enjoy using BASIC. This is especially true where BASIC was the first language learned. A programmer may eventually marry another, yet retain a certain fondness for the first—true of love, and languages.

All-purpose: BASIC is very commonly used for business and commercial purposes on time-sharing systems, with many users interacting with the computer. Although less powerful than ALGOL, FORTRAN, PL/1, or others, it is often adequate for both business data processing and machine process control applications.

Algebraic-Symbol: A definite genitive relationship can be inferred by comparing BASIC to FORTRAN. Both languages favor expressions in arithmetic form, and numerous facilities are provided for high-level mathematics. For a totally mathematics-committed environment however, BASIC is the lesser of the two. There is no FORMAT statement (a favorite in FORTRAN), and most implementations fail to distinguish between real numbers and integer numbers. However, the algebralike syntax and the math-macro instructions do permit greater ease of arithmetic expression than the pure business languages such as COBOL and RPG.

Symbolic Instruction Code: Each line of BASIC begins with a line number that identifies the line and specifies the order in which the statements should be executed. The line number then serves not only a sequencing function, but is also used as a symbolic reference within programming logic and control statements. Working storage locations, tables, constants, and literals (stored as constants) may also be assigned symbolic tags using the letters of the alphabet singly, or letters in conjunction with numbers. Keywords and commands are either mnemonic abbreviations or full English words, lending a degree of narrative context to program documentation.

Interpretive Compiler: The BASIC language was developed at Dartmouth College under a National Science Foundation grant by Professors J. G. Kemeny and T. E. Kurtz. The compiler was originally designed for the GE-234 computer and the GE DATANET 30, which is a data communications-oriented processor. Many time-sharing implementations permit highly humanistic dialogue, such as initial contact commands like HELLO,'' or HOW DO YOU DO.'' Some of the other characteristics touted for BASIC include the following:

- Conversational statements.
- Free-style formatting.
- Segmenting of complex statements.

- Six significant digits of accuracy.
- Easy program modification.
- Editing functions.
- Simple linking of two or more programs.
- Facilitates keyboard real-time debugging.

Most of the reasons listed above indicate the appropriateness of BASIC in a support role in a software in research lab, and also why it is a popular teaching language. The significance of the word *interpretive* should not be missed either. BASIC is a high-level language: It is procedure-oriented, artificial in the sense it is not machine-sensitive. It is symbolic address and mnemonic command based: simplistic parsing and minimum constants storage dependent. The relatively few *real commands* are readily distinguishable from the *macrocommands:* Subsetting the language by excluding unneeded commands is natural. This *real* and *macro* delineation is important: Language extensions are easily implemented as macrocommands. These arguments for modifications capability (of the language itself) causes us to broach the subject of standardization and conformance next.

Some measure of the popularity of a programming language can be gleaned from various attempts at standardization. Without any overt mention of the parentage of BASIC, the American National Standards Institute circulated a draft proposal in January 1976 for a four-month period of public review and comment. This draft of an intended standard was prepared by their Technical Committee X3J2-BASIC, American National Standards Committee X3—Computers and Information Processing, and bore the subtitle, "Programming Language Minimal BASIC." The purpose of the proposed standard is set forth in the introductory paragraphs:

This standard is designed to promote the interchangeability of BASIC programs among a variety of automatic data processing systems. Subsequent standards for the same purpose will describe extensions and enhancements to this standard. Programs conforming to this standard, as opposed to extension or enhancements of this standard, will be said to be written in "Minimal BASIC."

Although the BASIC language was originally designed primarily for interactive use, this standard describes a language that is not so restricted.

Written in almost legalistic jargon, a programming manual this document is not, a commercial sanctimony it is. To be able to advertise full compliance offers a vendor certain sanctity, and the users of their products may expect a familiar dialect of the language. Whether it is programs or programmers that must move from one system to another, both benefit from the use of standard languages.

In the case of implementation for a research lab, the likelihood of transporting programs to another system is small, and commonality is not given great importance. The possiblity of student programmers encountering BASIC on other systems is very real, however. This, then, is the guiding principle on which this BASIC is described. To achieve machine transportability requires too explicit conformance—machines are too

145

inflexible. To maintain programmer familiarity, the spirit of BASIC prevails—in anticipation of the purely human trait of mental agility.

The following guidelines apply, not only in this instance, but equally to other attempts at standards compliance for any language on any system.

Subsetting—meaning fewer provisions than the comparisons model or definitions document. Certain features, commands, or syntactical units may not be supported, recognized, or permitted. That which is included is syntactically correct for upward migration to more expensive implementations. Downward migration from the greater to the lesser is only viable in the instance of avoidance of restricted features of the latter.

Nucleus—all of the commands, features, and syntactical disciplines common to the standard should be in accord with the standard. By convention, the implementor may constrain or restrict the use of features or functions, but that which is included must conform to not only the content, but the intent as well, of the guiding standard. Expressed more pragmatically: That which there is must work just as stated, perhaps not as fully, but certainly what does work, works exactly.

Extensions—above and beyond the letter of the law. Two types of language extensions are senctioned: (1) additional commands, keywords, or other features, that seek to fulfill a supposed omission of the standard; and (2) a greater capacity or form of expression for features or facilities already provided for by the prevailing standard. Again, more commands may be added, or the system may provide greater limits or precision during execution than was originally stipulated.

10.3   The Application Requirements

The equipment configuration described in Section 10.1 was assembled to support research efforts in software technology. The system serves as a test vehicle on which to conduct experiments for both task techniques and function concepts. Whether seeking to improve a search algorithm or to prove a theory applicable to artificial intelligence, the test specimen is usually prepared in machine-language code.

As in other fields of scientific endeavor, the pure research work constitutes a proportionally small part of a given project. For many, a considerable amount of time must be allowed for preparation of test data, and for analysis of the test results.

A prime requirement, then, in a global form of description, is for a software system that facilitates rapid and easy development of utility-type programs. Many such programs, as used in these activities, are of a one-shot nature. That is, test data is needed, a program is written to create it, and the program is soon discarded since it is of no further value. Similarly, many programs are general enough in nature that they are retained in the library, to be modified on an as-needed basis to suit particular requirements.

Another class of utilities is also necessary. These share an anology with test bench equipment. Most are, in effect, front-ends. They are incomplete programs in the sense that they have only the rudiments of procedural logic, usually akin to the start-up or housekeeping tasks that typify much programming. The advantage of these programs is that much of the rote work is already done—the statements are syntactically clean, and the functions provided have been debugged in previous use.

No experienced programmer enjoys the high degree of repetition that often occurs—repetition in the sense that certain functional requirements must be provided for again and again with each new program to be written. That is the purpose of both utilities and front-end partial programs: to alleviate redundant design, coding, and debugging efforts.

Some of the attributes of a good software laboratory system include the following:

- High-level procedure-oriented language.
- Real-time compilation—source statements entered in an on-line mode, and immediately available for execution.
- Easy modification to already existing programs.
- Ability to add additional functions to reusable partial programs.
- Simple-to-use system, requiring only minimum effort to recall operational sequences.
- A highly consistent and comprehensive scheme for system messages and error condition recovery options.
- Highly volatile job mix—processing jobs vary considerably and are changed frequently, speed of execution is of a lesser priority.

There is one additional requirement that tends to be specific to the software development shop: being able to revert to machine-level coding from a high-level language and back again. Save for this unique requirement, the attributes thus far listed can equally apply to a software system for a teaching lab. Our colleagues in the teaching profession assure us that learning is considerably enhanced when students experience immediate cause-and-effect stimulation. Such is a special attribute of a source language interpretive system. And, certainly, an easy-to-use, conversationally assisted operations philosophy lends itself to student use. The self-confidence of the novice programmer is not nearly so apt to wane when the system prompts for that which is expected next, and provides for intelligible feedback when things go amiss.

With this background in mind, recognize that the following requirements are more specific to the hardware configuration and the BASIC language implementation used.

- Machine-language macroroutines must be accommodated, to be called by use of a symbolic name.

147

- An on-line keyboard entry facility must be provided to facilitate direct-to-memory entry of machine object code.
- Single-step execution of BASIC program statements is a must, with the ability to examine memory contents on the trailing threshold of execution of each statement.
- Program overlaying must be supported to permit segmentation of programs that are too large to be fully resident.
- Reasonable precautions should prevail in the interpreter design to preclude BASIC attempts to overrange application program memory.
- In the event of abnormal termination of a BASIC program, the statement line number then in process of execution should be announced to the operator.

In conclusion, much of what is described here as applicational requirements for this system can be said to apply equally to many other types of environments. It would be a false assumption, however, to say that this system can satisfy all seemingly comparable situations. A glaring omission here, inexcusable for many processing requirements, is the lack of protection provided for a volatile memory system. And even though this system could otherwise satisfy certain business-type data processing functions, its very flexibility (dynamic programability) could be disadvantageous if not adequately safeguarded.

Such cautionary comments may seem superflous to the reader, but the intent is to advise why some features are present and others are not in the software model that is to be dissected in the following chapters.

Chapter

11 The Architecture

This chapter discusses problems that can be resolved by the designer when planning the basic software architecture. As a global concept, this model addresses the space problem (of the two dimensions of space and time) by architecture design, and depends on internal coding techniques to satisfy execution speed requirements.

This concept is appropriate since the general theme of the usage scenario is for considerable functional features, with no special demands for optimum execution speed. With regard to speed, it is also assumed that greater degradation at program load and set-up is preferred over slower in-run execution. The basic philosophy applied, then, is to exclude from main memory residence any functional routines that are not subject to concurrent usage. A time-cost factor must be suffered by the operator when exchanging exclusive functions, but these design trade-offs have proven acceptable.

Software loading is discussed first, since a stored program is required before a computer can operate. Media and memory allocation of the software components is discussed next—where modules are stored is a function of the architecture. The final subject, program execution, is also sensitive to the basic design, especially interprogram linking and internal program operation.

11.1 Software Loading

As mentioned briefly in Chapter 10, the processor is designed so as to depend on a cold-start boot program that is stored in ROM (read only memory). The absolute address of the ROM (512 bytes) is hexadecimal 00. Contained in the ROM is a relatively small program that provides CPU initialization service and a cassette transport driver and read-to-memory sequence.

System power-up conventions first expects power on to the main frame, then power on at the terminal and cassette transport. Whether the printer is powered up at this point is unimportant during the cold-start process. With a systems software cassette mounted, the console RESET button is depressed to begin the software boot-up.

The hardware RESET logic causes the memory address decoder to identify the ROM as address 00 and the processor program counter is set to instruction address 00. As the ROM stored program begins execution, all interrupts are disabled and the CPU registers are cleared. The last function of processor initialization is to set up an interrupt for cassette drive-1, and control transfers to the driver routine. Data transfer to memory begins at location 1024 (hex 0400), and data is transferred on a byte-at-a-time basis to memory the read-and-store loop continuing until an end-sentinel is encountered (the end-sentinel for this purpose is a full 128-byte buffer load of zeros).

When the end-sentinel is encountered the ROM boot program generates an interrupt to a specially dedicated I/O address which causes the main memory decoder circuit to alter such that what was address 1024 (0400 hex) now becomes address 00. The boot program then executes a branch to this new address 00, which is the program that has just been loaded. This feature of the hardware logic effectively *deallocates* the ROM memory from the system. It can be deduced, then, that the boot program is incapable of reentrant execution, and is accessible only by way of a hardware logic RESET.

It is also significant that control passes to the main memory program while the cassette tape forward movement is still in progress. Because of this hardware architecture, software loading is accomplished in a leapfrog fashion, initially by the ROM-based boot, with the balance of the loading accomplished by the first incoming software routines.

The tape-based portion of the software load program is designed according to whatever conventions are established for the software system to be used: in this instance, the BASIC software interpreter system. Accordingly, the software tape next contains three more 128-byte records of all zeros (timing consideration) followed by the interpreter software.

The first module stored is the program loader. The first instruction of the program loader is a branch instruction (3 bytes) with a 2-byte address header next following. This address header will contain one of three possible values, which indicate the memory load starting address for, respectively, the interpreter software, a software system utility overlay, or an application program (or application overlay). Since according to the convention for module placement on the tape, the first module is the program loader, it is addressed to be loaded into memory in its ultimate location when the entire software system is resident.

The balance of the software contained on the master software cassette is the interpreter system, and each module is loaded under control of the program loader. For the purposes of the program loader, the entire software system is considered as one continuous module and the beginning memory address is word 00. As the interpreter is loaded, then, the boot link loader that was temporarily stashed starting at 00 is now overlayed.

The chief advantage of this leapfrog loading concept is to permit complete relocatability of the program loader, and in essence, there is no hardware dictates for memory allocation of any of the software system. Should it be necessary for any reason to relocate the program loader, for example, by changing the base address header value of the first tape stored module, all else is under control of the software for memory allocation, with no insistence that the loader be located at 00.

Once the software system is loaded, the program loader passes the active tape transport status to the generic files manager and transfers control to the executive routine, thereby relinquishing system control, and the system is ready to operate.

During normal operation of the system the program loader may be invoked by either of two methods. With processing suspended and control trapped in an idle state by the executive module, the operator may enter on the keyboard any of several system commands. To load a program the command typed should be LOAD, followed by the *name* of the program desired. The keyword LOAD is syntaxed to ensure that a valid task is intended, and if valid, control is passed to the loader module. Cassette reading is then initiated, searching for the appropriate *named program.* Program names can be up to eight characters, and begin in the sixth byte position of the first tape record of each program. (The first 3 bytes are reserved, and the second 2 bytes are the base address for load purposes.)

The second method by which the program loader is activated is somewhat similar, except that it occurs as a result of an application program commanding link up with another. The BASIC macrocommand LOAD (an extension) is used to initiate the program name search. The *name* of the program being called is a programmer-supplied argument following the LOAD macro.

Notice that, by reason of this design, programs may call other applications, utilities, or overlays to either. No validation of the base address for the called program is attempted by the loader, however, and run-time fatalities are possible if the tape does not contain valid address headers. If an entire tape is searched with negative results, control is passed to the executive's load point and an idle occurs, awaiting the operator's exchange of the cassette (assuming that the wrong cassette was mounted).

When a *not-found* trap-out to the executive occurs, the name of the program being searched for is displayed on the CRT along with the error code denoting that the file is not available. This error trap is the same for either type of program loader access. If the operator called for a program, the *name* to be searched for is already displayed, and if a program search was initiated, the program name is supplied to the CRT by the loader error routine.

One more aspect of the loader architecture should be noted. Although all programmed loading operations assume that drive-1 is to be used, programs may be located anywhere on the tape including being interspersed with data files. A throughput gain can be planned around this feature by copying software routines adjacent to data files to shorten the program search times, as appropriate.

It is also possible to queue successive job runs by chaining programs and files using single-statement programs that contain only the *LOAD macrocommand.* An enhancement potential for this system also exists: As an option, an additional parameter

151

of the LOAD macrocommand could specify *which cassette drive* is to be searched.

A block diagram depicting the cold-start and boot-up process is provided in Figure 11.1.

11.2   Software Storage

Reviewing the usage scenario of this system, certain requirements tend to dictate the software storage strategy. One of the key factors is the predicted *volume of real-time programming.* It may be fairly assumed that the interpreter itself is to be fully resident at all times. The alternative methodology of calling into memory selected interpreter routines on an as-needed basis is precluded here because of lack of a random access, mass storage device.

The adopted storage architecture does employ a form of memory conservation, however, by providing that selected support functions be treated as mutually exclusive, each sharing the same storage allocation. Generically referred to as *system utilities,* the space sharing routines include the following:

- Keyboard source entry.
- Memory modify.
- Dump to printer.
- Dump to cassette.
- Run-time trace.
- Cassette copy and modify.

Main memory allocation basically employs a scheme of low-order address assignment for the interpreter software, immediately followed by the *system utility* reserved space, and the balance of main memory reverts to applicational use. The space reserved for the *system utilities* is 512 bytes exactly, whether a given utility requires full use of the space or not. So that the reader may appreciate why it is possible for this space to be shared by these different support modules, each is briefly described.

Keyboard Source Entry

It is this module, when resident, that supports keyboard entry of BASIC source program statements. Included in this module are the syntaxing and parsing subroutines necessary for editing and qualification of operator entries. This functional module depends heavily on services provided elsewhere in the software system; viewed separately, this module does not really resemble a program. Included in this overlay are those discrete subroutines that are not otherwise needed by the interpreter system when running or loading BASIC applications. The decision to allocate the functional capability for source program entry as an overlay depends on the premise that when an application is being executed in a production mode the keyboard and display are committed to the application and not available for source entry.

Memory Modify

A prime user requirement is for machine-language object code entry capability. This

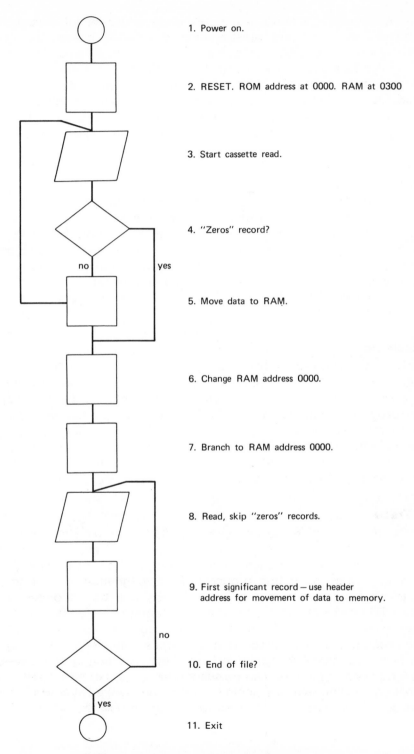

1. Power on.

2. RESET. ROM address at 0000. RAM at 0300

3. Start cassette read.

4. "Zeros" record?

no   yes

5. Move data to RAM.

6. Change RAM address 0000.

7. Branch to RAM address 0000.

8. Read, skip "zeros" records.

9. First significant record — use header
   address for movement of data to memory.

no

10. End of file?

yes

11. Exit

Figure 11.1 Diagram of the *leapfrog loader* principle.

153

permits referencing any location of memory (byte addressable), displaying memory content, and keyboard entry and transfer of keyed codes to memory, selectively. Since any area of memory may be accessed by this feature, a considerable responsibility rests with the operator to maintain the integrity of the software system and any resident program. It is also obvious that BASIC application program code may be altered, entered, or deleted by using this feature, but against caution: no validation, editing, or syntaxing services are provided by this utility. This feature is a practical choice for shared storage because of its low volume requirement, and its use by novice programmers is on a permissive basis.

Dump to Printer

The obvious value of this module is for printed documentation of program contents. A full range of options are provided as to what to print through the use of keyboard-supplied parameters. The resident BASIC program can be printed in its entirety, or selectively, by naming the beginning and ending statement line numbers. Systems software memory can also be printed, with the beginning and ending address specified by the operator. Memory addresses may be specified as decimal, hexadecimal, or octal values, and the printed listing is formatted with references according to the selected numerical notation.

Dump to Cassette

Basically this module is the same as the *dump to printer*; the most significant difference is the output medium. When first initiated, however, a programmer-supplied *file name* is requested (any eight characters), which is written into the header record on the cassette for program identification. For BASIC programs the load-address portion of the header is system generated. When other areas of main memory are to be written to tape it is incumbent upon the operator to format the data content of the header record. To facilitate this, a free-format keyboard entry routine is provided, and entries assume the numerical notation base specified by the operator.

Run-Time Trace

To invoke the trace function the operator keys TP or TF as a two-letter mnemonic following the RUN command. When invoked, Run-Time Trace will cause the BASIC statement line number (*TP—partial*) to be displayed on the CRT on line 16, position 1, during running of the application program. The designation TF will cause the full statement to be displayed, but only as much as can be accommodated by the 32-character CRT line length limit; any excess characters are truncated (not displayed). In the trace mode, as each BASIC statement is fetched it is immediately displayed, then interpretive execution occurs. Immediately after statement execution the system halts, awaiting a keyboard signal to continue, and thereby effecting single-step program execution. Single-step operation can be suspended by use of a CONTROL key, SHIFT key combination and line return. Tracing can again be invoked at any programmed halt point that expects keyboard entry. To restore the trace mode, the CONTROL key should be used in conjunction with whatever entry the program provides for. This highly useful debugging aid is most appreciated by the novice programmer, and it is a natural for shared memory usage with other system utilities.

Cassette Copy and Modify

This module provides for copying data or software cassettes from drive-1 to drive-2. Copying options include the entire cassette, selected files (*by name*) or selected blocks *by relative record number.* The record buffer may also be optionally displayed during copying, and as each record is displayed (input), it may be skipped or written to the output cassette as indicated by the operator's decision. While a record is displayed on the screen the operator may alter any character position by selective movement of the cursor and overlay keying of the desired modification prior to specifying the write output. Data are displayed in either hexadecimal or octal notation as optionally specified when the module is initiated. This feature is provided to permit minor changes to cassette files and to allow data repairs to cassette records that have been corrupted. Although the functional routines of this module share the system utility common area, main memory (applications area) is used for record buffers, so no application program can be resident during use of this module.

The memory allocation diagram in Figure 11.2 shows the relative location of the *system utilities* overlay area.

This same diagram shows the memory assignments for the other major software components. Location of the interpreter software in low-order memory is based on the assumed stability of its design and size. All memory addresses beyond the artificial boundary represented by the end of the systems software are available for application program storage. To reiterate: Application programs are stored in a split fashion, with the procedural code and data areas separated.

The BASIC program statements are stored serially, beginning with the first available address beyond the systems software area and continuing toward high-order addresses. Working storage defined by program statements (either *explicit* or *implicit* definition) is allocated in reverse sequence from the upper physical limit of memory downward. With the software system loaded and an application program in residence, any unused memory is relegated by this architecture to the approximate middle of the application's area of memory.

The actual midpoint address of uncommitted applications memory varies as a function of the user program structure. The ratio of procedural instructions to data storage definitions determines the blocking of unused space. Thus a program that is largely procedural (as opposed to being predominantly working storage) will cause a relatively higher midpoint address. At any given time, however, the amount of unused memory available can be derived by computation. The last available address preceding the data storage area, less the first available address following the procedures storage area, is the remaining available bytes of memory.

As the remaining memory is allocated during program statement entry, either procedure source lines or data-defining statements may finally exceed the space available. If a space contention occurs., favor is allowed the program statement rather than

155

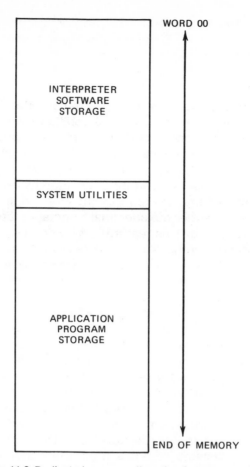

Figure 11.2 Dedicated memory allocation for *system utilities*.

work area assignment. Memory management assistance is provided to the user also by means of a system command (SPACE) that returns to the display the available memory as a total unused-bytes figure.

The method by which the system maintains advice as to the logical and physical allocation of memory is discussed in the next section. The mechanism is dependent, however, on a feature of the storage architecture: a *memory resident index* (MRI) table. Pointers are maintained in this table to argue the physical location of all working storage assigned, based on the symbolic tags used by the programmer. Additionally, *base address registers* provide notation of the beginning address of procedural memory and the last used address (ending of) application working storage. The MRI pointers are relative offset values from the base registers rather than actual physical memory addresses.

The significant aspects of this storage architecture, then, are that (1) application programs are split, with procedures and working areas allocated from upper and lower user memory, respectively; (2) a *memory resident index* table is maintained by the system to denote the physical location of data areas; (3) a *system utilities* area is provided for common overlay usage by mutually exclusive routines; and (4) during real-time programming activity, contention for the last remaining user space favors storage of procedural statements over any further allocation for working storage.

11.3   Program Execution

The following list of parameters dictates the primary design principles of this software system.

- The amount of memory to be allocated for an application program may be specified—up to the physical limits of main memory.
- BASIC permits use of symbolic identifiers for variable data fields locations.
- Data-defining statements (either explicit or implicit) may occur at any time within program sequence.
- Program control statements (such as GO TO) reference the statement line number of the intended branch destination.
- Programming statements may be keyboard entered in any line number order—correct sequential execution is a system responsibility.

The first of these requirements—memory for the application—is relatively easy to satisfy. Two base registers are maintained in interpreter working storage to indicate the beginning and ending addresses of user memory. A system command (MODIFY) is provided to permit operator specification of either the BOM or EOM registers (BOM IS *BEGINNING OF MEMORY* and EOM is *end of memory*). The only logical restriction imposed is that the EOM must be greater than the BOM. And, of course, the physical restrictions are that the BOM must start after the end of system software memory, and the upper limit for EOM cannot be greater than the end of the machine's actual memory.

Storage locations for the program's use for variable data are allocated by the programming statements and tagged for repeated reference by programmer-supplied symbols. In coining unique tags for each such working area, the programmer may choose from the following possibilities.

1   For NUMERIC fields:
   (a)   Any of the letters, A through Z; or
   (b)   Any letter in conjunction with a single digit (0–9), for example, A1, A2, A3, . . ., Z7, Z8, Z9.

2   For ALPHANUMERIC fields:
   (a)   Any letter (A through Z), followed by a dollar sign($); or
   (b)   A letter and digit pair, followed by a dollar sign, for example, A1$, A2$, A3$, . . ., Z7$, Z8$, Z9$.

157

3 For tables:
   (a) Either a letter only or a letter and digit pair (as above) immediately followed by a subscript integer in parentheses;
   (b) Again, alphanumeric data is distinguished from numeric by use of the dollar sign. Some examples: A(1), D2(4), F$(33), J6$(99). The subscript value in parentheses may itself be a variable, such as P(R), or an expression such as T2$(V+13).

4 Multidimensional arrays (limit is three levels):
   (a) Similar to tables, except subscripts are one, two, or three integer values, separated by commas, and the complete offset enclosed by the parentheses;
   (b) Either numeric or alphanumeric arrays are possible, again distinguished by use of the dollar sign. Some examples of array referencing symbolics are A(2,2), C(1,3,5), F2$(4,X,V), and M5$(R+2,V−16,Y3).

Even though the 26 letters of the alphabet may be used repeatedly for various storage designations, individual uniqueness is determined by the parser by the following rules.

- A letter followed by other than a digit, a dollar sign, or a left parenthesis denotes a single numeric value field.
- A letter followed by a digit, followed by other than a dollar sign or a left parenthesis, is also a single numeric field.
- If the character immediately to the right of a letter or a letter-digit pair is a dollar sign, but the next adjacent character is not a left parenthesis, the tag references a simple alphanumeric storage location.
- Any of the tagging possibilities—a letter or letter-digit pair, with or without a dollar sign—followed by parenthetical expressions with no imbedded comma denotes a tabularized working storage area.
- The significance of a comma within a parenthetical subscript definition determines array dimensioning—the comma separating the field level offsets within the array.

Programming statements may define storage allocation by explicit statements such as

DIM X(2,4)

or an implicit definition can be derived by the interpreter from a program construct such as

LET Z= 5Ø

158

where the letter Z is inferred to designate a simple numeric field location, even though the letter Z was not previously encountered in any other programming statement.

The processing algorithm by which the system is able to tolerate implicit storage definitions depends on two rules: (1) Repeated uses of a given tag (B1, and again later, B1) refer to the same location—the first occurrence of which dictates storage space allocation; and (2) in the absence of a dimension, value, or DEF (definition) statement, all tables and array storage is assumed to be not greater than ten elements deep. For tables (single-dimension arrays) the total fields reserved is ten. For arrays, ten fields are assumed to be needed for each subscript stated. Thus the expression

LET X=J4(A+1,B,C)

assumes an array storage area of 30 fields, in the absence of any explicit statement providing for a different memory allocation.

Actual memory space for the storage of data required by an application program is allocated by the interpreter in the user's memory area. The table (the *memory resident index*), which is contained within the interpreter's working storage, is used by the interpreter to contain pointers that identify the physical location of data in user memory. That portion of the MRI that pertains to user-variable data storage consists of three sections (table words are 2 bytes).

- *Letter section:* 26 words for letters denoting numerics, and 26 words for letters denoting alphanumerics.
- *Letter-digit section:* 260 words each, for numerics and alphanumerics [26 letters, times the digit range (∅–9), that is, $26 \times 10 = 260$].
- *Table and array section:* 26 words for numeric tables, 26 words for alphanumeric tables, 26 words each for (alpha and numeric) two-dimensional array, and 26 words each for three-dimensional arrays, both alphanumeric and numeric.

The total working storage space for this data within the interpreter is 1144 bytes. Each 2-byte word of the table is used to contain the actual memory address within user memory where the programmer's data is physically stored. Notice that regardless of the size of a table or an array specified by the programmer, only a single MRI word is necessary to support symbolic referencing. In the *table and array* section of the MRI, the address pointer is actually the address of the beginning of the table working storage in user memory. The offset parameters supplied within the referencing program statement are effectively added to the MRI *base address* table value to obtain the correct location of the user variable.

Thus far described, then, is the mechanism by which programmer supplied variables and constants are stored in applications memory. The space for storage of the data is allocated based on a counter maintained to reflect the next available unused memory area as each new value is put away. Advice as to the absolute location of all such stored

159

data is obtained by referencing the MRI for the *relative offset* value (byte position count) which, when added to the base address register, indicates the *starting position* of stored data. For all arrays the absolute address of an element must also include the dimensioning parameters in addition to the table starting address indicated in the MRI.

A somewhat different device is used to maintain reference to DATA statement values. Sequential strings of constant data values may be described in a BASIC program, accessible by use of the READ command. A program example defining DATA is

100 DATA 1, 14, 36, 100.25–, ABC COMPANY, " TAX / 4%"
110 DATA BILL TO, SHIP TO, DATE, INVOICE NUMBER, ACCOUNT NUMBER

Program DATA statement lines may occur anywhere within a program, including being interspersed with procedural instruction lines. In concept, all data values established by use of DATA statements are considered to be logical extensions of a sequential (serial) list of all such items. The comma is used by the parser to distinguish the length of each field or data element. Space characters preceding a constant value are not stored unless confined within quotation marks. (In the above example, the spaces in front of TAX are stored as data values).

During entry of DATA statements, the parser argues the field length necessary to store the data value described using the trailing comma as the variable length indicator. As each successive field of data is moved to applications memory, the comma is discarded and each character string is placed contiguous to conserve memory space. The facility to denote the logical end of each element for the stored result depends on the criterion that all characters stored as data values normally range from 01 to 7F in hexadecimal notation. The software routine that moves DATA elements to user memory sets ON the *high-order 8-bit* of the last character byte.

To illustratre this technique, if the programmer provides

200 DATA ABC, DEF

the internal contents in hexadecimal is

```
A   B   C   ,       D   E   F
41  42  43  2B  20  44  45  46
```

and the hexadecimal string of bytes stored in the application's area of main memory is

```
41  42  C3  44  45  C6
```

The character C is the ending character of the first field of data ABC. The normal (ASCII) value for C is 43, or in binary notation, 0100 0011. With the 8-bit of the high-order half of the byte set to ON, the binary value is 1100 0011, or hexadecimal C3. Continuing with the character scanning of this example, the next statement position is an insignificant space, thus the parser ignores it and proceeds to the data element DEF.

160

The character F is determined to be the ending character of this element (nothing follows), therefore the 8-bit of the normally 46 code is set to ON, resulting in C6.

Since constants stored by use of DATA statements may be intermingled with other data in main memory (variables, arrays, etc.), and no prescience can be assumed as to the amount of memory ultimately required to contain DATA values, it is necessary to signify the end of character strings after processing each DATA statement. The unique hexadecimal byte code of 00 is used for this purpose. In the above example, the string

    41 42 C3 44 45 C6

is followed by a 00 code. Two additional bytes are immediately reserved next. This 2-byte word is used by the interpreter to store an address counter to link to the address of any later stored DATA string.

During program statement processing the first DATA program statement encountered sets up the chaining sequence. A dedicated word of storage in the interpreter's working storage area is used as a DATA *base register.* This software register is loaded with the *absolute address* of the first DATA value stored.

Assume the following sequence of activity. The programmer enters a DATA program statement. The DATA *base register* initially contains zeros. The beginning address of the just entered DATA string is loaded into the data *base register.* The DATA string is then parsed as previously described, a NULL (00) is generated as a final marker, and a 2-byte word is reserved immediately following the NULL. The programmer may now enter other statements, and their various processes are invoked as appropriate. The need for another DATA statement now occurs.

The interpreter references the DATA *base register* to determine the starting of DATA in memory. A scan of the DATA addressed begins, to find the NULL. If the reserved word following the NULL is zero, only one DATA statement has been processed thus far. Any value other than zero implies that other DATA statements exist, and the value contained here is a byte positional count to the location of the start of the next DATA block. As successive DATA statements are processed, the offset value to enable chaining must be calculated and appended to the end of the last previously stored DATA string.

The mechanics described so far pertain to the allocation of DATA memory and the composition of the character strings stored, as well as the rudiments of the accessing algorithm. During execution of the BASIC program, DATA elements are retrieved from main memory and presented for processing by use of the command READ. The first iteration of a READ brings forth the first DATA element. Each successive READ accesses the next sequentially stored element of DATA without regard to where within the program DATA was stored by the programmer. An attempt by the program during execution to READ past the end of data is trapped by the interpreter as a run-time error. The READ interpretive is responsible for noticing the logical end of DATA values. Although strings of DATA are stored at various locations and they may be chained together for processing purposes, the final such string is the only one that logically ends

161

with a reserved word count of zeros, and it is this condition that enables the interpretive to ascertain the end of DATA.

In the interest of completeness, it is necessary to mention here the use of the restore command. All DATA values are constants as originally presented within program statements, and they are not subject to alteration by programming procedures. However, it is possible in BASIC to reuse DATA constants. To reinitialize program access to DATA values (begin again from the first element), the command RESTORE sets the DATA *pointer* back to 1. The DATA *pointer* is a working storage word in the interpreter that is maintained by the READ interpretive string, and its content always points to the beginning location of the next DATA value.

Described to this point is working storage memory management for a BASIC program. Included are the architecture (space allocation) and the execution (access reference) design principles. Again, briefly, the working storage areas required by a program are relegated to high-order memory and space is allocated on an as-needed basis beginning from the upper limit of memory downward toward low-order memory. The need for space (and sometimes the value to be contained there) is gleaned by the interpreter software as programming statements are encountered, parsed, and stored. Actual data to be stored in working storage may be derived from the program statement during parsing (*literals, constants,* and *DATA constants*), or only a space allocation determination is possible and the values (*variables*) are generated as a consequence of program execution.

Another aspect of the execution architecture remains: the storage of, and actual execution of, the program. Program statements are stored as they are entered serially in program memory. Program memory begins immediately following the interpreter software system area. All statements are parsed as they are entered, any working storage assignments prescribed are allocated, the statement is reduced to a coded character string, and finally the string is moved to the next unused space immediately following the previous statement. Notice that statements are stored serially in the order they are presented, regardless of any execution sequence implied by their respective line numbers.

A chaining mechanism, conceptually similar to that of DATA values, is used to effect sequential linking of program procedures. Two addresses must be ascertained from which this statement was accessed (assuming straight-line sequential execution). The address of the next in-line statement is appended to the end of each statement as it is moved to program storage, and the appropriate appendage of the last preceding statement is amended to reflect this insertion.

The chaining value appended to each statement string is a byte positional counter, used as an offset from the *program base register*. This offset, when added to the *program base register,* becomes the *program counter* value during sequential execution of program lines.

Since the before and after statement line numbers must be argued as each new statement is moved into program memory, on sizable programs the searching process could be time consuming. To minimize the total amount of memory that must be scanned to locate the next smaller and the next larger (if any) line number, a paging scheme is employed to preclude having to start the scan from the very beginning of program memory each time.

A 32 two-word *page stack* is maintained in interpreter working storage. Program memory is artificially subdivided into blocks of 1024 bytes, each such block deserving of an entry in the *page stack.* Each of the word pairs in the *page stack* contains, respectively, the lowest and the highest line numbers contained within the particular page block.

The complexities and overhead burden of the *page stack* would not be justified if it were used only for locating the before and after arguments at statement entry time. The *page stack,* however, also serves an important speed-motivated execution-time purpose.

Four BASIC commands affect program flow control: GO TO, GO SUB, RETURN, and, optionally, THEN. The syntax for GO TO and GO SUB dictate that a statement line number must follow. The keyword THEN may be followed by a statement line number (or an expression or a function). The only use of RETURN is to effect a branch-back to the program step next immediately following a GO SUB (an implied GO TO, effectively).

The practical effect of any of these control commands requires the interpreter to locate the referenced statement in program storage. An interpreter macro routine is used by either of the interpretive strings that processes control commands to argue the location of the referenced statement line number. The *line search* macro routine tests the word pairs in the *page stack* to check whether the sought-after statement line number can possibly be within a given page-block. If the test of the *page stack* entry is affirmative, the page block is scanned for a match on the line number being searched for. An affirmative test does not necessarily ensure that the referenced line number will be contained within a given block, but a negative test result does exclude searching any page areas that do not contain the line in question.

In practice, then, successive *page stack* word pairs are tested and *no-go* entries are skipped. When a *possible-go* is found the page block is scanned. The scanning process is exited if a line number match occurs, or if the *scan-count* exceeds 1023 bytes, and control is transfered back, to test the next *page stack* entry. Of course, when the entire *page stack* is exhausted without a line number match, an UNDEFINED LINE NUMBER syntax message is triggered to the operator since an attempt was made to pass control to a nonexisting program statement.

As can be perceived from this description, several page blocks may have to be searched to locate a line number. The algorithm does preclude scanning any pages that cannot possibly contain a given number, but it does not preclude *multiple possibles.* Examine closely the following fictitious *page stack:*

    Entry 1:   00010-00204
    Entry 2:   00106-00770
    Entry 3:   00780-01400
    Entries 4 through 32 are all zeros

A call for line number 00005 is quickly determined to be invalid, requiring only testing for each of the three active *page stack* word pairs. Similarly, any called-for line number greater than 01400 is equally an error. An attempt for a number between 00771 and 00779 inclusive is also determined to be a bad choice because of the high limit in entry 2 and the low limit in entry 3.

Suppose a reference to line 100. Entry 1 parameters will initiate a search of page-block number 1, and if the scan is successful control will be transferred accordingly. A *no-match scan* of block-1 requires a further test of the remaining *page stack* entries, and a *no-go* test is quickly accomplished on entries 2 and 3, hence an erroneous line number attempt was invoked.

A call requirement for line number 110 could necessitate a double search, however. Entry 1 reveals a *possible-go* for line 110 in the first page-block. If the scan of the first page proves futile, however, the second *page stack* entry indicates that the number 110 may yet exist, therefore the second page must be scanned. Figure 11.3 shows the PAGE-STACK scanning routine for the BASIC program.

Knowing full well the intracacies of this paging scheme, a programmer could calculatedly defeat its optimizing capabilities and enter program statements in such a way as to dictate a complete search of active memory for every reference—the consequence of which would be to degrade the run-time performance of the BASIC program. Although perhaps such an effort would be an interesting academic exercise, no worthwhile practical result would be achieved and the entire paging architecture and searching algorithm are devised in anticipation of more conventional programming practices.

Laboratory use of this model has proven the overall validity of the mechanism as described here. The actual number of page-blocks that must be scanned for a given circumstance varies according to several factors. The total number of different statement line numbers, both for the whole program and the number contained within 1024-byte strings, has a direct influence. More significant, however, is the order in which program statements are added to program memory.

A program statement numbered as line 00000 and added late in the day will only be found within one block. Line 00110, inserted after several pages of memory are full, could require scanning of multiple pages.

A performance test was run using 20 different BASIC programs in the early days of implementation of this model, and the page-scanning process was tracked by a performance tuning routine, patched into the *line search* macro. This somewhat limited evaluation revealed that, as an average, less than three page-blocks had to be scanned to locate a line number reference. This average applies only to those occasions when a match is not located within the first page-block scanned. The ratio of attempts for lines that were not located within *page stack* entry limits was on the order of less than 1 in 100 such calls.

The potential for degraded performance due to multiple page-block searching is applicable only during real-time programming operations. The utility overlay routine to SAVE a program from memory unloads the program statements in line number sequence, thus when a program is loaded into memory the *page stack* is newly generated with no overlap between word pairs.

It remains only to look at the effect of changing and deleting program statements. Appreciate first that if a program statement is deleted, two gaps are potential. If

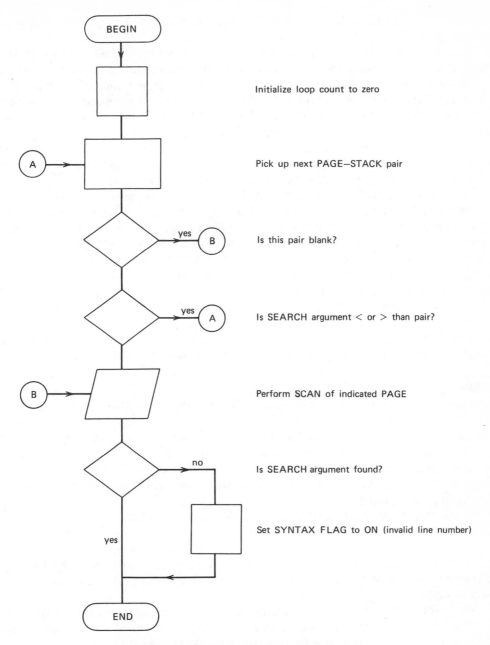

Figure 11.3 The PAGE-STACK scanning routine.

a deleted statement explicitly or implicitly reserved space in the working storage area of program memory, when that statement is deleted a waste area results. In this case there is waste in working storage and in program memory where the statement string itself is

165

stored. For those statements that do not reference working storage, the only waste is that associated with statement storage.

Reclamation of the freed space that contains program statement strings is fairly straightforward. A memory-to-memory block move macroroutine is used by the interpreter to relocate the higher-ordered program blocks, as a collective group of bytes contiguous to the remaining valid area, thus overlaying the vacated space. The number of bytes reclaimed is then used as an adjustment figure to the software register that denotes the address of available (unused) memory. Exit from this process is then through the routine that builds and maintains the *page stack,* since it must now be regenerated to reflect the new contents (line numbers) of the respective page-blocks.

The mechanism for reclaiming freed-up working storage is somewhat comparable to that for program statement memory. However, it is necessary to make individual adjustments to the *memory resident index* table as each deleted space is accounted for. At the instant of line number deletion by the operator, only those working storage areas that are explicitly defined are salvaged by this process. Statements that implicitly allocate working storage do not permit immediate reclamation since it cannot be readily determined whether or not other statements also use the same area. A potential for waste does exist because of this, but no special problem occurs in most normal use.

During the program loading operation the MRI is built "on the fly," and any previously wasted space is automatically eliminated. If in the event excessive entry and deletion activity does create an out-of-memory condition due to this particular waste potential, a SAVE and LOAD operation will serve to clean up memory.

Changes

A statement entry using a line number that already exists arbitrarily assumes that the existing line is intended to be overlaid with a new construct. If the newly entered statement is shorter in length than the previous one, it is placed into the same location and any unused space is reclaimed as in a delete operation. If the statement just entered is longer than the previous one, it is placed onto the end of the program memory area thus far used (as if it were a new line) and the previous statement is deleted using the delete scheme.

In summary, then, the execution architecture of this model depends on several schemes. The interpreter maintains advice on the actual memory address of the programmer's need for working storage by use of an index table (the MRI). Program-supplied constants (by use of DATA statements) are stored in program working storage as presented, and individual statement strings are chained together by use of a pointer value appended to each discrete string.

Program statements are reduced to a codified form and stored in program memory in the same order as introduced during keyboard entry. Each coded statement string is appended with a pointer to indicate the next statement to be accessed in-line. To benefit reasonably rapid location of line numbers addressed by control transfers, a *page stack* is maintained for vectoring the line-search process into artifically defined page-blocks of 1024 increments.

Gaps occurring as a result of changing or deleting previously entered program statements are reclaimed by a memory management macro process. In program statement memory, block moves are accomplished to compress remaining statements and overlay vacated space. Explicitly defined working storage is salvaged when the defining statement is deleted by updating the MRI entries that denoted the allocated space.

A *quick-parse* macroroutine is employed during program loading to generate both the *page stack* and the MRI afresh with each load, thereby negating any inefficiencies suffered during highly volatile real-time programming activities.

Chapter

12 Interpreter Interfacing

*I*nterface is used here to refer to the common boundary points between physical components of our model. There are internal interfaces within the interpreter software (between modules); and there are interfaces between the software system and the hardware, between the interpreter and the user's program, and between the system and the operator.

This chapter begins with the design rules that ensure successful interfacing of various discrete routines and modules of the interpreter software. Internal binding principles are followed here by external interfacing conventions—from the software system outwards.

In the second section we take the point of view of a BASIC program that the *interpreter* is itself an interface, permitting cross-talk between the programmer and the computing system. While the language syntax of BASIC provides finite rules for communication to the system, the programmer also assumes certain operational conventions and services of the software. Some of these assumed services are described here with supporting rationales for their implementation.

The final section of this chaper deals with human-computer dialogue. An important part of human-computer interfacing is its double meaning—conversation with the software and hardware, and interaction of an operator with an application program.

12.1   System Interfacing

Call them as you will: rules, conventions, disciplines, whatever. My preference is habit. Established early on and cultivated to the point of rote, the dividends are immense. It is often easier to envision conceptually what a program routine should do than to write the first line of code. Operating from an established habit pattern has the benefit of getting you going before indecision can occur.

Habit also makes debugging easier. Analysis of a routine that you wrote yesterday or even several weeks ago is simpler when you can glance over large areas of procedural code with the assurance that it isn't necessary to double-check the details of housekeeping chores. At times, of course, errors will happen in the things done automatically, and when all else fails clerical detail must be confirmed. But even here, habits pay off. If you expect the norm, an error is many times glaring, if only by reason of deviation.

The examples that follow form a case in point. These conventions were applied in the design of our tutorial model. Though not formal legislation, most of these rules have evolved with programming practice, and apply often to other software designing efforts.

Zero: The *insignificance* of *something*, and the *significance* of *nothing*. Searching a table? When zeros are encountered, the search is over, regardless of whether the loop count indicates that the bottom has been reached. Being able to rely on this assumption requires that a rule be adopted to ensure that all table areas are preinitialized to blanks in all fields. Of course, there is an overhead burden in the time required to do the housekeeping. Permit, then, some optimizing techniques.

Do housekeeping and cleanup chores at start-of-run whenever practical. The time delay when a program first begins execution is usually more tolerable than it is in-run. This is especially true in an interactive-type operation; the operator doesn't appreciate having to wait for you. And this suggests another convention.

Human reaction times are infinitely slower than the execution times of a computer; capitalize on this fact. The later section on human-computer dialogue discusses this possibility more fully, but the point here is that when you output a message that expects a response, before trapping out to the keyboard for input, jump to a table cleanup process. Sizable tables can be cleared in the several hundred milliseconds time lag that is bound to occur between operator *awareness* and operator *action*.

Table areas are already clear when software is loaded initially. This is not just an assumption, but rather an intent of design—and another convention. Before unloading the software system to storage media, clear all table areas, and *capture the blank areas as significant memory*. When the software system is loaded to memory, the zeros are copied to memory, effectively: *cleared tables.*

To reiterate the rule of significant zeros: By convention, you may assume that zeros encountered in a table search indicates that nothing follows. The rule to support the convention is that *table areas are always preinitialized to zero.*

In the previous chapter we described the *page stack* and the *memory resident index* tables. Religious application of the *bottom-is-empty* convention facilitates maintenance of these tables and benefits interfacing of the servicing routines that depend on the values in these tables. Linear search functions against the *page stack* arbitrarily assume an *end-of-search* attitude when a zero element is encountered. Similarly, a vectored access to the MRI, returned with a zero value, indicates that a variable data symbolic tag has not been used.

Mentioning the linear search introduces the topic of looping. Loop processes abound in any software design, and some specific rules apply here. First there are the possible types of loop. There is the *finite loop,* or *continue until done,* for a specific number of iterations. Another type is that which either continues for *n* repetitions or exits on a condition. The last, really an expansion of the second, loops for *x,* quits on a condition, or may be interrupted to permit servicing of a higher-priority task.

For the sake of habitual design, *for all loops,* the count is set within the routine, and within the first few instructions. Exit tests, whether arguing the limit or a condition, are coded at the beginning of the loop and *before* incrementing (or decrementing) the loop count. Multiple conditional tests (more than one exit condition possible) are always coded *in-line* and *contiguous,* with *no* intervening procedures.

As a general rule, *finite loops use decrementing counters,* exiting on zero. Loop processes with *conditional-exit* potential use *incrementing iteration logic,* the counter value indicating the number of iterations completed when an exit occurs.

Any loop process that is capable of being interrupted by the processor for I/O servicing must assume the responsibility for flag and register settings in wholesale. To ensure success of the loop function, the interfacing conventions place no burdens on the I/O drivers for restoring integrity of data partially processed by unidentified routines.

Again, a rule: All loops exit with the iterative count value remaining in the *accumulator.* Another register could have been chosen, of course; the significance here is that all loops end with the count in a common register—again to benefit interfacing of other modules. The status of the accumulator upon any return from a loop process, if zero, indicates that the loop was a finite process (decrements to zero), and a positive value indicates the iteration count on exit (all incrementing begins with 1).

Application of this rule does require presaving accumulator contents on occasion, and loading of the accumulator with the counter on exit for some cases, but the procedural overhead is compensated by the assumptions that can be made when interfacing various modules.

A final word on loop processes: *Nesting of loops is routinely avoided.* Certain instances do exist where nesting of loops within loops is chosen because of economies of space or time, but where reasonable alternatives are possible nested loops are avoided. Interfacing complexities occur with nesting; that is, which loop counter should be retained in the accumulator on exit? A common philosophy for this case is to use a finite loop within a loop that permits conditional exits; the saved count reflects the exit-iteration, since the finite loop must have been completed or the exit wouldn't have occurred.

Structured programming, top-down design, and *hierarchical design* are among the terms that have been coined over the years to suggest diciplines for the composition of programming routines. The degree and extent of application of any of these remains the option of the individual, and no personal favorite is touted here. Ease of interfacing software modules is the goal, however, and at least one structuring convention is appropriate: Go in the top, and come out the bottom. For a specific routine the entry point (branch into) is at the first instruction, and the exit from (subroutine return or branch from) is the last instruction on the program listing.

Branching into a routine at the top requires no special effort other than to bring

170

all entries to this common point. It may be tempting at times to branch into a routine at some later point, but consider various alternatives of design, *both* of the accessing routine and the subject module.

Getting to the bottom requires an internal branch to that point for all instances of premature or conditionally satisfied escapes, but the double-branch sequence is not a serious speed degradation problem.

Consider some arguments in favor of the common entry point. First, *"if you remove the module,"* what happens? At the point of entry, substitute the common exit command (a branch or a return), and now there are no loose ends. The alternative (permitting midpoint entries) requires identification of the accessing routines to divert the access.

Using a common instruction point (at the bottom) to exit, no matter the internal algorithms, also facilitates module binding and debugging. To readdress the flow from a given module through different services than originally planned requires only that the *final command* be changed. The alternative, escapes permitted from random points within a module, will later require isolation of each of these if you change your mind. And if relative branching is used to enforce exit from the common last instruction, moving the module intact is facilitated since internal (to the module) branches need not be changed. When absolute addresses are used they must each be modified if relocation of the module is necessary.

A final argument is offered in support of the top-in, bottom-out rule. Modifications to the initial housekeeping tasks are easier when it's all done up front, and patches to cleanup chores are simpler when they are all appended as a group to the bottom of a routine. Localization of these common procedures ensures that all accesses and exits produce comparable results at run time. The result is *software reliability.*

Touched upon lightly in the immediately preceding discussion was the subject of flags. Whether called flags, switches, indicators, conditionals, or something else, consider the case of the *dangling pennant.* Assume that, by reason of design convention, no flags are on without purpose.

Application of this principle decrees that he who acts upon a flag setting is responsible for turning off the flag that stimulated the access. Examine the following logic:

200 IF A > B THEN 400

The interpretive string that compares variables will set ON a flag to record the results of the comparison, indicating either a greater than, less than, or equal condition. If the condition is TRUE (A is *greater* than B), control passes to the THEN interpretive for execution of a branch function. Within the THEN interpretive string the comparator flag is immediately set OFF. The usefulness of the flag setting has been realized when the THEN string is invoked and no further need of comparator status is required. (THEN logic is only accessed in the event of a TRUE comparison.) To ignore the *dangling pennant* serves no purpose, and the risks of promiscuous flag combinations can be severe.

171

Software debugging operations depend heavily on observation of the state-of-the-system at various checkpoints in an execution sequence. To have to spend hours isolating the cause of an ON flag setting only to learn that the system doesn't care whether a particular flag is on or off is frustrating and needless. Much of this type of wasted effort can be eliminated by adopting rules to ensure that status indicators are routinely cleaned up.

Sloppy flag maintenance can adversely affect module interfacing also. As a general statement of concept, control transfers from one module to another are a result of conditional logic flow. Before a given module can be accessed it is necessary to anticipate whether any carried-along flag settings will cause incorrect execution. In the absence of any disciplines to preclude *dangling penants,* it is difficult to predict what flag conditions may be carried along indefinitely.

Mentioning conditionals and comparators leads to suggesting another convention of design for ease of interfacing. Develop a habit of consistent use of either negative or positive conditioning logic. Indiscriminate or arbitrary switching from IF GREATER to IF LESS testing can be confusing to both a programmer and a computer. In the case of the programmer, pencil tracking of logic flow can be tedious, and seemingly confused execution results are difficult to analyze. Although the processor is not really confused, run-time operations may run amok because of accessing a default sequence that the programmer never anticipated. Module interfacing is simplified when the assumption is valid that the sender and receiver are designed with common appreciation of the significance of data or statuses.

Several conventions are applicable to *data,* and very specific rules are necessary to ensure data integrity at all times. At the top of the conventions list is the definition of data. Our model is an 8-bit system, therefore the data bandwidth is 8-bit bytes. There are no restrictions on the content of a byte, meaning that any byte is capable of the full range from 00 to FF (hexadecimal). The significance of the bit configuration within a byte is a function of logical interpretation by the user routine. All transporter routines are designed so as to permit movement of data from one location to another without regard to the contents of the bytes being moved. That is, the data is *transparent* to the routine affecting movement, and all bits are moved intact without alteration.

There is a categorization of data types, defined according to use characteristics rather than specific content. Of the highest-priority enforcement of interfacing rules are the user program data bytes. In addition to the strictest adherence to the rules of transparency is the insistence on indirect addressing techniques. No user data is ever moved or examined by use of *absolute* addressing. Application of this rule for accumulator moves generally allows the use of the B and C registers for pickups (memory-to-accumulator moves), and the D and E registers for moves to memory. For data movement tasks between memory locations using the *accumulator* as an intermediary, the D and E registers are used exclusively.

User data bytes may be transported between the user's storage areas or between the user's storage and interpreter work areas, and of course user data is subject to movement between respective interpreter work areas. Full application of the preceding rule pertains to the relocation of data *within user storage* and for all movements *into* or *out of* user storage.

172

The rules pertaining to data movement within working storage of the interpreter are formulated on the basis of propinquity. Once a user's data is absorbed by the interpreter, the interpreter assumes propietary rights for the duration. By reason of this assumption the autocratic rules for *indirect addressing* are tempered somewhat. The extent of relaxation of the rule is constrained according to module interchange requirements. Data resident within interpreter working storage on an interim basis is relocated by *indirect addressing* techniques when intercommunicated by various software modules. The tempering of the rule applies *only* to instances of addressing within the confines of the procedures *of a given module.*

To reiterate these rules in a slightly different fashion: Data addressing for working storage between software modules, or between software modules and user program storage, is accomplished only with *indirect modes.* During the time that data is *exclusively owned* by a particular software module, that module enjoys the license to address it by *whatever mode convenient.*

Another category of data is that of exclusive interpreter ownership. This data may be constants or literals imbedded within the interpreter, or it may be intermediate worker values generated by processing tasks. Such data may be the sole responsibility of a discrete module or it may be subject to interchange with other software routines, and some are eventually transmitted to the user's application program.

No interfacing rules are enforced for *interpreter-owned* data that remain within the exclusive domain of a given module. All data subject to exchange between interpretive processes are permitted the benefit of a firm rule, however. Interpreter working storage is localized and contiguous within interpreter memory, and a single base address worker reflects the beginning of that area. Thus the rule is that *exchange of interpreter data between modules is by use of indirect addressing using a common base address.*

The interpretive strings that accomplish function calls (SQUARE ROOT, TANGENT, etc.) transmit interpreter-generated data values to the user's program. At the time of transmission, ownership of the data is *relinquished* to the application, and as of that point, the foregoing rules concerning movement of user data apply.

The remaining category of data is that of converted user data. This data does not require additional conventions or rules, but is mentioned here separately to clarify its posture. This category Includes all of that data received into the interpreter in one form and returned to the user in a different form. The responsibilities of the software system for data integrity in these instances is no less than for simplistic operations where the data is massaged, yet returned without alteration. By reason of this philosophy, then, the preceding rules of indirect addressing modes apply.

The scope of interfacing conventions to this point has reached only so far as to include software system components. Mentioned also were certain eristic processor and memory rules. There are, in addition to these, conventions and rules necessary for interfacing the software to the hardware. In this context, software means the interpreter model, and hardware includes the cassette transports, the CRT, the printer, and the keyboard.

To reiterate the central theme: *The interpreter is an interface between the BASIC application program and the computing system.* Hence the total responsibility for I/O device management is vested in the interpreter. From the top, the priorities are (1) *cassettes,* (2) *CRT,* (3) *printer,* (4) *keyboard.*

Of the various peripherals, the cassettes are unique to the extent that two-way data interchange and communication is necessary between the device and the computer. Data may be moved from memory to the tape, or data may be read into memory, depending on whether a BASIC command for INPUT or PRINT is interpreted. Data input or output activity may also be accomplished as a system support service of the interpreter system upon the direct request of the operator for a LOAD or SAVE task. In a similar vein, tape I/O processes can be invoked by utility functions such as COPY and DUMP.

The conventions concerning data for cassette storage are limited and apply equally regardless of whether the service request is of BASIC, the operator, or a utility. Again, a byte is 8 bits, with the range potential of 00 to FF (hexadecimal), and character conjectures are transparent to the peripheral and its associated electronics. The READ and WRITE electronics do provide certain qualifications to avoid possibly corrupt strings, but in every case, *that which is read is communicated,* thereby permitting software abjudication of validity.

By reason of hardware design, tape blocks are always 256 bytes in length, but the interpreter supports *variable length records,* defined by the application programmer or as a function of usage by the software system. To the tape drive electronics, character positions are serial from 0 through 255 (decimal). The transport buffer exchanges with a software buffer a full 256-byte block in any instance of input or output. The delineation of less than a physical block of characters to represent a logical record block is a function of the interpreter software. To ensure that the unused space of a physical block is padded with *nulls,* the driver algorithm clears the software buffer with *zeros* preparatory to each block transfer.

Physical management of the transport device is provided by a specific software module: the cassette driver. Cross-talk between the processor and the transport includes interrupt signaling the peripheral to engage the read-head, directional movement of tape specifics, and head drop-out to revert to a passive state. An *echoed status signal* is generated by the device and made available to the CPU for acknowledgment and an indication of readiness. Additionally, the drive electronics perform a *quality check* on data transmissions, and the results of this check are provided to the system.

The rules for software and cassette peripheral interfacing accommodate these hardware attributes and embrace the following. Data to be written to tape is prepared as a *concatenated string* of characters in the output buffer. The cassette driver is invoked by either the BASIC I/O interpretives or the system command processor. The driver assumes command of the system and disables all interrupts. The status of the transport is qualified and the requested I/O transfer is invoked. A completed function with no status exceptions permits the driver to relinquish autocratic dominance of the system to the interpreter's process control module. The only exception to the system-ownership-until-done convention is the tape REWIND instance. A tape drive may be commanded to begin rewinding, the driver tests only for acknowledgment, and the function is assumed to be complete from the *instance of initiation,* thereby permitting a degree of overlapped operations.

174

During the time of systems control by the software driver, a drive status indication of a *read* or *write error* causes the driver to attempt up to five retrys of the commanded task. On the sixth iteration (original plus five retrys), by design convention, the assumption is that a corrupt block has been encountered, and this condition is error-trapped back to the interpreter for advice to the operator and the application. (Notice that even though an ERROR status is announced, the buffer will contain an *image of the bit patterns as read,* permitting a software scrutiny for contamination.)

The CRT driver module is less complex than the cassette routine, and the interfacing rules are less demanding. The basic driver contains two submodules, one each for *character output* and *cursor control.* Two separate I/O data lines are used, one for each, and the *base driver* first checks the readiness of the total device, then branches to output either a character or a cursor vector. Data to be placed on the screen is moved into an output buffer and the relocation process includes stripping the high-order 2 bits of each byte, leaving 6 bits significant (00 to 128, hex). Assuming that the CRT is ready, the driver transmits each character of the buffer in series. The submodule for driving the cursor transmits a 2-byte data word to indicate the desired *line* and *position* address on the screen. The interpreter qualifies the cursor positioning request to ensure that the first byte (*line*) is within the range 0–15 and the position value (second byte) ranges 0–31. In testing the *leftmost* byte the high-order bits are ignored, permitting a bit value for the hardware decoder to cause a clear-screen function in conjunction with and immediately prior to cursor positioning.

As data is transfered to the CRT on a serial character basis, the byte value 07 (hex) is compared for by the electronics and when encountered the audible alarm (buzzer) is triggered and the data character is culled from the string passed to the CRT refresh circuitry.

For the sake of simplicity, the CRT driver software depends on the basic concept that whatever is sent to the CRT is properly displayed by that device, and the driver attempts *no audit of function.* Each invocation of the driver begins with a CRT readiness check, but no further echo or acknowledgment is anticipated on the assumption that all is well.

The software module that serves as a printer driver adopts a similar posture as well. Character transmission of the printer buffer is asynchronous, and each character is processed by the driver as a complete task. The *printer-ready* interrupt is monitored continuously during the time the driver is in command, but the driver assumes accurate receipt by the printer in the absence of a *not-ready* status. Line space control for the printer is automatic as a function of electronics when column 81 is attempted. A character value of OD or OA (hex) is used to command print-head return and line spacing (single space), triggered solely by the character decoder in the printer. And electronics within the printer decoder will sound an alarm tone on the printer in the event an 07 code is received, and a space is printed.

The keyboard is listed as the lowest priority, not because of relative unimportance, but rather because of its unique role as an external command stimulus. Viewed from within the software system, the keyboard is a passive device. The application of this concept requires that keyboard signals be acknowledged only on an *as-permitted basis.*

To see the reason for this, assume that the processing system is in an idle state, fully powered, initialized, and that software execution is suspended, trapped in a tight loop awaiting a keyboard stimulus. In this state no processing is underway and no work is being accomplished. A character key is depressed by the operator. The keyboard driver accepts the 8-bit code generated by the depressed key, the byte is stored in interpreter working storage, and the CRT software driver is invoked to display the character on the display. With the key value stored in memory and displayed on the screen, the system is returned to the idle state to await further keyboard signals.

Depression of the *line return* key by the operator causes the keyboard driver to assume the logical end of transmission of a message from the operator and the *command processor* module is invoked. The input message is qualified for validity of command, and control of the system is transferred accordingly. If the command is illegal or unintelligible to the software, an ERROR is announced and control returns to place the system in the idle state awaiting further input.

On a valid command the necessary software process is addressed and command of the system is relinquished by the operator. Hence the passive posture of the keyboard. Regardless of what may be attempted by the operator through key depressions, the system at this point is under control of *some* program routine and the keyboard driver is not active.

The called routine continues in force until completion, utilizing whatever system components are required. In order of priority, then, if the cassette transport is needed it is used, nothing further occurring until the task is completed. Output to either the CRT or the printer occurs as necessary, again generally under the philosophy of *transmit and assume immediate receipt* and continue. With all I/O (if any) functions completed, and all memory storage maintenance tasks completed, system control reverts to the operator.

The keyboard interfacing conventions to support the passive character of this device are relatively simple. A single buffer area within working storage of the interpreter software is used for keyboard purposes. This buffer is 256 bytes in length and is maintained by the keyboard driver module. Any message-complete status such as key depression of the *line return* causes the driver to call upon service modules to determine the appropriate use of the data entered. Depending on the processes required, the buffer is cleared by the driver as a final service before transferring system control to the intended function. Thus, by convention of design, the keyboard software buffer is always clear when the system again reverts to operator control.

And although the operator may own the system, by reason of software design *the operator may only command when permitted to do so,* and permission is only granted *when the computer has nothing better to do.*

12.2 Application Interface

Introduction

To use a computer requires a program. To write a program first requires a definition of the data processing task to be accomplished. Second, knowledge of the language provided is necessary. And then the computer—its configuration, peripheral capabilities, memory size, and, to the point here, system software provisions—prescribe definite programming conventions.

Programming commands for the model described here are categorized basically into two groups, according to what is being commanded. *Procedural instructions* written in the BASIC language comprise one group, and they are used by the programmer to direct the computing system through logical problem-solving steps. The second group of command facilities allows interfacing of the BASIC application program to the system. This section describes this second group of command capabilities, referred to collectively as *system commands.* Although in certain instances some of these commands are available to the programmer for use within BASIC program sequences, they are generally used in a DIRECT mode, the operator communicating directly with the software system. Direct-mode operations contrast with interactive communications of the operator and an application program written in BASIC. To reiterate less formally, in the one case the operator talks to *the system,* in the other the conversation is with *the application* program.

Program Storage

To cause a program to be loaded into system memory, the command LOAD is provided. This command may be typed on the console by the operator (DIRECT mode), and it may also be used procedurally within a BASIC application (PROGRAM mode). In either event the services provided by the software interpreter system are identical. When the LOAD command is detected by the command processing module, a qualifier is expected immediately thereafter, to argue what is to be loaded.

An alphabetic character string of not more than eight characters is expected, and this string (PROGRAM-ID) will be used by the loader module to compare with label records on cassette tape. If the LOAD command construct is syntactically correct, system control reverts to the software routine that manages the cassette transports. The tape is read sequentially, and all label records are tested for comparison to the program name called for.

If LOAD was entered in the direct mode, the tape cassette is rewound to the beginning before the search is commenced. When a programmer uses the LOAD command in a program sequence he or she may assume that the search begins immediately, and if it is logically necessary to rewind the tape before searching, it is the programmer's responsibility to do so. Another system command (UNLOAD) is available to cause a tape rewind to occur. It may be used by either the programmer or the operator, in a direct mode. Notice, however, that UNLOAD infers nothing about program storage operations. Rather, it is used to advise the system that the cassette is to be UNLOADed from the transport; and it should be rewound in preparation for removal. Whether or not the operator actually removes the cassette is incidental to the system and is a function of operating procedures.

The LOAD command is useful for loading to memory either application programs written in BASIC or utility programs written in machine language. The LOAD function is

177

considered an imperative task and the loader module, once invoked, promises no salvage opportunities in the event of an incomplete or unsuccessful attempt. By design convention, any already-resident program or data remain secure until the point that a match on the program name being searched for is complete. If a new BASIC program is called for, when the program is located, the loader routine jumps to a subroutine that clears the entire user program memory area in preparation for the incoming program. Whether user memory is violated by calling for a utility program depends on which specific utility it is and whether it is capable of coresiding with an application program.

The loading process is a discrete, distinct, stand-alone task. Memory is cleared, the requested program is copied from storage to memory, all work areas are initialized, and system control returns to the command mode to await further stimulus from the keyboard. The cassette tape unit stops and remains steady at the point of the *last read block,* assuming that the operator or the programmer will manage further tape movement.

The correlative to LOAD is SAVE. Whenever desired, from the command mode, SAVE is typed on the console followed by an alphanumeric *name* to be used as program identification. As discussed in Chapter 11, however, to be able to use the SAVE command depends on having the DUMP utility program in residence. If a SAVE is attempted and DUMP is not in memory, a message to the operator appears on the display, requesting that DUMP be loaded. Just as with the LOAD logic, when a program is SAVEd, tape positioning on the transport is abandoned in place, and the operator and the programmer share responsibility for further movement of the tape. On the tape, immediately following the last block of data written, a tape mark is issued by the software system to mark the logical end of the saved program.

As can be gleaned from the preceding, the ability to chain programs and files on cassette tape depends on the system conventions for tape positioning following LOAD and SAVE processes. Chaining of one program to another is possible with LOAD, but recognize that when a LOAD is completed, system control reverts to the DIRECT mode, therefore starting of an application program requires operator stimulus.

Execution of Application Programs

To start a program, use RUN. To restart after a BREAK, use CONT (continue). From the command mode, to make a vectored start at a specified line number, use GO TO *nnnn* (where *n* = line number). To attempt a system-managed continuation after an I/O error-trap, use RESUME.

The command RUN is similar to LOAD but more extensive. A RUN command with no operands implies that a program is already in memory and the desire is to execute it from the logical beginning. By convention of design, RUN will cause complete initialization of all working storage, counters, variables, and so on. If a program name is typed immediately following the RUN command, a LOAD process occurs first, and the conventions are identical to that described for LOAD. Use of RUN as an alternative to LOAD is appropriate for chaining of successive programs since execution of the application program is automatically invoked as soon as the program is loaded. RUN may be used in either a DIRECT mode or in PROGRAM mode.

There is one other variation of the RUN command usage. In the DIRECT mode (only), a line number may be entered as an operand to cause a vectored start. Initialization of work areas takes place before execution begins, but instead of beginning with the first program statement, execution begins with the line number specified. It is also permitted to provide, in this same manner, a suspense-limit to cause program termination at a specified point. Observe:

RUN 100-730

This construct typed in the DIRECT mode will cause the program to be initialized and execution to begin with statement 100. Normal interpretive execution of the application will continue until line number 730 is encountered. The BASIC statement numbered 730 will not be attempted; rather, the interpreter will trap-out, back to the command mode, when 730 is matched with the program counter. If the logical flow of the application never procedurally references line 730, *no trap-out will ever occur.*

Either of the two numeric operands may be omitted as desired. A single number implies a vectored start and the run continues until the logical completion of the program. A hyphen followed by a number tells the interpreter that execution should begin with the first program statement (physical, lowest numbered line in memory), but the run should be permitted to progress only until the *suspense-limit* is encountered.

The command CONT (continue) may be used to resume execution of a program that was suspended using the delimited RUN as above, provided that no other DIRECT mode operations are performed while the system is in the suspended state. The command CONT never requires (nor tolerates) any operands. The suspense-limit provided with the RUN command remains intact regardless of the use of CONT, and a trap-out will occur every time the specified line number is encountered. Use of CONT causes program execution to resume with the delimited line number; in the above example, line 730 is next executed following CONT.

From the console, the operator's use of the BREAK key will cause program execution to be suspended at the point of pickup of the next BASIC statement number immediately following that point at which the break function is acknowledged. Similar to the RUN-*limiter,* a BREAK-invoked suspense-limit can be resumed by use of CONT. The BREAK-*limit* is transitory, however, and CONT will cause the suspense-limit to be abandoned, and no recurrent or automatic trap-out will occur (except of course, any predefined RUN-*limit*).

As a reminder, the model interpreter system being described is expected to support programming learning activities, hence the emphasis on program debugging aids. The ability to execute a portion of a program with start and stop delimiters is provided specifically as a debugging tool. The BREAK key is normally used to escape perpetual loops, and CONT permits resuming in-place. LOAD brings a program into memory from tape storage, but the program does not immediately begin execution; it is especially useful for restoring to memory a partially completed program that was previously SAVE in an earlier programming session.

The key word GO TO belongs to the BASIC language but it is also useful as a system command. Used in the DIRECT mode with a line number, GO TO permits a vectored start at any valid line number. Notice the subtleties. When CONT is used the

179

system already knows a line number—either a temporary vector generated by BREAK, or a static suspense-limit that was provided in a RUN construct. The RUN command also permits a vectored start, but working storage is automatically initialized before execution begins. The GO TO used in the DIRECT mode permits a vectored start anywhere, and working storage is *not* initialized automatically. The RESUME command is similar to CONT. Where CONT is used after BREAK, the RESUME is used after a trap-out due to an I/O not-ready condition; for example, if BASIC tries to PRINT and the printer is off, the system halts. Turn the printer on and RESUME. There is another use of RESUME as a program command, which is described later in conjunction with *error trapping*.

Keyboard Source Statement Entry

In the DIRECT mode, and assuming that the proper utility is in place, the command processor determines input of source statements by reason of the leading characters being numbers. The only permitted use of numerics as the first characters in a typed string is for program statements.

If only a number is entered, program memory is searched for a match, and by convention, a line number with nothing following is accepted as an intention to delete the statement of the same number. If a number followed by syntactically valid character sequences is entered, memory is searched for a match. A match on the line numbers is assumed to be a request to replace an existing statement with the string just entered. If the memory search finds no match, the statement just entered is considered a new line, and it is added to those already in memory.

Statement deletions may be accomplished *en masse* by use of the DELETE command. Examples include:

```
800 DELETE 150
820 DELETE 150-200
840 DELETE -100
```

Statement 800 deletes a *single line,* statement number 150. A *series of statements* is cleared from memory by statement 820. Beginning with 150, all statements up to and including statement number 200 are deleted. Line 840 in the example will cause *all lines numbered less than 100* to be erased in memory; line 100 is also deleted, and control returns to the DIRECT mode. Notice that even though DELETE may be used in the PROGRAM mode, control of the interpreter returns to the DIRECT mode immediately following execution of the DELETE function. The software system does *not* support dynamic deletion of source statements during program execution.

Program statements stored in memory may be examined by use of the LIST system command. Parameters are permitted with LIST, and the syntax rules are the same as described for DELETE. A single number following LIST will call forth to the CRT the requested line. A pair of numbers seperated by a hyphen will display the inclusive statements, and a hyphen followed by a number is accepted as meaning "from the beginning . . . through." If the statement text requested exceeds CRT capacity, bottom-up scrolling occurs, and what remains displayed is the lower range of state-ments of the inclusive block asked for. Although normally used by the programmer in the DIRECT mode, LIST may be used programmatically with BASIC. When used within an application, LIST enjoys the same parameter capabilities, display conventions are identical, and program execution continues without interruption. This capability is use-ful during debugging; one can insert a temporary LIST to provide visual assurance that a line or a routine is being accessed during program execution.

Another source statement entry convenience is SPACE. Used in either the DIRECT or PROGRAM mode, SPACE is a function request of the interpreter to provide advice on the remaining number of bytes of program memory available. During entry of program statements, the programmer may be concerned whether sufficient memory is left for more statements. Type SPACE and terminate. The interpreter accepts this com-mand as a request for advice, and the number of bytes remaining for program use is displayed on the CRT. A SPACE request within BASIC during execution will return the space value to the CRT or to a variable argument depending on the statement con-struct. This capability is provided to enable the management of memory in all instances of dynamic allocation of space during execution of a BASIC program.

Memory Management

The ERASE command is provided as an aid to the programmer in controlling allocation of program working storage. Although useful in a DIRECT mode *preceding vectored starts,* ERASE is more commonly used in the PROGRAM mode to manage dynamic reallocation of work areas. The interfacing conventions provide that ERASE will cause a MRI (*memory-resident index*) entry to be abandoned. The work space associated with a variable indicator is also relinquished, and that space is immediately available for real-location. The argument supplied with ERASE may be *any valid variable name,* including simple variables, tables, and arrays.

Another system command, CLEAR, is used for initializing work areas. Useful *prior to vectored starts,* the real advantage of CLEAR is within a program. If no parame-ters are supplied, CLEAR causes all I/O buffers within interpreter working storage to be initialized. An argument appended to CLEAR is interpreted as a request to initialize a specific application work storage variable.

The clearing of I/O areas with CLEAR can be device-selective. A simple CLEAR INPUT or CLEAR PRINT clears the keyboard input buffer or the CRT display, respec-tively. Printer or cassette buffers may be cleared by providing the FILE number as an argument with the CLEAR command.

In simple review, then, ERASE works to relieve *an assignment of working storage* and CLEAR services *initialize workers* or *buffers* but the *space allocation remains.*

File Processing, Setup, Cleanup, and Labeling

To announce to the system the need for a file, use OPEN. With the command OPEN supply the *name* of the file (eight alpha characters), the *device number* (printer, cas-sette drive number), and the number to be used for *logical reference* to the file with INPUT or PRINT commands. The OPEN command is accepted by the software system as an imperative to allocate a buffer area. For cassette files only, a FILE-NAME is required, and this name is output on execution of the OPEN command to the tape as a *label record.* Interfacing rules include the following:

1 For a given file name, OPEN may only occur once, unless a file is subsequently CLOSEd.

2 Only *one* file may be OPEN on the printer at a time, and only *one* file may be OPEN per cassette drive.

3 For cassette files, OPEN must specify whether the file is intended for input or output; necessarily only one or the other is logical.

To remove a file from active status, the command CLOSE is used. The only argument required with CLOSE is the logical file number. Execution of the CLOSE command will cause a *tape mark* to be output to cassette tape in the event of an OPEN-*for-output* file. In all instances of CLOSE, the file device is logically removed from the active resources list and the peripheral is abandoned *in-place,* and tape or paper remain *stationary.*

Whether or not an implicit CLOSE is executed by the software system depends on the interfacing conventions associated with initialization. As an example, a RUN attempted from the beginning of a program that had been interrupted with open files will cause those files to be automatically CLOSEd by the interpreter as a function of prerun initialization services. Similarly, a vectored start beyond a line that OPENed a file will cause run-time errors if I/O attempts are made and the file was not logically OPEN. To state another convention, it is illogical to CLOSE a file that was never OPEN.

The commands OPEN and CLOSE, then, are used to allocate and deallocate buffer space and to advise the software of file assignment attributes. The software system will automatically service a CLOSE for any file abandoned in an OPEN state whenever the application is reinitialized. Tape positioning is the responsibility of the programmer, however, and multiple files with matching names are potential due to successive aborts and restarts. Care must be exercised in the use of vectored starts to ensure that file-active statuses are logical.

ON ERROR GO TO: Run-Time Error Trapping

The key word ERROR is a system command provided to advise the interpreter of a declarative process provided by the programmer for handling system-detected error conditions. The construct ON ERROR GO TO *nnnn* (where *n* = line number) is passed over during interpretive execution when encountered. The line number specified is saved by the interpreter for subsequent use whenever a syntax or device conditional error occurs. The convention for programming use, then, is to insert an error trap statement early in the program flow, before any error conditions are anticipated.

During execution of the BASIC program, syntax efforts are attempted against each statement, and peripheral statuses are monitored on an as-needed basis. At the point of program execution where an error condition is detected, the interpreter will execute an implied GO TO function for which the destination address is the line number provided in the ON ERROR statement. The declarative process at the error-trap may be ended with a RESUME command. The parameter possibilities with RESUME are (1) *none*—program execution is resumed at the same statement that triggered the trap-out; (2) RESUME NEXT—causes a return to the statement next following the statement that triggered the trap-out; or (3) RESUME *nnnn*—the program resumes execution at the specified statement number. This last option is directly comparable to a GO TO imperative.

Two key words are supplied in the system command list to benefit logical operations in error-trapping routines. They are ERS and ERC. The mnemonic ERS refers to *error statement,* and ERC is for *error code.* In all instances of system-detected error conditions the interpreter automatically provides ERS and ERC advice to the operator on the system message line of the CRT (the bottom line). Procedurally, within BASIC programs, ERS and ERC may be called forth to permit conditional logic flow. The value returned on ERS permits the program to determine which statement number was being executed at the time of an error, and ERC can be used to determine the specific nature of an error condition.

The ON ERROR system command provision is a design convention to service error trap-outs. The two mnemonics, ERS and ERC, provide an interface from the interpreter to the application to advise the program execution point at which the error occurred, and to define the exact nature of the error condition detected.

To summarize this section, let us review the system commands that allow interfacing the interpreter and the application program.

- Program storage: LOAD, SAVE, and, for tape rewinding, UNLOAD.
- Program execution: RUN, GO TO, CONT, and RESUME.
- Source program entry: DELETE, SPACE, LIST, and line number.
- Memory management: ERASE and CLEAR.
- Files operations: OPEN and CLOSE.
- Error trapping: ERROR, ERS, and ERC, and RESUME.

12.3 Operator Interface

This section discusses human-computer dialogue. Entire texts have been written on the art of human factors engineering of operator consoles, and James Martin's *Design of Man-Computer Dialogues* is especially recommended. This section is not intended as a complete treatment of the subject; here we describe only the specifics and conventions of design as applied to the system model under study.

Communication with the system is exclusively through the keyboard, and with only one exception, always at the request of the system. Advice to the operator that input is expected is by way of prompting with messages on the CRT display. There is an audible alarm unit mounted in the console, used by the interpreter software and available to the programmer for enhancing the quality of operator advice.

Although all input is controlled by software, the effective throughput of operator-interactive processes is paced by the operator. The significance of relatively slower reaction by the operator as compared to execution time of the system has been capitalized on wherever practical in this model. A case in point is the prompting stimulus on the CRT that precedes input of a source statement. Upon completion of the parsing and syntaxing processes, the *prompt character* (a question mark) is displayed on the CRT—signaling readiness for the next input—but before the keyboard input routine is invoked, the necessary movement of the last input from the buffer to main storage is carried out. To wait until all processes are accomplished, including relocation of the previous line of input, would serve no advantage, and overall throughput may be slightly slower.

The example just cited serves as a base for describing an important category of operator dialogues. When in the command mode the system awaits direction from the operator. The variety of inputs possible requires deliberation on the part of the operator. Input is not possible until the software is ready—*until it is prompted*—but *what* is input is decided by the operator. Whether what is typed in the command mode is *intelligible* to the system is determined only after the entry is terminated.

This category of activity contrasts with programmed requests for input that anticipate very *specific responses.* For example, an input requirement that tolerates only a *yes* or *no* decision of the operator conventionally permits only a Y or N character. In this instance the time required for operator deliberation is expected to be short, and in cases of recurrent operations, the operator's decision is often made *in anticipation* of the input prompt. Such is the case when the COPY utility queries the operator with "READY?"—meaning, "Are the required cassettes in place?"

A note is appropriate at this point regarding the use of the audible alarm tone by the software system. As a matter of convention, the alarm is sounded *after* any visual message on the display. In most cases, the ear is quicker than the eye. Time is required, albeit sometimes very little, for the operator's eyes to be attracted to a displayed message and for mental decipherment of the content. Sounding the alarm after output to the CRT tends to cause the two stimuli to be synchronized; sounding the alarm first may cause confusion—*seemingly* two separate notices.

As indicated earlier, line 16 of the CRT (the bottom line) is used by the software system for advice to the operator of *system statuses.* The illustration in Figure 12.1 shows an example of the possible output on line 16 with descriptions of each message field. The first item of data displayed to the operator is a single character advising the type of data expected to be typed. When the system is in the DIRECT mode the letter C is displayed here to indicate that a COMMAND is expected. Similarly, when the expected input is restricted to a numeric entry, the letter N is displayed, and, alternatively, the letter A indicates that alphanumeric data input is permitted. The number in parentheses immediately following the input mode indicator reflects the remaining number of consecutive inputs expected when multiple entries are required. The nature of this message deserves a more exact explanation.

In the BASIC language it is possible to request multiple entires from the operator

184

with a single program statement. For example, consider

    330 INPUT A$, B, X$(V)

When this statement first begins interpretive execution the letter A appears following the message MODE to indicate that an alphanumeric input is expected. In the parentheses, the number 3 is displayed to indicate that three fields of data are to be input at this programmed acceptance point. By convention of the BASIC language, multiple inputs per programming statement are typed consecutively, each field of input is separated by a comma, and only the final field is terminated with a carriage return or line feed key signal. As these fields are typed, use of the *comma* character will cause the field counter to be decremented by one and the MODE character changes according to the expected input indicator. Referring to the above example, then, the following displays occur in sequence: MODE A (3), then MODE N (2), then MODE A (1).

Within the interpreter it is the CRT display INPUT driver module, which has the responsibility for managing the MODE and field counter. As each character is typed it is examined by the driver for a match on the ASCII value for a *comma*. All characters entered are concatenated in the buffer until a comma is detected, at which time the buffered data is moved to working storage, the buffer cleared, the field counter decremented, and the MODE indicator updated.

During execution of multiple INPUT fields, a carriage return or line feed, signaled by the operator at any point during entry, will cause the interpreter to space-fill (or zero-fill) all nonaccessed fields, and program execution will proceed to the next program statement. (The convention for automatic space or zero blanking of input fields applies absolutely, in all cases, for any programmed INPUT, throughout the software system.

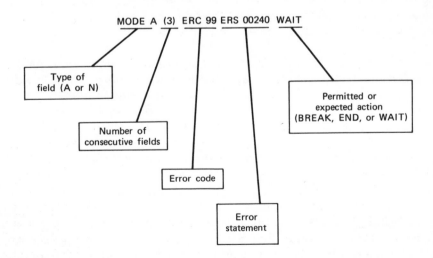

Figure 12.1 The bottom line: system status message area.

Nothing entered—simple termination with no characters typed—generates *null charac-ters* in the keyboard buffer area, thus blanks or zeros are transferred to the receiving field in memory.)

Returning to the system message line on the CRT, the caption MODE, the indica-tor following, and the field counter are displayed only when keyboard input is expected, and these data are extinguished immediately upon termination of an entry. Effectively, the line is blank until a programmed requirement for typing occurs, and the message is erased when typing is complete.

We continue now with a description of the remaining fields of data on the system message line. The next two fields are used to advise the operator of error conditions detected by the software. The abbreviation ERC (*error code*) is displayed, followed by a two-digit code to denote the type of error detected. The following field is similar, ERS (*error statement*) reflecting the BASIC statement number being executed at the time of error. These two fields are also self-blanking, and normally this area is blank during routine running of the system. As each BASIC program statement is executed it is edited by the software syntaxer, and any violation of the language conventions is trapped and an appropriate code is generated with the ERC message. Peripheral status conditions that prevent completion of any requested I/O function are also trapped by the software, and a code is communicated to the operator at this point to advise the nature of the problem.

Two other conventions pertaining to operator interfacing need explaining for the use of the ERC and ERS message area. In the previous section the BASIC capability for ERROR trapping was described. Recall that the programmer may use an ON ERROR GO TO statement to cause program execution to branch to a declaratives routine for error-recovery steps. Before the software displays ERC and ERS messages, the ON ERROR conditional flag is tested to determine whether the programmer has provided an error-recovery routine. If the flag is ON, the branch to the error routine takes preced-ence over the error message driver and this area remains blank on the CRT momentarily.

The steps taken by the programmer within the error-recovery routine should fall within three possibilities. Do *something different* (as an alternative); do *nothing* at all (ignore the problem); attempt to *reexecute* the error-causing statement. In all cases, by convention of this BASIC implementation, the only proper exit from the error-recovery routine is by use of a RESUME command (either RESUME, RESUME NEXT, or RESUME nnnnn, to retry, continue at the next statement, or continue with a specific line number, respectively). Depending on which of these alternatives was chosen, the ERC and ERS message is held in abeyance until the RESUME statement is encountered. If, because of the recovery technique provided, the condition is overcome, the ERC and ERS message is abandoned by the software as being unnecessary. At the time of interpretive execu-tion of the RESUME, however, any unsatisfied error condition takes procedural prece-dence and the appropriate ERC and ERS values are announced to the operator.

The second advantage of this convention for the use of error status messages is the provision provided to the programmer for displaying his or her own advisory notice. From within an error-recovery routine only—the ON ERROR conditional flag is ON—a

186

special construct of the PRINT statement is permitted. The form is PRINT ERROR *"xxxxxxx"* (the *x* values being any permitted character string; the length of the string is limited to 16 characters). The string-literal or string-variable used with the PRINT ERROR form of statement is output by the software on the CRT in the ERC and ERS message area and the 16-character string length limit is enforced automatically; any excess characters are arbitrarily truncated.

Let us review what happens when an attempt to output to the printer is encountered in a BASIC statement during program execution. The printer is OFF. The software detects the nonready condition of the printer. An ON ERROR statement early in the program file provides a GO TO to an error-recovery routine. The interpreter is routed to the error-recovery routine and immediately encounters IF conditional logic, and the conditions being tested are ERC values. A *true* condition occurs in the statement that tests for a printer not-ready situation, and a branch to a simple subroutine occurs. Here the construct PRINT ERROR "PRINTER OFF" is encountered. The message to the operator appears on line 16 and the program stops awaiting the operator's response. The programmer assumes that the operator will turn on the printer and terminate the temporary halt condition, and the next BASIC step is a RESUME. When the operator depresses the line feed key the error message is erased and the program continues by attempting to reexecute the statement to output to the printer.

In the sequence portrayed here, the need to stop the program to await an operator response is worth noting. A special system command available to the BASIC programmer in this model is WAIT. The WAIT command is a special extension to BASIC and may be used anytime it is desired to suspend program execution and trap-out to the keyboard driver. When used, the message WAIT is automatically output as the last field on the system error message line (line 16). Not only does WAIT provide an automatic *output message,* it may also accept *single alphanumeric input* characters, the typed character appearing immediately adjacent, and to the right of, the word WAIT.

By providing an argument, such as a variable field identifier, with WAIT, the programmer may conditionally test for codes to determine alternative logic paths based on operator-permitted responses.

This same area of the message line at the bottom of the display normally contains the simple message OK, followed by a single character to denote the type of program in execution. When the software system is in the command mode the message on the bottom line, to the extreme right, is OK S. The intent of this advisory is that all is copacetic and the system software is in charge. When running a utility program the OK message carries a U identity, and BASIC programs in command reflect OK B. The OK message normally appears as the only data on the message line, and it alternates with any WAIT function supplied by either the software system or BASIC.

Two other messages are possible outputs in this same area. They are END and BREAK. The END message occurs only in conjunction with interpretive execution of the BASIC command END, used optionally to designate the logical and physical end of a program. When END occurs on the message line the software system reverts to the system command mode of operation and any keyboard input at this point will cause END to be replaced by OK S. Similarly, BREAK appears if the interpreter attempts to go

187

beyond the physical end of the program statement file. In this instance an ERS message is also displayed to indicate the line number of the last statement of BASIC executed. This type of condition prevails when the programmer failed to provide any END statement and sequential execution terminates as a result of having no further statements to execute. In this case, control reverts to the command mode, just as with the use of an orderly program ending.

We complete the description of the operator-to-system interfacing by reiterating that, for this tutorial model, most conventions depend on the use of a single message line on the CRT to communicate with the operator. The primary use of this line is by the interpreter software to advise the type of input expected by the operator, the status of any error conditions, and the state of the system as well as which type of software is in command. Certain language extensions are also provided to the programmer to assist in interfacing BASIC programs with the operator. The motive for enhancing BASIC is twofold: easier programming, and consistency of operator interactive procedures and messages. Again, novice programmers and operators are anticipated, and *consistency* and *simplicity* are at least somewhat analogus.

Chapter

13 The Design Template

very author of technical texts is confronted with the dilemma of depth of detail. One dimension of this problem is how much detail to give in describing a tutorial model when it will be copied only with regard to concept, not implementation. For the reader who by this point perceives the overall and wishes not to labor through greater detail, a branch is in order:

```
IF COMPREHENSION IS EQUAL TO COMPLETE GO TO PART-V
    ELSE NEXT SENTENCE.
```

In the above, the syntax of COBOL is employed for the sake of brevity. So, too, the balance of this chapter is a compromise between succinctness and completeness. The software template from Chapter 9 is repeated here, and serves as a point of reference for discussion. In the succeeding sections the components of the software are described on an individual basis. The intent for each is to describe at least three attributes: (1) the functional reason for the module, (2) from whence the module may be accessed, and (3) exit point and direction of flow from the module.

We begin with a glance at Figure 13.1, recalling that the software system is composed of four major sections. In Figure 13.2 a further subdivision of each of these is suggested. Figure 13.3 is a breakout to *task level* of the model template. Each of the sections of this chapter is divided according to the major template components, and within each the narrative defines the detail.

13.1 The Monitor Section

The name *Monitor* is apt, since the role of this major group of software modules is predominantly one of *supervision* and *regulation* rather than task accomplishment.

189

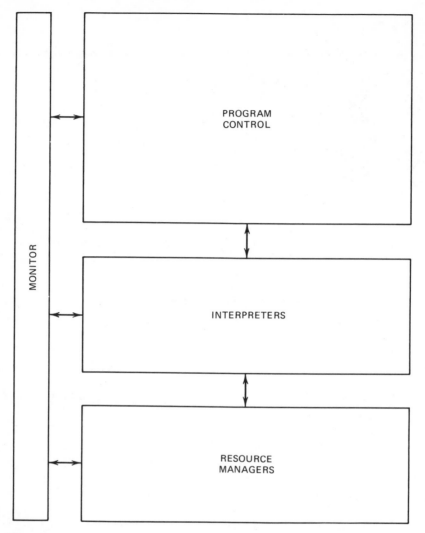

Figure 13.1 Major components template.

Although physically separated from each other in memory, the logical and philosophical orientation of the three subdivisions of the Monitor relate to control of other modules.

On the template the central group is named the *Executive*. Notice also that the only interfacing possibilities of the Executive are to the other two Monitor members, and for a single purpose, to the *Operator Communications* section of the *Program Control* group. Rather than digress at this point, note for later discussion that the reason for the *operator-to-Executive* direct link is for BREAK key signals.

The *Class Manager* group and the *Sequencer* are the other two members of the

190

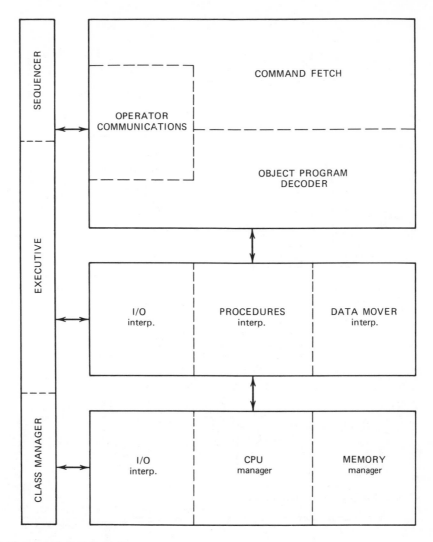

Figure 13.2 Major modules template.

Monitor classification. Notice also that the Class Manager tends to be hardware-oriented, the Sequencer pertains to the running of the interpretive processes, and the Executive largely serves as an overseer and arbitrator of these two.

The Executive

Software system synchronization is a major responsibility of the Executive. The nucleus of the Executive is a series of conditional branches, and any true conditions will cause continuous looping through this test series until all status codes will permit continued operation of the system. The predominant flow of execution through the Executive is

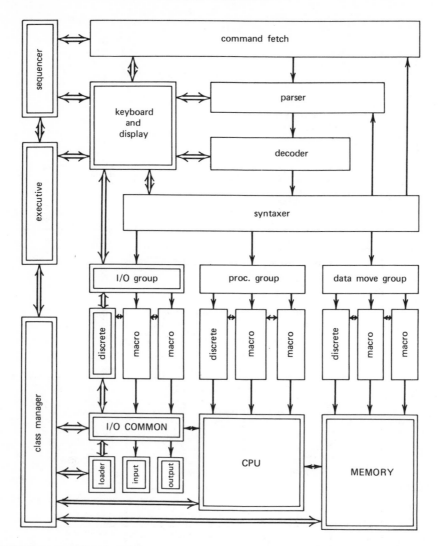

Figure 13.3 Major subroutines template.

from the Class Manager areas, and when all is copacetic, control transfers to the sequencer for interpretive execution of the next BASIC statement or diversion to the keyboard for system command operations.

The only reverse-flow potential is when the Executive finds it necessary to branch back to the Class Manager. Two categories of testing are carried out within the Executive, one for hardware and one for software. Hardware statuses (I/O interrupts) are generally serviced and completed prior to accessing the Executive, and software routines depend on the Executive to secure all housekeeping chores. The Executive then, tests, a series of soft codes, and any indication of incomplete functions will cause a branch back to the Class Manager area. This algorithm depends on the design technique that each major routine sets ON a bit within a code word when a routine is first entered. It is this bit that is tested by the Executive to ensure that all is ready. Bits within bytes, and bytes within words, are assigned positional significance such that a last-at determination can be made according to which are set ON.

Conceptually, then, as each interpretive execution sequence begins, signals are turned on as routines are accessed and are extinguished as functional tasks are completed. These trail markers serve to enhance software reliability, provide a control mechanism, and not least significant, are highly useful in fault diagnosis when anything goes awry.

Lest we forget—the BREAK key exception. As a last act of the Executive process, before control passes to the Sequencer, the keyboard interrupt is tested for an operator attempt to BREAK. If ON, it is at this point (and only at this point) that the operator is permitted to usurp control of the system. The logic of this scheme is to ensure that all processes are sufficiently cleaned up and an orderly, programmed-for interruption can occur. Since each interpretive cycle channels through this test block, BREAK is possible between any two BASIC statements, but only after full execution of any in process.

Since it is only the Executive that can acknowledge a BREAK, it is also incumbent upon this module to service a request to continue. If the operator enters the system command CONT and the BREAK flag has not yet been set OFF, the Executive can pass control to the sequencer and interpretive execution can proceed. While the system is in a BREAK-*suspense status,* use of any system command that alters the BASIC program status will reset the BREAK flag; thus a CONT is not permitted by the Executive. As described just previously, the Executive process of looping through a series of conditional status checks, and the provisions for BREAK monitoring, ensure the integrity of the system for the benefit of both the operator and the programmer.

The Class Manager

Conceptually, the location of the Class Manager is between the Executive and the various modules that manage hardware resources. Hardware in this context includes the processor, the main memory, the printer, and the cassette peripherals. Notice the exception: The keyboard and CRT are not within Class Manager jurisdiction.

The primary role of the Class Manager modules is housekeeping. The various routines claimed by this grouping include those for clearing buffers, interpreter working storage, program work areas, and all tables and arrays. The general architecture of this model system depends on relocatable software techniques, and it is within the Class Manager group of routines that base registers are maintained. Although individual processes and interpretives have occasion to alter pointer values (such as in the *Data Movement group*), it is incumbent upon the Class Manager to ascertain the validity of the values of all base registers on completion of each cycle.

The normal sequence of flow during interpreter execution is from the I/O, CPU, or Memory Manager routines to the Class Manager, thence to the Executive. Either of the *discrete managers* (I/O, CPU, or memory) may intercommunicate through the Class Manager, however. An example of this type of process is a system command request to

LOAD. The I/O group is first invoked where a determination is made that user program memory should be cleared. A subroutine jump sequence occurs then to the Class Manager where the BASIC base registers are initialized. Intermediate jumping results to the Memory Manager for the clearing routine, and return is back to the Class Manager. A memory CLEAR status is determined by the Class Manager, and control returns to the I/O Common module to complete the load task. As a final act before passing control to the Executive, the Class Manager ensures that the cassette device is secure, the CPU is initialized, and memory pointers are set.

The Sequencer

Physically the smallest generic module, the Sequencer is the real heart of the interpreter system. It is this routine that manages an address pointer to indicate the memory location of the BASIC program instructions. As each instruction is executed, this pointer is adjusted to compensate for the length of the instruction in process. The Program Control section calculates the amount of all offsets and reloads the program counter based on control statements. It is the Sequencer routine that actually adjusts the program counter, however, using work values provided by the other modules. Once adjusted, the program counter represents the correct memory address of the next instruction, and the Sequencer zeros all workers that are used for program counter calculations.

The Sequencer may be invoked by either the Executive or the Program Control Group (Keyboard and Display module). Exit from the Sequencer is direct to the Command Fetch routine of the Program Control Group, and the only instance of reverse flow is via the Syntaxer-to-Command-Fetch route when servicing ON ERROR logic.

The Monitor, then, consists of the Executive, the Sequencer, and the Class Manager software routines. The Sequencer, a single module, maintains the BASIC program counter, the Class Manager provides housekeeping services, and the Executive interfaces and supervises software and hardware interaction. The categorization of the Monitor modules is based on generic and functional reasons, and the various routines are not necessarily contiguous in memory.

13.2   The Program Control Section

One of the four major levels of the design template is for the control of the internally stored application program: the Program Control Section. Minor-level descriptors relate to command fetch, object code decode processes, and operator requests to alter programmed operations. Specific software subroutines are designed to satisfy each of these requirements.

Command Fetch

An instruction retrieval routine is used to access main memory, pick up an object code command, and transfer it to a work area. The address of the next program instruction to be executed is denoted by the program counter, which is maintained by the Sequencer.

The program counter indicates only physical location; it is the task of the Command Fetch subroutine to ascertain the word length of the pseudo-code and to move the operation code and the operands to working storage. Prior to exiting the Command Fetch routine, the length of the instruction is passed to the Sequencer for use in incrementing the program counter on the next cycle.

Entry into the Command Fetch module can be from three possible points. The most usual entry is from the Sequencer. During program execution the Sequencer sets up the next instruction reference and transfers control to the Command Fetch routine. A possible alternative entry is from the Syntaxer. In any event of an invalid ranging attempt (an illegal address in the program counter), this error status is trapped by the Syntaxer. Either the operator or an ON ERROR conditional may attempt continued execution of the BASIC program, but in no event can the Command Fetch process act on an invalid or nonexistent address.

The third possible entry directive may come from the operator's console. A feature of this software system permits the operator to load a next-do instruction address directly into the program counter. This facility is provided as a program debugging tool and can also be used to overcome abnormal operations problems. It is assumed, of course, that the operator is responsible for the procedural correctness of any such vectored start.

Exit from the Command Fetch procedures is normally direct to the Parser. An indirect path to the Parser (through the Console and Display module) is used when executing in a trace mode. Program tracing is that mode which provides a running display of the program counter and BASIC statements, in a step-by-step fashion, during sequential execution of the user's program. The intermediate subroutine jump to the Tracer does not alter the method of sequence of execution of the interpreter however.

Parser

The pseudo-object command consists of several elements. The first component is a header, the second is the operation code, and the remaining parts are operands. It is a function of the Parser to separate the user's program instructions into these individual components. Parsing is accomplished by moving each of these several parts to respective work areas. Normal entry into this routine is from the Command Fetch process. The Parser assumes that the input is a valid user instruction set up in working storage area especially for the benefit of the Parser. No actual validity checking is attempted by the parser, since qualification occurs as a function of the decoder routine. Although small in size and scope, the Parser is essential to prepare the pseudo-object instructions for the Decoder.

Normal entry to the Parser is from the Command Fetch module, and exit is always to the Decoder. An exception to this is inherent to a unique debugging facility. This feature permits the programmer to enter an object code instruction directly into Parser storage from the keyboard and effect immediate execution. Any command thus entered is a *one-shot*, since it does not occur anywhere in memory except in the working storage area. Access to this special facility is on a highly controlled basis, permitted only from an error trap managed by the Syntaxer.

Decoder

As the name implies, the Decoder routine is responsible for decoding the stored BASIC instructions. The ultimate exit from this routine is to the appropriate interpreter string, as indicated by the operation code portion of the object instruction. Before control is transferred, however, the decoder is responsible for certain other decoding operations.

Decimal literals may be appended to an operation code, encoded in binary but to be used as a decimal numeric operand. A special code in the instruction header serves to identify a format such as this, and it is the Decoder's task to accomplish all conversions.

Another function of the Decoder is to intercept all system commands, and to distinguish directional control requirements. Exit from the Decoder may be to a system service routine or to an appropriate interpretive process.

Notice that control passes from the Decoder to an interpreter routine through the Syntaxer. Assuming that no syntax condition occurs, the transfer of control to an interpreter string is seemingly transparent to the Syntaxer. This is accomplished by the design of the front end of the Syntaxer. The entry point into the Syntaxer immediately tests for a conditional flag. If ON, the Syntaxer procedures are entered to effect control of the system for operator and user program advice. If the conditional is OFF, the Syntaxer is effectively bypassed. The Decoder places the address of the selected interpreter string into the operand area of the instruction immediately following the conditional branch at the beginning of the Syntaxer. Therefore, if the flag is not set, sequential execution causes a drop-through, and a branch to the selected routine is encountered.

This seemingly devious routing technique is required to support the requirement for a consistent error-reporting scheme. Since a variety of opportunities exist throughout the software system that can necessitate error reporting, this common trap point is provided. As a convention of this model, suspended operation of the interpretive process is accompanied by advice to the operator of the statement in error and a code to denote why. Operationally, then, any software routine wishing to halt the run needs only to set the syntax flag ON and communicate its identifier to the ERC (*error code*) area. Execution of the interpretive process is then permitted to continue until the error trap point is reached at the beginning of the Syntaxer. As a result of this design, the software system is advised not only of the last preceding statement (perhaps in error), and the instruction next to be executed has already been decoded.

The ERC area is a *push-down stack.* Any software routine that turns ON the syntax conditional flag places an appropriate code on *top* of the stack. When the Syntaxer is invoked, the topmost code is displayed first. As each succeeding code is announced (when more than one error exists), recovery attempts pop the stack contents upward and when the stack is empty processing is permitted to continue. The normal exit then from the Syntaxer is to the selected interpreter string as previously defined by the Decoder.

As described earlier, however, it is possible for the programmer (operator) to cause the Syntaxer to exit by returning to the Parser (one-shot keyboard commands) or to return to the Command Fetch routine to effect redirection. Depending on the nature of the error condition, this redirection may in fact be to attempt the next, *already decoded,* BASIC program step.

Operator Communications Module

In the detail template (Figure 13.3) this component has a double-line outline to portray better its executive-level posture within the software hierarchy. (All such double-lined components enjoy a similar distinction.) Operationally, however, the operator interface module is more correctly considered as a member of the Program Control group.

While it is approximately correct for the system operator to assume a proprietary position, the onus for logically correct operations is on the software. With the exception of an absolute takeover of the system by the operator, all input is qualified and is normally permitted only as a response to a system-generated message or condition. The nature of the ultimate control that may be imposed by the operator is to abort a process or program in favor of loading a different job, or more usually, to call up the next job upon terminal completion of the one in residence.

Keyboard input resolution is the responsibility of a subroutine within the console interface functions. The basic concept here is explicitly to compare key codes with any that may be logically permitted at a given acceptance point. In essence, this process is one of delimitation—if the keyed code is not contained in the list of those permitted, it is disallowed or ignored. Since a variety of options must exist, and specific options vary according to conditions, the permitted choices are defined by the message output routine.

Message output control is localized in a single software module. The need for the system to communicate with the operator can be triggered from a variety of points within the software environment. As a design philosophy, however, actual dialogue tasks are managed *exclusively* by the operator communications module. Recalling briefly the description of the Syntaxer, the technique of a single dialogue driver is better appreciated.

Assume that a peripheral error condition occurs. The I/O driver routine places its identification code in the ERC stack and turns ON the syntax flag. Execution continues and control is passed to the Command Fetch routine. (Since the route to the sequencer is bypassed, the command that is fetched is the same one that is entrapped.)

With the flag ON the Syntaxer is invoked, and the peripheral *ID code* is output to the operator. Program execution is now halted and the operator is advised as to the condition for the halt and which BASIC statement is entrapped.

If, as an example, an out-of-paper condition was sensed and the printer *ID code* was displayed, the permitted choices for the operator include correcting the condition and resuming operation, or aborting the run, or ignoring the problem and attempting to continue with the next program statement. The subroutine that is selected to qualify the operator's input will exit down through the syntaxer, back to the I/O driver, to ascertain whether processing may continue.

To review, the Program Control section includes the Keyboard and Display routines, within which all human-computer dialogue is managed. This physically large section consists of several modules, and collectively they interface with the Command

Fetch routine and the Parser, Decoder, and the Syntaxer. Pseudo-object commands (BASIC statements) are fetched from memory and separated by the Parser. The Decoder determines the appropriate interpretive routine for each type of BASIC instruction, and the Syntaxer is invoked in the event of an error, either with the syntax of the user's instructions or any failure of software or hardware.

13.3 The Interpretive String Section

String selection is accomplished by the Program Control Section of the software system, as described in the previous section. The strings are comprised of machine-code instructions that execute discrete microprocessor tasks, and there is one such string for each BASIC *command*.

According to the template, the *interpreter section* consists of all of the strings, grouped according to major functions. The three groups are (1) the I/O Group, (2) the *Procedures Group*, and (3) the *Data Movement Group*. The architecture of each of these groups is similar, consisting of group-level tasks, followed in turn by individual sequences for subordinate (unique) tasks for support of specific commands. This design concept permits translation of program commands that require use of more than one string-group for total interpretation.

Group-level entry is, normally, from the command Decoder (via the Syntaxer), preparatory functions are carried out, and control is then transferred to the targetted string. An alternative entry route into a group is possible when, depending on the program command involved, control is transferred between groups. Exit from a group-level task is always direct to a string, however, and the string exit point is also constant; *all strings branch to respective Resource Managers.*

Group-to-group linking is accomplished by a preconditioning technique at the group level. At time of entry into an interpreter string group, determination is made as to whether more than one group is required and an indicator is set ON or OFF accordingly. All branches within groups are *subroutine jumps;* within strings they are *unconditional branches.* Within resource managers a conditional test of the linking indicator enables using a subroutine return to return to the group level module, or if the indicator is OFF, linear execution prevails.

String-level management consists of the two tasks: (1) *group linking* (just discussed) and (2) *loop control.* Each string is designed to accomplish one complete task, usually on a per-byte basis. The housekeeping function of preloading loop counters is accomplished at the group level before control is passed to a string. To ensure continuity and string operation integrity, the last step prior to entry into a given string is to disable all peripheral interrupts.

Two types of interpreter strings are employed: discrete and macro. Discrete strings, as the name implies, are *machine-code routines*, and macros are *series of subroutine jump instructions.* The routines that are referenced by jump-series macros are discrete code strings, or in some cases they may be other macro strings. All such routines are designed as subroutines (ending with jump-returns) so that, in effect, only a single level of jump-nesting is ever involved.

198

Although string-to-string transfers are used (macros), such activity is restricted to include only strings within a group. The orientation of the group-level managers is to satisfy housekeeping functions of the strings within the respective groups. It is this design concept that determines the three groups described.

The I/O Group

At the user program level it is INPUT and PRINT command activities that decode to this group. Device driver tasks are accomplished within the peripheral Resource Manager module (described later), but it is at the interpreter level that user command functions are managed. Cross-communication is usually required between the I/O Group and either, or both, the procedures and the data movement groups.

As an example of the scope of the interpretive tasks within this group, consider a user-programmed request to print data from memory. The I/O Group manager is the module that sets in motion the sequence to carry out the programmer's request. In this instance, the PRINT operation is fairly straightforward. Other types of I/O operations are different in scope, but they are similar in design concept.

The first consideration is *what data.* The memory address at which the data is stored is moved to the PRINT interpreter string.

The second consideration is *how much data.* The *data-string length delimiter* is also passed to the PRINT string. Interrupts are disabled and control passes to the string. Characters are now transferred, a byte at a time, from memory to the printer buffer, the string loop being repeated according to the length of the data string to be output. If, as in many cases, any *editing* of data is required, the PRINT interpreter string uses other I/O Group subroutines during the character-by-character loop process. Control ultimately passes to the peripheral manager. When the entire data string has been set up in the printer buffer area, the process of command interpretation is complete, save for the actual print function.

The Procedures Group

The Procedures Group of interpreters accomplish full translated execution of two types of programmed commands. The least complex of these are those involving program control, that is, GOTO, GOSUB, and RETURN. The second category of user commands accomplished by this group are those involving arithmetic. Seemingly dissimilar in function, these two types of commands are common enough in the context of processor usage.

The individual string processes within the Procedures Group involve nearly complete dominance of the ALU (arithmetic logic unit) of the microprocessor. A partial reason for the inclusion of these two types of tasks within this group *is the arithmetic steps necessary* to carry out a programmed branch or jump (incrementing of the program counter, etc.).

At the group level, housekeeping chores include conditioning of arithmetic registers, accumulator flags, address identification (either *data* or *next-do* program step location), and loop counter initialization. Both macro and discrete routines are used in the interpreter strings of this group, with the greatest emphasis on macros to support arithmetic tasks.

199

The Data Movement Group

The primary responsibility of the *Data Movement Group* is to effect all *data movement* in main memory. Data is defined in this context to include variable-length blocks of words of *program constants*, and data that is brought into main memory by the *application program*. There are two users of the Data Movement Group: either of the other two *interpreter groups*, or the *user's program*, whether the requirement is explicitly or implicitly defined.

Some of the various tasks managed by these strings include the foillowing:

- Alphanumeric character string moves with space code filling, overflow truncation, and ETX (end-of-text) null code insertion.
- Concatenation and deconcatenation, juxtapositioning, and word boundary justification.
- Replication (repeated character sequences), including clearing of table areas, etc.—actually space values.
- Table access support: index maintenance and table element format parameters.
- Code set conversion operations; character string scans and replacement functions.

Again, at the group level, housekeeping operations are performed for all tasks that are common to more than one string *prior to* passing control of selected strings. Both the SEND and RECEIVE base addresses are predefined for the benefit of string execution, and loop limits are established prior to entry into a string. Cross-string operations are used, but nesting of subroutines is limited to single occurances within a group. Exit from the individual interpretive strings is either direct to an appropriate Resource Manager or, by way of a *subroutine return*, back to the group level for transfer to another string.

The responsibility of the *Interpreter Strings Section* is for functional execution of BASIC program instructions. There are strings for each possible BASIC *imperative*. Strings are either of *discrete* design or they may be *macro* sequences. Discrete strings are series of machine-language instructions that carry out the intended functional task. The macro strings are series of jump instructions that use combinations of discrete strings for task accomplishment. Strings are selected by the Decoder (control transfer is indirect, through the Syntaxer) and exit from strings is to Resource Managers. Cross-string transfers are used, but only at the group level, and all strings are contained within either the I/O Group, the Procedure Group, or the Data Movement Group.

13.4 The Resource Manager Section

The remaining portion of the software system depicted by the design template is the *Resource Manager Section.* Resources as intended here are, respectively, *peripherals, main computer memory,* and the *processor* itself. There is a direct relationship between these module categories and the Interpreter String groupings. The I/O Group of strings

200

relate to the I/O Manager, the Procedures Group interacts with the CPU Manager, and the Data Movement Group depends on the Memory Manager module.

Each of the Resource Managers may cross-communicate, and they are all conceptually under the control of the Class Manager module of the Monitor section. The largest and most complex of these three sections of the software system is that dealing with I/O devices, but all of the Resource Managers are similar in concept. One intention of this architecture is to separate as much of the software system as possible from the *mechanical* aspects of the system. In theory at least, if a peripheral device is exchanged for another, only a nominal effect is experienced by a majority of the software system. The net effect of any such exchange should require substitution of the I/O driver module involved, and perhaps minor changes will be necessary at the group level.

The I/O Common Resource Manager

Separate routines are grouped here based on *functional tasks.* The *Loader* series of routines include all tasks associated with program loading to memory; programs for this purpose include the *software system, utilities,* and BASIC *programs,* as well as program *overlays* to any of these. This management module includes a unique cassette driver specifically designed to support program loading. Entry into this driver area is from the I/O Resource Manager, and exit from the loading process is to the Class Manager. The loader routines are dependent on services provided by the CPU Manager and the Memory Manager, and all cross-talk between Resource Managers is at the *manager level.*

The remaining routines of the I/O Manager are classed according to *directional flow* of the data. The Input driver module has a counterpart—the Output driver. Common housekeeping chores for either of these is accomplished at the Resource Manager level. Both discrete and macro techniques are employed within these routines and, again, interaction with other software modules is possible only at the manager level. Exit from either of these tasks is to the Class Manager, this route being taken *only upon completion of the requested service.*

The CPU Manager

The CPU Manager suffers from a slight misnomer problem. It is within this area that management of the *I/O stack* is performed. A table is contained here that denotes the physical assignment of all I/O ports, and DMA (direct memory access) assistance is provided by the CPU Manager. Since either of these two types of activity involve use of *or suspension of* the CPU resources, the name is only slightly indistinct.

Entry into the CPU Manager is predominantly from the I/O Resource Manager or the Procedures Group, and only occassionally from the Data Movement Group. Exit from the CPU Manager may be to the Class Manager, but more commonly, an *I/O-complete* returns control to *the requesting module.*

The Memory Manager

The Memory Manager consists of several rather small, discrete subroutines. These routines are designed for specific tasks relating to initializing base registers and for maintenance of interpreter working storage. Clearing of the MRI (memory resident index), as an example, is performed under the control of the Memory Manager. It is the manager's responsibility to set up the loop counter for all routines that clear continguous sections of memory, and this responsibility includes validating for size all such clearing requests.

Exit from the Memory Manager, in the absence of an explicit subroutine return, *implicitly defaults* to the Class Manager. The Memory Manager module is *independent in function* and does not require the services of any other software group. It is instead, a *servicing module,* and is depended upon by other software groups.

Resource Managers are, then, the *I/O Common, the CPU Manager,* and *the Memory Manager.* The I/O management group contains the peripheral drivers and the CPU group maintains port assignments, I/O stack addresses, and DMA pointers. The Memory Manager modules provide memory maintenance services and function as an auditor for all requests for memory allocation and deallocation. Exit from these procedures areas is always back to the Class Manager, it is there determined whether or not resource service requests have been satisfied.

PART

Optimization Techniques

Optimize . . . to make as perfect, effective, or functional as possible.

Technique . . . a method of accomplishing a desired aim.

The next two chapters are necessary and yet, in a sense, they are only complementary to the basic theme of this book. The material presented is not intended as a primer or treatise in programming technology—what has been included is relevant to software interpreter designing. As mentioned in the introductory chapters, interpreters are often cited as being inefficient because of their speed and overhead burdens. It is a contention of this author, however, that these inefficiencies can be minimized by skillful design and judicious balancing of system resources.

When compared to their larger EDP brothers, microcomputers are slower and have smaller main memories. So, too, peripheral adjuncts tend to be slower and provide fewer features than those usually costing many thousands of dollars more. It is for these reasons that the software designer must apply his or her skills more expertly when confronted with the modern micro.

The two parameters of x speed and y bytes are prescribed for any system by the design of the hardware. And this two-dimensional problem must be considered by all software writers, on whatever system. Never have I met a programmer who didn't wish at some time for more memory or a faster processor—or both! There is an analogy, however, that is especially applicable to the microcomputer. You must fit 5 pounds of sand into a 4-pound sack. In the case of software interpreters, the sack is often stitched to a limit of only 2 pounds; *some room must be reserved for the user.*

203

Although the x and y axes of the speed and space problem are not congruent, neither are they exclusive. There is a strong tendency for any technique that favors one to be at the expense of the other. Thus the next two chapters focus on the *speed of execution* and *storage conservation* methods.

The analyst examining an existing system may appreciate the design rationale that prevailed, and for the newly commissioned project designer this data should assist in making trade-off decisions.

204

Chapter

Execution Speed

The subject of this chapter is *speed*—speed of execution of software *interpretive processes.* The arguments for optimization have been offered elsewhere, and it is stipulated that *performance success is a function of design.* The correlative is also assumed: A *lack of success* is *equally a function of design.* With regard to successful performance in terms of speed, this chapter is based on the premise that what is *unnoticed* is *acceptable,* and what is acceptable is *successful.*

If credence is permitted for these basic assumptions, attention to detail in the design of software routines should focus on execution speed considerations for those processes that portend *visible* degradation—in a word, *bottleneck analysis.*

To labor over choices of coding technique to achieve savings of 100 milliseconds during a system initialization routine is ill-advised effort. However, the savings of a hundred mills for a sequence that is imbedded within a reiterative loop that must be executed 100 times produces *a net optimization of 10 seconds*—well worth the effort, especially if this same routine is encountered frequently. And the value is even greater if the operator is in a standby mode during that 10 seconds. From the Sage of Systems: *"Aggrevate the operator and suffer the risk of unacceptable performance."*

This chapter has three parts: procedural technique within individual routines, tasking priorities between multiple routines, and memory addressing schemes. The implicit definition here is that a routine is a *sequence* of programming instructions that, when executed, comprise a complete, but discrete, *single processing task.* Multitasking by the software engineer's definition means that multiple tasks are seemingly performed *concurrently.* And, of course, memory addressing embraces memory allocation and utilization as well as the specifics for transferring data to and from memory locations.

As a preamble to the material that follows, the qualifiers concerning variation among microprocessors is offered. The different commands for a given processor often vary considerably in terms of execution speed. So, too, similar commands provided by different manufacturer's products vary considerably. And the fact that a given CPU chip provides *single command* capabilities that may require *use of several* by another to accomplish identical functions must not go unnoticed.

With this in mind, then, consider the following techniques as tutorial. The concepts described are valid, and the methods suggested are nearly always useful. Whether or not specific techniques are applicable for a given design circumstance remains the choice of the architect. And so it should be, for therein lies the real pleasures of programming—the matching of techniques and tasks, and the realization that *optimum performance is possible only by superior design.*

14.1 Linear and Reiterative Functions

This section is dedicated to the principle that the *fastest* programming routines are those with the *fewest* instructions—that is, fewest in terms of *execution*, not in terms of *quantity* of code. The reason is that it takes less time to execute 10 instruction steps than to do 20. Of course, some commands are faster than others—it is the *principle* we shall discuss, not the absolute or specific.

At the risk of oversimplification I offer the postulate that *linear sequences* are faster than *reiterative.* Straight lining is faster than looping. It must be: To accomplish a loop requires more instructions. A loop requires, as a minimum, initializing of a counter, incrementing the counter, conditionally testing whether or not the process is complete, and at the bottom a branch is required to direct the sequence back through another loop. Depending on the command set available and the programming technique employed, probably five instructions additional to the process at hand must be used to carry out the loop function.

Assuming that the estimated five instructions is correct—one for setting the counter to begin, the other four commands contained within the loop for control purposes and executed repeatedly—they each require time to execute. The alternative, of course, is to code the task steps repeatedly.

Consider as a task example the need to move a string of 5 bytes from one memory location to another. One technique in 8080 machine language is to use a *load* and *store* instruction sequence. Pick up from memory into the accumulator with one instruction, and copy the accumulator to memory with another. In a linear fashion, then, two commands are used for each byte—5 bytes require a linear sequence of 10 instructions.

Compare this to a looping method: Set a counter to zero—one instruction. Add the counter to the pickup address and load the first byte to the accumulator. Add the counter to the send address and store the accumulator in memory. Add one to the counter. *Done?* (Test for a total of five iterations; the counter should equal four.) Branch back for another task sequence until all 5 bytes are moved, *then* exit.

Six instructions are required for each iteration, and one command was required to initialize the loop counter. A total of 31 program steps must be executed *to do the task example.* The loop technique is three times slower than the linear technique—not quite, but close enough for our purposes. Again, not all commands have the *same*

206

execution timing factor, nor are all commands of *equal* length. If we *assume* that all are of equal length, however, the linear sequence requires ten words of program storage space and the loop requires only seven. *The loop enjoys approximately a 30% space saving advantage.*

The real power of the loop technique is in its *variability*. The linear technique in this example always moves 5 bytes, *no more and no less.* By *varying the conditional* that tests for the number of loop iterations, the loop technique can move from *1* to *n* bytes— quite an advantage.

And so, the art of designing programs. Whether to use linear or looping techniques requires balancing memory conservation requirements, speed considerations, task requirements, and whether or not iterative variability is required.

It is pertinent to summarize by suggesting that, for the sake of enhancing speed, due deliberation be allowed for applying the principle that *linear is faster than looping.* Be especially alert also for the compounding effect of *nested loops.* A reiterative process *contained within a reiterative process* can be guilty of severe degradation. Albeit, there are times when that is the optimum overall choice. Bottleneck analysis generally centers on nested loops, however, for when execution *speed is long,* it is typically in the *shortest routines* (coding wise).

And now for the case of the *careless conditionals.* Within sequences of procedural code it is common to use a conditional branch to alter program flow. It is also usual to place several conditional branch tests in immediate succession. Figure 14.1 is an example of multiple, successive conditional testing. The essence of this optimizing suggestion is to arrange multiple tests in the order of *most likely first.* The alternate design in Figure 14.2 permits changing the search hierarchy based on presentation probability, and if tables are used for the LOAD function, multiple (different) tables may drive the same routine.

Application of this principle depends on having done a *probability analysis.* Assume that five possibilities must be tested, one after another. Jot a list of the conditions that must prevail for each to be executed. In reviewing the list, which conditions are likely to occur with the greatest frequency? Next most likely? and finally, the least probable, necessary to be tested, but only infrequently active?

Consider the circumstance of these five theoretical tests, and assume that each conditional branch requires 1 millisecond to execute if false. If the *most routine exit* was placed last and the series were contained within a loop that typically runs for 100 times, 500 mills are consumed for *just these conditional tests.* Placing the *most-likely-to-occur* conditional at the beginning of the series would save nearly half of a second. This is a substantial saving, especially when compared to the relatively nominal analysis effort necessary to achieve it.

This is an opportune point to amplify the idea of the probability analysis. When doing linear search algorithms on strings or tables, order the list of data by *descending precedence.* Examine the *Keyword List* in the BASIC interpreter. The word LET is the most frequently used keyword in BASIC. Placed as the first constant in the memory table, execution time for the search for matching words is the bare minimum when the comparator is LET.

In the model system described in Part 4 of this book the use of LET *is optional.* In

Search a 100—character string for an A, G, L, X, or Z

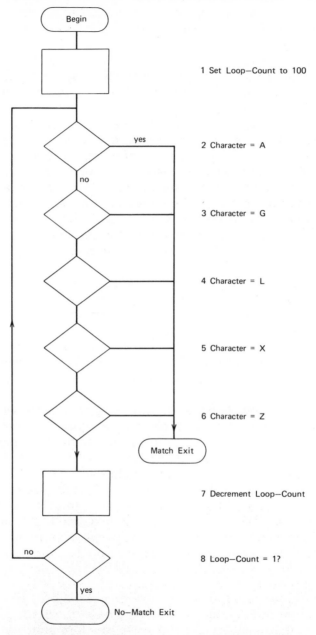

Begin

1 Set Loop—Count to 100

2 Character = A

3 Character = G

4 Character = L

5 Character = X

6 Character = Z

Match Exit

7 Decrement Loop—Count

8 Loop—Count = 1?

No—Match Exit

Note: A memory cycle is required to fetch each TEST—CONSTANT —
each iteration of the loop.

Figure 14.1 Character string scanning for multiple constants.

Search a 100—character string for an A, G, L, X, or Z

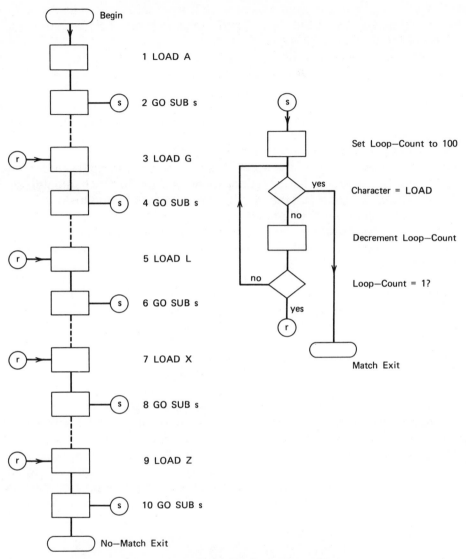

Begin

1 LOAD A

2 GO SUB s

3 LOAD G

4 GO SUB s

5 LOAD L

6 GO SUB s

7 LOAD X

8 GO SUB s

9 LOAD Z

10 GO SUB s

No—Match Exit

s

Set Loop—Count to 100

Character = LOAD

yes

no

Decrement Loop—Count

Loop—Count = 1?

no

yes

r

Match Exit

Note: Memory—fetch of test constant occurs but once per LOAD.
Order of characters tested is governed by rules of probability—
most likely first, next likely second, etc.

Figure 14.2 A faster technique, assuming a wide disparity in probability of occurence of constants (see Figure 14.1).

this case the keyword LET is probably the *least* frequently used, since it need not be used at all. Therefore, in this implementation, LET is actually placed as the last element in the Keyword List—so as not to slow down the search process, because a match is *highly probable* long before LET is encountered.

The technique mentioned next is the real forte of the bit benders. When practical to do so, use *bits* instead of *bytes.* A dual saving is realized here: less memory required for variables, and significantly enhanced speed of execution. The principle on which enhanced execution is based is a function of memory-to-register movement timing. The slowest commands of a microcomputer set are those for transfers between *CPU registers* and *main memory.* Once a byte of data is captured from memory, however, it may be *repeatedly* messaged within the various registers at optimum speed.

Reflecting momentarily on the earlier discussion of looping, notice the need for an iteration counter. If otherwise practical to do so, use a CPU register as a loop counter. For the rare instance that the counter must be maintained instead in a memory word, a serious degradation must be suffered. In an actual test on a laboratory system (8080-based), using an otherwise identical test model, a *1000*-count loop differed in timing by nearly 3 seconds. In the first case a register was used for the loop counter, and in the second a memory word was used.

As a parenthetical note: *To count to 1000 using a 1-byte word requires four iterations of 256, the maximum decimal value in binary using only 8 bits.*

Again, consider the possibility of using bits for variables. Supposing the earlier instance of *multiple conditionals,* if each test is on the same byte content of a given register, the optimum speed of execution is possible. By arguing on a different *bit* of the *same byte,* each conditional needs only to test on the register, and no memory-to-register transfers are necessary. Even complex algorithms may employ shift commands to rearrange the *bit pattern* of a register. And the timings of the shift functions is considerably faster than to have to fetch individual bytes *from memory.*

In review of this section, the concepts mentioned may be summarized as follows. Fine tuning for speed optimization depends on *bottleneck analysis* and *probability theory.* The design methods suggested include using *linear* sequences instead of *reiterative* where practical, and *preclude nested loops,* or at least constrain them to the fewest compounds. Avoid having to execute any more steps than the absolute minimum required to accomplish a task. And, finally, use *bits for variables* rather than *memory bytes,* a technique that capitalizes on the optimum execution of the CPU using registers in lieu of memory transfers.

14.2 Multitasking Operations

This section centers on the word *task.* Speed optimization suggests getting the most done in the least time, and multitasking implies concurrency or simultaneity. We begin with a short discourse on the power of definition—adjectival flexibility serves to the advantage of programmers *and* authors.

A task is a unit of work, and it is characterized by having a starting point, an ending, and a result or achievement. In the most discrete sense, then, a single machine-language instruction is capable of performing a task, albeit the achievement factor is only nominal when compared to the global tasks of the processing system.

In the more usual context a task within a software system is a *series of program steps* arranged in a sequence so as to accomplish a specific *function* of processing. The characteristic of having a distinct beginning and ending for a series of task steps tends to denote a routine. The various routines of a program serve as logical subdivisions of the total program, and generally, each routine is designed to accomplish some major subtask of the overall. Subroutines are also used, and the usual connotation applies to a subtask series of instructions that enjoy universal usage by one or more major routines.

Notice in the preceding the apparent lack of finite definition. So be it. And more is the power of application in programming. In what follows, concept and principle are portrayed by description of example and technique.

Prioritized Tasking

Prioritized tasking is the application of priorities to tasks within a process or routine as a design principle. Assume, first, that all procedural sequences within a given routine are necessary. Second, the complete routine is capable of subdivision into small groups of instructions, each group comprising a subtask. Now, what is the requirement for *order of execution* of each subtask? Often, within the design of major routines some latitude is possible as to which subtasks need to be executed first, second, and so on.

Consider as an example a requirement to accept input from the keyboard into a buffer area, and by design convention, this buffer is empty when the input function is invoked. When is the buffer cleared? *Immediately prior* to INPUT? Or *immediately following* any input, in anticipation of the next access? Whether to invoke a subroutine to clear the buffer before or after keyboard entry is a function of *deciding priorities.* The buffer is clear when the software is first loaded, therefore it is empty immediately prior to its first use. Notice the requirement is that the buffer be cleared, it is inconsequential to the logic *when* it is cleared.

Having to clear immediately prior to permitting the operator to type may be observed as a delay, however. Conversely, a nominal pause following termination of an entry may typically go unnoticed. In either case, collectively the same processing time is required, although the illusion may be of enhanced speed of execution.

Extensive application of prioritized tasking techniques can save *real* time, however, as opposed to illusory time. The time saving can be a result of *not executing* steps that become unnecessary due to changing circumstances while processing. Assume the need to invoke two different subroutines in a serial fashion, one after the other. If as the result of a conditional test the second routine is not necessary, the time required for execution of the second can be saved *by not doing it.*

One very interesting technique for varying the priority of access of successive subroutines is by use of a parameter table. Consider the example requiring the use of five subroutines, identified here by the letters A through E. For one purpose these routines may be accessed in ascending sequence, for another in descending order; and yet in another, some other order is required. By preconditioning a table or list of the preferred sequence, a simple *conditional caller sequence* can be used to control the order of execution. For one circumstance routine B may be apt to terminate early, and in another the D routine is required only if A is accessed.

Although this example is theoretical, the concept is accurate and this method is useful for prioritizing the sequence of execution of tasks. Speed degradation is also minimized by ensuring that only necessary tasks are undertaken, avoiding any that are summarily redundant.

Alternate Tasking

The essence of the principle of alternate tasking is the factor of *when* to choose alternate execution paths. In many instances the expedient of relocating a conditional test to the *earliest point practicable* will save time by precluding unnecessary steps in execution.

As a case in point, argue the requirement for determing if alphabetic characters are typed into a numerics-only field. At least three opportunities for editing of the data input exist. A character *scan-and-test* loop can be invoked after the data is moved from the buffer to memory. The qualifying can be done prior to the move to memory, or optimally, each character can be tested as it is entered into the buffer. In the latter case, an immediate branch to an error-handling routine will avoid execution of intermediate steps. Equally significant to the operator is the immediacy of error detection. To have typed a string of data only to learn that the *first character is wrong* not only wastes time, it is aggravating.

Another example of alternate tasking is that of parsing of command input. When in the command mode, the first character typed may be either a number or a letter. *What* is typed first is significant in terms of *which* major software routines will be employed after the full entry is typed. A command line that begins with a letter must be, by design convention, a system direct command. When a number is entered as the first character, the BASIC source program entry mode is assumed. Which major routines are invoked after the complete entry is made can be argued on the significance of the *first character entered.* The sooner this determination is made, the greater the opportunities to avoid unnecessary procedural steps.

Concurrent Tasking

Concurrent tasking means combining within a loop the commands to do several tasks rather than just one. There are variations possible for this seemingly obvious technique. In a preceding example notice the serial consideration for designing two routines, one for *transferring* buffer contents and another for *clearing* the buffer. Concurrent tasking techniques transfer and clear at the same time.

In actual practice the method works like this: Pick up a byte from the sending location, clear the sender, then transfer the accumulator to the receiving location. Whether the sender is cleared prior to the copy to memory is not important, but notice that each sender byte is cleared *as it is picked up.* By combining the transfer and the sender-clearing steps within a single routine, the entire overhead for a *second* loop process is saved—both a speed and a storage saving advantage (fewer total instructions are needed).

212

There is also a more subtle speed enhancement, but of almost equal value. By commanding the clear function in immediate succession to the pickup, the *varying address pointer* is useful for both tasks, saving the overhead otherwise necessary to increment the pointer.

A variation on the use of this principle is to clear two areas with a single loop. Assume that the requirement is to clear two memory areas of equal length. Increment the loop counter, clear one address, then one in the second area, using the same offset for each of the two commands; then loop. Again, the loop-control overhead for a second routine is saved.

This principle can be applied to more than just clearing tasks. It is also practical to combine a clearing task of one area within a loop that relocates data between *two other areas* as well. And, obviously, dual transfers can be accomplished in much the same manner.

In the preceding section an example was given of a loop requiring 1000 interations, and it was noted that 256 is the decimal capacity of a single 8-bit counter. To save the overhead of dual byte management for a counter, do this: Within the loop use four *addressed commands*. The first uses a relative offset of zero, the second +250, the third +500, and the fourth uses relative +750. Only *250 iterations* of the loop are necessary to affect a *1000=element* area. Perhaps a few more instructions are needed, but the net execution time may well be less because of the fewer repetitions of the *loop control instructions*. There is, of course, a finite limit to the application of this technique for saving time. The trade-off delta is at that point that time of execution of the additional instructions totals more than the combined effect of the loop-control overhead. An exact analysis is necessary for each case, including the timings of the individual commands involved, and the CPU architecture used.

The ultimate optimization is possible using a combination of these two variations for concurrent tasking. Argue the possibilities of clearing two different 1000-byte areas, combining the addressing of each, within a single loop that uses multiple relative offsets. The combined effect of these methods can achieve a speed enhancement on the order of five to ten times better than for simpler, serial tasking methods.

Overlapping Tasking

Start the cassette to rewinding . *Then,* initialize the cassette input buffer area and complete any other miscillaney. *Now* begin tape data I/O operations. The time saved can be considerable, since multiple tasks may be accomplished in an overlapped fashion—*true simultaneity.*

In the strictest sense, simultaneous processing techniques are not possible with a microprocessor. Only one machine-language instruction can be executed *per machine cycle.* There are opportunities to accomplish overlapped execution of multiple processes, however. Witness the case of DMA transfers. Direct memory access electronics permit *bus-to-memory* movements without idling the CPU. The principle again is to initiate the start of the transfer, then resume execution of procedures that are *not dependent on* the data being moved at that exact point in time.

The last point deserves repeating: . . . . *execution of procedures that are not dependent on the data.* . . . True multitasked operations are those that enjoy *mutually*

213

exclusive data dependencies. It is not logical, for instance, to overlap the procedural sequence that acts on a string of data with the input function that acquires that data.

A greater aspect of consideration in deciding processes that may be overlapped is the potential of *incompletion.* What are the interdependencies involved? If the first of two tasks is aborted prematurely, what is the effect on the second, overlapped task? Is it possible of completion? Is it logical of completion? These questions are especially applicable when overlapping internal processing with I/O device operations. Peripherials are prone to malfunction or temporary suspended operation due to media problems. The logic of what may or must occur for each predictable circumstance can influence *what processes* may be overlapped.

Consideration must also be allowed for the error-recovery choices. The analysis must contend with the effects of data processed by the overlapped tasks. Some of the possibilities include reexecution of the multitasked steps, or skipping of those caused to be redundant by reason of an error in an overrlapped task.

In any event, the designer should be alert to the possibilities for overlapped tasking. Speed enhancement results from concurrent task accomplishment—*more work in less time*—but few things are without price. The cost in the case of overlapped tasking, especially with I/O devices, is in the greater analysis and design required.

Reviewing this section, we have *prioritized* tasking and *alternate* tasking—in effect, the *when* to do and *whether* to do principles. *Concurrent tasking is the technique of combining into a single routine several tasks to save the overhead of multiple loop-control processes. And overlapped* tasking is a resource management technique that depends on activation and control of other than CPU tasks so as to allow CPU activity at the same time.

14.3   Addressing Algorithms

The different procedural methods of addressing suffer varying amounts of overhead, both in execution time and the space required to contain program instructions. Discussed here are certain topics oriented toward minimizing the speed impacts for various addressing requirements. For purposes of organization, the subject of addressing is divided into three types. Procedural sequence control is first: the types of branching from one routine to another. Second is the matter of addressing memory storage for data. The final discussion also, concerns data but it is limited to table and array processing.

Since the subject of addressing covers extreme variety and scope, discrete selection was applied in determining the material included here. We discuss here only those aspects of value in the design of interpreters, for *source entry* BASIC on a *microcomputer.* Second, examples are discussed that are pertinent to time savings for those processes that are especially prone to degrading performance. At the conceptual level, however, the techniques described are viable for application in many other areas of software designing.

We begin with a look at command decoding. From a point in the execution of the interpreter program it is necessary to direct the sequence to a specific routine for interpretive execution of the BASIC command at hand. An average implementation of BASIC has 100 keywords. Theoretically at least, each of these keywords requires an interpreter string. Determining quickly which string should be branched-to is important. The logical function of decoding these keywords is highly repetitive, occurring at least once for each BASIC program step. Any minor ineffeciency experienced at this point is subject to compounding by reason of multiplication of the excess time by the number of program step iterations.

The ultimate in speed is possible by use of direct or absolute addressing. Assume that the keyword XOR is available (used for Boolean logic operations). In ASCII the letter X is coded as 58; the character value could be appended to a branch command and direct, absolute, addressing would be possible—probably the fastest method of getting there. Notice also the savings by reason of the simple parsing required.

There are at least two pitfalls to this method, however, from a design viewpoint. This technique assumes that only one keyword begins with the letter X, and that no code 59 will be encountered. (A code of 59 would cause a branch directly into the second byte of the beginning of the routine that supports XOR.) Not very tenable.

The proximity problem can be solved, however, by the expedient of factoring the code. By shifting the binary bits of 0101 1000 to the left by three positions, effectively multiplication by eight occurs, allowing intervals of eight bytes between relative branch points. And a shift command requires miniscule time in most processors.

The problem of multiple keywords beginning with the same letter can also be simply solved. *Multilevel indexing* is the jargon for describing successive levels of indexed addressing. Given the keywords IF and INPUT, branch first on the value of I (49 in ASCII). At the address 49 use the second character (F or N) to determine further branching in a similar manner. Obviously this method can be used for as many levels as required to distinguish the uniqueness of virtually any keyword of a command set.

In actual practice, though, consider some other alternatives. The shift instruction could be relocated to the routine that stashes the source command in memory at keyboard entry time. The speed enhancement value of preencoding the keyword at entry time rather than at program run time is very significant. The point of this example is to emphasize the advantage of the slower execution times tolerable during source program entry. Quite extensive mastication algoritms can be processed at entry time, all to the benefit of favoring enhanced speed during interpretive execution. In short, the greater the effort of designing the encoding process, the less the degradation and overhead of decoding.

A word is in order here concerning integrity problems of using codes as effective addresses. The risk potential is inherent to using an invalid code, thus causing a branch to an iilogical location. One obvious solution is to qualify the code conditionally before use to eliminate illegal codes. Instructions for conditional qualification require time to execute, however, and depending on design, they must be executed every cycle, before using the code. A time-saving solution is to construct the code set such that no qualification is necessary.

Use a 128-byte string. Each byte contains the address of a routine. The pickup vector is used to address one of the 128 bytes. The address stored in each of the bytes that represent illegal codes causes a branch to an error-handling routine. The address stored for each legal code is the address of the appropriate supporting routine. The speed-saving argument here depends on the fact that at least one indirect branch is necessary for decoding legal values. Use of an indirect branch for the illegal codes also, as in this example, reduces the procedural code necessary for conditional testing; hence speed of execution is enhanced.

One of the most time-consuming tasks of nearly any process is the movement of data between memory locations. A speed technique is offered here for the benefit of those systems that have particular attributes—not all systems of course, but true of an overwhelming majority of microcomputers. If DMA is supported for I/O transfers, but not for memory-to-memory moves, take advantage of the relatively faster speeds of DMA by this method. Transfer blocks of data to an I/O buffer (depending on capacity) using DMA—but do not invoke peripheral control. Relocate the data to the receiving memory address as a DMA transfer from the I/O buffer, just as if it was input from the device. Again, this advantage is sensitive to particular systems, but where applicable a considerable speed enhancement is possible for especially large data string transfers.

Another technique is suggested for addressing constants in main memory— again, it is useful only in selected cases, but can be applied successfully with error messages to the operator in these cases. By convention of design, use only 26 messages. Each begins with a different letter of the alphabet. Error codes are the same as, or a derivation of, the ASCII character values for A through Z. As can be surmised, the minimum procedural code is required to equate a given code with the appropriate message—minimum code, fastest speed.

Table management technique is another area possible of lengthy dissertation. Here it is assumed that the reader is acquainted with the subject and with methods of binary and linear algorithms. Many texts are available that argue the merits of each, and the formulas popular for arguing the appropriateness of each. The cautionary advice offered is that, without the effort of calculation, linear techniques are often discarded prematurely in favor of binary. This tends to happen because of a lack of thorough analysis of the ways for increasing the speed of linear tasks, some of which are offered next.

First, a favorite in other sections of this book: *probability ordering.* Stack the constants in a table in order of most likely encounterance. As in poker, stacking the deck has a tremendous influence on the odds of what comes up next.

In determining whether to use binary or linear, consider the effect of *halving* the table. Split the linear table in two parts, and arrange the data of each on the basis of probability of need. Decide which data belongs to either half-table according to the first character of each element. The accessing algorithm can discern which of two tables with a single conditional, testing on whether a byte is *odd* or *even*. If half of a table is faster with linear than the whole table would be using binary techniques, speed can be further enchanced with a stacked content of each half.

For large tables it is possible to carry this logic at least one step further before resorting to binary as a faster mechanism. Initially argue two halves on the basis of odd and even for the first character. Do it again on the second character. In effect, the large table is divided into four parts, each of which is searched by use of linear techniques. The commands required in 8080 machine language for the *double byte odds and evens* test is fewer than for the most efficient binary search method. Fewer commands means faster execution speed. This rationale is often valid for other systems as well. Binary search algorithms require a procedures loop, usually of greater overhead burden than for a simple linear search loop.

Whether binary or linear table accessing algorithms are employed, there are some techniques worthy of mentioning that can be applied for either. Before pursuing these in detail, however, realize the possibilities of a hybird idea using binary *and* linear methods. Use binary for a major-level decision, then revert to linear for a segment of a table, or, perhaps use an odd-and-even test to argue which of two tables should be accessed using binary. *(Notice also that determining odd or even character for a byte is equivalent to one iteration of dividing by 2.)*

Specifics will vary, but as an average overall, 50% of all table accesses are to the *same address* as the last previous access. Although the percentage factor can be debated, the estimate is valid enough to substantiate a concept. Before any procedural steps are executed in support of a search process, test first against the data referenced by the last vector. Application of this principle merely requires saving the last vector used in a convenient storage location. Upon entry to the search routine, use this saved address for an immediate test of the new argument. At least for all of those instances of repeat occurrence, no time is wasted in locating the same data twice.

Progressive qualification of bytes within elements. Save time by not belaboring table element comparisons for all of the characters of each element for each test. Discern equality of the *first character*—if there is no match, increment the search sequence to another element, and avoid the redundancy of testing the next character of the same element. This suggestion may seem elementary, but it may be honestly contemplated for the sake of simplicity, without due deliberation for the speed degradation potential.

In summarizing this section, review the potential areas for enhancing speed of execution by efficient design of addressing algorithms. The area worthy of the greatest effort of design for procedural controls concerns command decoder logic. The first opportunity for optimization is in the design of the codes themselves. Second, remove the overhead of decoding by placing the greater demands on the process of encoding. Considerable execution time is frequently spent in relocating data between memory areas. Use of innovative methods here can include those similar to the suggestion to use DMA via I/O buffers to avoid character-driven transfer loops. And finally, management of table processes can have significant consequences at run time. Careful selection of the primary technique is important: whether to use binary, linear, or a hybrid search. A large majority of searches into a table are to the same address as was used last, so the technique of looking there first upon reentry to the search routine may save time. And saving execution time for a software interpreter on a microcomputer is worth the effort of optimum design.

Chapter

15 Memory Utilization

The main memory of a computer is a finite resource, and there is no greater chagrin in programming than to run out of memory before the job is done. During the early stages of designing a software system it is necessary to estimate the amount of space required for various purposes, and it is at that time that trade-offs can be made as to whether or not specific features can be included. Once the basic architecture is committed, however, it is difficult to give up any capability that was originally planned or promised.

The programming of a software interpreter for a microcomputer is doubly demanding in the need for memory conservation—not only are relatively small memories typical of such systems, but not all of the memory is available for the interpreter. Some space must be reserved for the user's program, else there is no need for the interpreter.

Memory optimization methods depend on one of three basic principles. So, too, this chapter is divided into three sections. Packing of data is first. Condense what is to be stored so as to require the minimum of space. Overlaying is next. Use a given storage allocation repeatedly, for a variety of purposes. And finally, the simplest in principle but often the most difficult in application, the ultimate alternative to the use of memory—nonuse. Consideration should be given for alternative solutions, and of all the features provided, sometimes it is not necessary to provide them all concurrently.

15.1 Data Concentration

This section ponders some possibilities for condensing data to save storage space. In considering the appropriateness of these or other techniques, however, the designer must be alert to two variables. Packing algorithms require *time for procedural execution,* and the program instructions for encoding and decoding also *require storage space.* Detailed analysis is often necessary to determine whether any real or theoretical

218

saving is cost-justified. The cost in some instances may be in degraded performance, or perhaps an innovative technique consumes more space for programming than would the otherwise expanded data.

Two basic methods can be applied to nearly all data concentration algorithms. The first is to remove or eliminate unnecessary bit or positional values, and the second is to substitute physically smaller codes for those representing expansive data formats.

A type of data that is particularly vulnerable to condensing techniques is ASCII. In a byte-oriented system it is usual to store one alphanumeric character per byte. A byte is 8 bits, however, not all of which are used for most character code sets. A 128-character ASCII implementation requires only 6 bits per character. It is often quite practical, then, to devise a processing routine for storing four characters per every 3 bytes. Typically such algorithms depend on the use of register shift commands, working in 2-bit increments to contract or expand character strings.

It is possible to apply this technique one bit further. A subsetted chart that includes only the alphabet can be devised using 5-bit characters. Attention to detail must be applied when adopting such a scheme, however. The odd number 5 in a binary environment usually results in some unexpened bit positions, so the added complexity is seldom justified.

There are some other possibilities for saving space for purely alphabetic data. Can the message content be constrained to using only 16 letters? Of the 26 letters in the modern alphabet, not all are used with equal frequency. Discounting of several is fairly easy. Letters such as Z, Q, J, and K are near the bottom of the frequency scale. To reduce to 16 a working alphabet does require imagination, however. Short messages can often be constrained to such a set by the expedient of using synonyms of various words for those words that do not fit the shortened character set.

The advantage of the 16-character alphabet is the ability to store two letters per byte. Four bits (a half-byte, or nibble) can represent 16 unique values; hence, two letters per byte are possible.

Before we leave the subject of alphabetic text, the obvious must be mentioned: *abbreviations.* Mnemonic forms of data representation are certainly not novel to the practicing programmer, but the intent here is to be sure that the obvious does not go unnoticed.

Another space-saver technique is to eliminate spaces. This technique dates back a number of years and was originally pioneered to optimize the use of storage media. Strings of consecutive space codes imbedded within data may serve no purpose other than for graphic output. These aids to human readability can be retained, yet in a manner that does not require individual character storage in memory (or on media).

Algorithms for space concatenation require two parameters, a marker character and a counter to indicate the number of spaces to follow. Application of this technique usually takes the form of a processing routine to scan a data string, substituting a marker and a counter for variable-length series of spaces. An example of this technique is shown in Figure 15.1. A single byte may serve as a marker and a counter, or for instances of very long series of spaces, 2 bytes can be used.

Assume that no printable character can be of the form 00 through 0F, hexadeci-

219

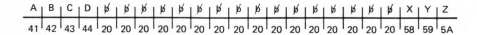

Expanded data string (β = space characters)

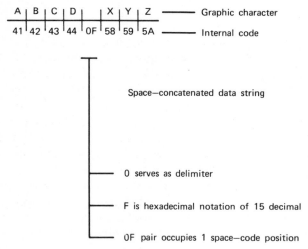

Figure 15.1 The effects of space-code concatenation.

mal. The left digit of 0 then serves as a concatenation marker and the right digit may range from 0 to F, serving as a counter to denote up to 16 spaces. The double-byte scheme works similarly, the left byte being the marker (any unique code) and the next byte being a counter with a capacity up to 255.

The practical use of the space concatenation concept for a source statement interpreter is in program storage. For documentation purposes the programmer may wish to use printable spaces for formatting program listings. Only two relatively small subroutines are required, the first to strip strings of space codes, and the second to replace them for displayed output.

One further suggestion applies to space-character savings for BASIC source statements. As a convention of design within the source parsing routine, any space characters typed by the programmer are eliminated arbitrarily. The source line display routine, then, automatically implants spaces between lexical elements at output time. The overhead for the procedures required is nominal, and execution speed is not significantly degraded for most systems employing this space-saving technique.

Packed numerics date at least from the days of Hollerith. This technique is recounted here in the interest of completeness. Two decimal numbers are possible per data byte of storage. Each half-byte is fully capable of 0–9 representation with 5 bits per half-byte unneeded, but also useful for arithmetic sign purposes. Assuming that all input text is in fully expanded ASCII (or some other 8-bit code set), decimal numbers may be stored by packing two digits per byte—a two-for-one space saving for numeric fields of data. In any event, all working storage for user program numeric quantities should be of the packed form. Conversion to other forms such as binary for internal processing requirements can depend on a corresponding pair of subroutines, designed especially for this purpose.

Let us continue with some further concepts concerning the use of half-bytes. By convention or otherwise, people are used to decimals. A predominant requirement of many supporting routines of a BASIC interpreter is to count to ten or less. Rather than devote an entire byte of memory storage for every decade counter required, use instead only a half-byte. A single byte of storage may then be shared by two different routines that require counting ability in the range from 0 to 15, inclusive.

Review of the model software system described previously evinced a savings of approximately 50 bytes by use of this single technique. While 50 is not a substantial number, when you are out of storage space and wishing for more, an extra 50 is sure to be handy.

We resort now to using the individual bits within bytes. Often it is a requirement in the design of various routines to establish an indicator that can later be conditionally tested by other procedures. And usually the need is to be able to distinguish nothing more than a true or false status. Use a bit and save a byte. A single byte is capable of containing eight such unique indicators—a saving of 7 bytes for every multiple of eight required flags or switches in main memory storage. Although additional procedural code is required to discriminate a specific bit, by mapping flag words contiguous, a single subroutine can service others in maintenance of the flag table.

In review, the essence of this section aims to save space by concentrating on data types that are especially space-consuming. Alphabetic text tends to consume storage at an indiscriminate rate, so it is highly vulnerable to condensing techniques. Packed numerics, a long-time favorite of software designers, should be exploited to the maximums of practicality in a BASIC interpreter. And finally, the significance of binary bits deserves the benefit of optimizing efforts. Using bits to save a few bytes may prove very worthwhile, especially when the memory runs out before the job does.

15.2 Overlay Schemes

This section is deserving of central placement within a chapter devoted to space-saving methods. Conceptually at least, the better memory conservation techniques concentrate not so much on saving, but rather on maximum utilization. And maximum utilization assumes continuous reuse of a given amount of memory, for a variety of purposes, and at various times.

To set the tone for what follows, the reader is cautioned that this author harbors no philosophical bias concerning the use of memory. It is considered fundamentally correct here, in the design of software interpreters, that anything that works correctly is legitimate discipline in favor of constraining the overall size of the software system.

There are, of course, those who refuse certain methods for reasons that cannot be discounted lightly. For those techniques predicated on self-destruct overlaying concepts, due deliberation must be allowed the complexities of software debugging that can result. Whether or not a designer should attempt some of the suggested techniques remains the choice of the individual. In any event, it is valid to recommend that a thorough risk analysis be made for those schemes that deliberately erase any run time auditability. Judgment as to whether or not to proceed must rest on a comparison of the memory-saving advantage versus the difficulties of implementation.

At the risk of belaboring the point, the greatest economies are bound to require the greatest effort. And every effort to constrain the interpreter to the least space is rewarded to the user by providing the maximum memory for an application program.

Fledgling airplane pilots are continually reminded by their instructors of two things most useless to them—the runway behind, and the altitude above. There is an anology in software. The memory space containing program instructions that have been executed is already nearly as useless as the airplane runway that has passed beneath.

Memory overlaying schemes are usually motivated by the realization that, at some point, the storage area containing program instructions for some routines is in effect wasted space. Notice that in nearly all large software systems, a number of procedures are seldom used. Yet, where these same routines are continually in residence, their storage space is wasted for all of the time that they are dormant. The suggestion is, then, to devise methods by which this space may be used for other purposes during those periods of dormancy.

One-Shots and Self-destructs

The first memory optimization attack should be aimed at the *one-shot* procedural sequences—those routines that are executed only once, usually following immediately after software loading. The suggested technique for reclaiming the space occupied by these instruction sequences is to cause them to self-destruct as a final act of performance.

A likely candidate for application of this suggestion is typified by the interpreter model discussed earlier. Immediately after the software system is loaded into memory, a branch is effected to a routine that, with display dialogue, the system queries the operator for certain parameters for initializing the system. Once executed, these procedures are impossible of reexecution, since some of the parameters are used to establish permanently the run-time environment. Not only are the instruction series no longer needed, the alphanumeric constants used by the dialogue driver are equally useless. Upon completion of the initializing process, then, a branch is taken to a serviceing subroutine that clears the areas of both the initializing sequence and its related operator lead-through messages. This reclaimed space may now be used for other purposes, perhaps as working storage for other software routines.

Two perspectives are possible for the designer contemplating use of this scheme. The preceding description viewed the problem as an opportunity to reuse the space that originated with procedural code. Another view is to borrow, temporarily, memory space that is allocated for working storage, *by encoding initializing procedures into that space.* This second perspective has the advantage that no particular instruction sequence is required for the cleanup chore, if, as a routine happening of progressive execution, this area is automatically cleared anyway.

Recognize, however, the difficulties that may be encountered in the early phases of debugging the initializing process. Once cleared, it is difficult to audit the specific performance of the instructions that are no longer visible. The counter argument, of course, is that once these procedures operate correctly it is no longer necessary to have them available for examination.

One further rationale is offered for these schemes, to counter those schools that disallow them. A much better job is often possible by adopting these methods. The area of design that benefits the most is in the operator interface. Routines that are bound to be always resident must suffer their fair share of criteria for space conservation. In composing operator dialogue that occupies space only temporarily, the rules for keeping such messages brief may be relaxed. And all operators, including programmers, enjoy full text messges more than symbolic codes and abbreviations that require mental exercise in decipherment. This is especially true of dialogue that is infrequently encountered, such as start-of-day porcedures.

Discussed thus far is an overlaying concept that is based on dual usage of a memory area by totally memory resident software, all of which was loaded at the same time. The next suggestion is for calling into memory software overlays on an as-needed basis. An example of this could be for that which immediately follows system initialization.

The software loading sequence can be designed so that the operator dialogue message and the driver are loaded first, then the load process is temporarily suspended while the operator interchange takes place. Assuming that the operator correctly enters all of the initializing parameters, the software loading process continues, overloading and replacing the dialogue procedures.

This design methodology does suffer from slower performance as viewed by the operator because of the delay after entry, while awaiting the completion of software loading and initialization. The trade-off advantages are in favor of the superior operator interface messages and the more thorough entry syntaxing that results. Having available vast areas of memory permits expansive design with no constraints imposed, since the entire area will be subsequently overlayed.

The two previous concepts for overlaying software presumed opportunities for sequential-only need of routines that are needed just once. The first suggestion preloads everything and depends on internal processing to eliminate no longer needed code and allow reuse of the space. The second suggestion breaks the software into parts, successively loading and executing each process as needed. In both cases the significance is that the procedures are needed only once. Overlaying techniques are possible, of course, for both procedures and data that are required repeatedly.

223

Swappables

Consider as likely candidates for swapping two distinct routines of approximately equal size, either of which is needed only occassionally, neither of which is required to support the other. With a random files storage device on the system (disk, perhaps), load either routine into a memory area that is allocated for their common use, and the time of loading and which of the two is argued at the point of need. Naturally, more than two routines may be managed in this fashion, allow though the criteria for the space-traders to be mutually exclusive and the overlay space allocation must be sufficient to accommodate the largest such routine. Bear in mind also the potential performance degradation suffered while awaiting callables to be brought into memory. Speed of access of the storage device is a paramount designer consideration here. Of course, the implied requirement for a random files device is not absolute. Serial media such as cassettes can be used with these methods, but, again, the greater is the significance of access times.

The foregoing types of overlays are referred to in some texts as *demand-destruct* overlays. They are called on demand, and they are destroyed by others when the space they occupy is demanded for other purposes.

The ultimate application of overlaying techniques is that of *roll-in, roll-out*. These are still called for on a demand basis, but before a newly required overlay is loaded its space-sharing companion is unloaded to media before the overlay loading is performed. Of course there is a greater speed degradation potential because of the need to output memory to media before the callable is fetched.

The decision as to which concept should apply, either demand-destruct or roll-in, roll-out, can be reduced to consideration of the need to save working storage values. If only procedural program code is involved, the obvious choice is for demand-destruct methods. Data constants areas may also be destruct overlayed, assuming that they will be refreshed during any subsequent call into memory from media storage. Not all of that to be rolled out to media is, then, necessarily the same as that subject to later recall. Intermediate working storage values are predominantly the memory areas that must be copied from memory prior to permitting the space to be overlayed.

Before leaving this subject, notice that there is one restriction imposed on the specific design techniques permitted for routines that are subject to demand-destruct algorithms. Procedural code that is altered by reason of routine execution will be in its original state on successive iterations of the call process. This is not necessarily a bad restriction; in fact, this tendency for self-repair can be exploited by not having to devise procedures for reinitializing altered instructions. Notice also the possibilities for using the same idea for working storage areas that need to be cleared prior to use.

In brief, then, overlaying of memory areas can be exercised from within as internal procedures, or required routines can be called as needed from storage media. Because overlaying causes that which was already resident to be eradicated, anything of value in a space subject to being overlayed should be saved prior to permitting the overlay process. The fastest methods are those that use internal exchanges of space, the next choice being demand-destruct types, and of course the slowest performance is experienced with roll-in, roll-out techniques. And for media-based overlays, access speed and type of file device tends to dictate the choice of method.

224

A background consideration must also be borne in mind as to the degree and extent of predictable difficulties resulting from the use of overlays. Because it is at times arduous to run-trace software logic that disappears after use, due consideration must be given and a comparison of memory saved over debugging and maintenance costs made. The fact remains, though, that memory-optimization opportunities are greater with overlay techniques—multiple use of a given resource provides benefits in excess of the best attempts at containment.

15.3 Memory Use Alternatives

At a point in recent history the U.S. Army supplied an ever-constant conservation reminder on vehicle trip request froms. *"Is this trip really necessary?"* Although the frequency of repetition of this reminder tended to be irritating, it did sometimes provoke evaluation of priorities. Borrowing freely from this and similar tactics, we suggest a prominent sign on the software writer's wall: "Is this *routine* really necessary?"

Thus we set the tone for what follows. The intent is to stimulate due deliberation for what is finally included in memory—for leaving anything out is bound to save space. The obvious alternative to omission is optimal design. "Is there any other way to provide the same or an equivalent feature that requires less memory?" And finally, we attack functions: In large software systems there is bound to be tasking repitition.

Let us consider feature evaluation. In the early design days of the model described previously, it was contemplated to provide a feature that was later discarded. As a feature of the software system, a special code character placed immediately after a statement line number would cause that line to function as an otherwise blank line (no command constructs) on program printouts. Desired for cosmetic purposes, it was thought that this feature would be useful to the programmer in enhancing the appearance of program documentation.

The decision to discard this feature was based on two arguments. First, some additional software overhead was necessary to support it, and second, if provided, it would undoubtedly be used. In terms of additional overhead, not a great deal of memory was necessary, and yet, if no discipline is observed there is a tendency toward escalating elegance. It is best to curtail the *nice-to-have* features in favor of doing a thorough job for the *need-to-have.* And as to the risk of use of such a feature, the programmer is afforded a gratuity by a simple act of omission. Each program statement number requires 5 bytes of user program memory. By not providing a facility for wasting memory, the software designer actually assists the user programmer toward more optimum use of the BASIC memory.

This brief example should suffice as a description of the concepts and arguments that apply in making judgments concerning feature omissions. Again however, remember to restrain the tendency to provide features of dubious worth in favor of doing a better job for those things having functional merit.

What about design alternatives? Data constants tend to consume large blocks of memory, as was discussed in the previous section. There are sometimes possibilities for substituting procedural algorithms for data constants, and the suggestion here is to analyze the alternatives.

225

As an example, assume the need for a table consisting of the letters of the alphabet. Use a *data generator* routine in lieu of a constants table. The procedural code required to initialize a counter at hexadecimal 41 and loop-increment for 26 times may approximately equal the space requirement as the table. But if this same counter subroutine can be used to support other, similar tasks, a real saving can be achieved. Perhaps there is the need elsewhere for a numerical series—you can use this same subroutine. The working storage location to contain these dynamically generated data constants can be anywhere convenient—the essence of this savings technique is not to require dedicated constant storage.

This discussion leads us to the consideration of tasking alternatives. To coin a phrase, use *multifunctional subroutines.* In the above example of a subroutine that loops and increments to generate an ascending series of codes, with only a minor modification this same subroutine is capable of supporting a variety of functional requirements; thus it can be *multifunctional.*

From several different locations within the software system there is the need to generate variable-length strings of space characters. By addition of a conditional branch instruction in the sequence that generates ascending codes, the instruction that increments the code constant can be skipped, thus generating a variable-length series of a given code. Not just space characters, but repetitions of any 1-byte values are possible—truly a multifunctional subroutine.

In actual practice, four initializing steps are necessary before this type of routine is invoked. Establish the beginning count and the reiteration limit. Set up the code character to be repeated (or incremented) and condition the flag that controls if the character is incremented.

The preceding relied on maximizing the use of conditional logic to enhance the multifunctional capabilities of software subroutines. There is another method for increasing the utility of both subroutines and main-flow procedural sequences. There is in the COBOL language a verb, ALTER. Microprocessor machine languages typically have no direct counterpart, yet the implied facility of ALTER suggests a viable technique of design for systems software.

A simple instance of application of the ALTER principle is for redirecting program control from one set of procedures to another. Consider the instance of a series of instructions that normally terminate with a branch to another routine. Assume also the need to conditionally redirect this branch to a different routine on certain occassions. A sequence of two branches will suffice, the first executing upon a specific condition, otherwise a default will execute the second branch. Usual and typical programming technique—no argument.

An alternative technique would be to ALTER a final, single-branch instruction by procedurally modifying the address portion of the stored branch command. Although less frequently used, perhaps, this technique is common enough. From another perspective, however, consider the use of the ALTER concept for virtually any program instruction. Thus, we have the essence of a concept for expanding the multifunctional capability of many routines.

As a cautionary comment, it is necessary to mention the risks of overenthusiastic use of these techniques. Any routine subject to being altered may also require restoration to its original design. Typically, then, there is an overhead factor associated with conditionally altering a series of instructions to more than one configuration. A thorough analysis is frequently necessary to determine whether the overhead burden is greater or less than would be the alternative of functionally parallel routines.

And, too, there are those schools that disparage the use of the ALTER techniques on the basis of software reliability and maintenance arguments. Conceptually at least, ALTER is not very different from program overlays; the latter concerns routines and the former is, effectively, overlaying at the instruction level. Consideration must be given, then, to the potentials of debugging of procedures that are difficult to audit. In the interest of memory optimization, however, it is often useful to consider the applicability of multifunctional subroutines.

The space savings to be realized by these methods assumes that the alternatives were several different routines, stored at various locations, supporting functionally similar requirements. It is appreciated that the practiced programmer may regard these methods as elementary, but perhaps the less experienced will benefit from the suggestions.

In any event, to summarily review most any software system, there are usually opportunities to salvage some space by nominally redesigning a given routine to increase its multifunctional usability, thus saving memory through optimum design. And to reiterate the beginning, space conservation considerations begin with the question: "Is this routine really necessary?"

Bibliography

SOLOMON MARTIN BERNARD, *System/3 Programming RPG II*, Prentice-Hall, Englewood Cliffs, N.J., 1972.

JOHN J. DONOVAN, *Systems Programming*, McGraw-Hill, New York, 1972.

IEEE 1975 Microprogramming, a Tutorial on the Queen Mary, 1975.

DONALD P. KENNEY, *Minicomputers: Low-Cost Computer Power for Management*, AMACOM, New York, 1973.

GEORGE K. KOSTOPOULOS, *Digital Engineering*, Wiley, New York, 1975.

KEITH R. LONDON, *Documentation Standards*, 2nd ed., Mason & Lipscomb, London, 1974.

JAMES K. MARTIN, *Design of Man-Computer Dialogues*, Prentice-Hall, Englewood Cliffs, N.J., 1973.

DANIEL R. MCGLYNN, *Microprocessors: Technology Architecture, and Applications*, Wiley, New York, 1975.

Minimal BASIC, American National Standards Institute, 1976.

NCR Century 8200 COBOL Student Text, NCR, Dayton, Ohio, 1976.

CHARLES J. SIPPL AND CHARLES P. SIPPL, *Computer Dictionary and Handbook*, 2nd ed., Sams, Indianapolis, Ind., 1972.

Index